499

Tank Battles in Miniature
5

Books in the same series published by Patrick Stephens Limited

Tank Battles in Miniature 1: A wargamers' guide to the Western Desert Campaign 1940-1942
by Donald F. Featherstone

Tank Battles in Miniature 2: A wargamers' guide to the Russian Campaign 1941-1945
by Bruce Quarrie

Tank Battles in Miniature 3: A wargamers' guide to the North-West European Campaign 1944-1945
by Bruce Quarrie

Tank Battles in Miniature 4: A wargamers' guide to the Mediterranean Campaigns 1942-1945
by Donald F. Featherstone

Tank Battles in Miniature

5 A wargamers' guide to the Arab-Israeli Wars since 1948

Bruce Quarrie

Patrick Stephens Limited, Cambridge

© Bruce Quarrie 1978
Chapters on aerial warfare and aerial wargaming
© Mike Spick 1978

All rights reserved. No part of this publication may be reproduced, stored in a retrieval system or transmitted, in any form or by any means, electronic, mechanical, photocopying, recording or otherwise, without prior permission in writing from Patrick Stephens Limited

First published in 1978

British Library Cataloguing in Publication Data
Tank battles in miniature.
   5: A wargamers' guide to the Arab-Israeli wars since 1948.
   1. War games
   I. Quarrie, Bruce
   793'.9   U310

ISBN 0 85059 304 2

Text photoset in 9 on 10pt English 49
by Stevenage Printing Ltd, Stevenage.
Printed in Great Britain on 80 gsm Supreme Book Wove
and bound by The Garden City Press, Letchworth,
for the publishers, Patrick Stephens Limited,
Bar Hill, Cambridge, CB3 8EL, England.

Contents

Introduction	7
Glossary	8
1 Prelude to conflict	9
2 What it was *really* like!	12
3 Chronology of the Arab-Israeli Wars 1948-1973	15
4 Israeli Armoured Fighting Vehicles	43
5 Arab Armoured Fighting Vehicles	58
6 Anti-tank missiles and recoilless weapons	63
7 Towed artillery and anti-tank guns	66
8 Rocket artillery	69
9 Infantry weapons	70
10 Organisation and tactics	73
11 Minefields	78
12 Helicopters	81
13 Playing rules	84
14 Skirmish-type games	99
15 Aerial warfare, by Mike Spick	106
16 Aerial wargaming, by Mike Spick	116
17 The naval war	126
Appendix Availability of model vehicles	130
Select bibliography	131
Index	132

Maps and diagrams in text

The Middle East	16-17
Sinai, 1967	23
Golan, 1967	28
Suez, 1973	35
Syria, 1973	39
AFV recognition silhouettes	61
Ground observation diagram	90
Artillery ranging device	95
The 'third dimension'	116
Aerial observation diagram	117
Low-level bombsight	119

Photographs

Centurion with 105 mm gun	49
M60A1 of the type supplied to Israel	49
Soviet T-62s on exercise	50
Egyptian BMP-1 on parade	50
Knocked-out Arab T-34/85	51
BTR-152s	51
M-110 8" SPG of the type used by Israel	52
French AMX-13 with 75 mm gun	52
Israeli M-3 half-track mortar carrier	53
PT-76 Model 2 leaving the water	53
BTR-60s leaving a landing ship	54
M-47 Patton	54
Soviet M-1938 122 mm howitzers	55
The unconventional 122 mm D-30	55
M4A3 Sherman	56
Russian 122 mm 'Katyushas'	56

'I believe that the tank was the backbone of the land forces during [the Yom Kippur] war, and will remain so in the future. All anti-tank measures, from mines to missiles, were aimed at reducing the efficiency of the tanks in the field and at limiting their success. Indeed, all in all they did succeed in one way or another to inflict casualties and slow down the impetus of the tank, but it is not in their power to defeat the armour; that can only be done by an armoured confrontation.'

Lieutenant General David Elazar,
Tel Aviv, October 1975

Introduction

This has not been the easiest of books to compile. Unlike World War 2, which encompasses a neat period of six years and about which information is abundantly available, the various Arab-Israeli conflicts span 30 years at the time of writing and involve modern weapon systems and vehicles whose performance, for obvious security reasons, is often shrouded in mystery. Nevertheless, such is the current popularity of Arab-Israeli wargaming that I have done my best to interpret the conflicting data, to resolve the widely differing campaign accounts, to synthesize the structures and to bring the whole into a reasonably tidy 'package' which can provide the basis for miniature tank battles of this period. The data is, unfortunately, full of question marks and what are usually referred to as 'intelligent guesses'. The actual battles are, fortunately, better documented, and can be reported in some depth, as can the tactical methods. The organisation charts also have some question marks hanging over them, and can only be taken as a guide, not a definitive statement of precise composition on any precise date(s).

The playing rules themselves are still somewhat experimental, although they seem to work in practice. For the first time in this series of *Tank Battles in Miniature* books they introduce percentage dice and (optional) morale rules. Otherwise, anyone who has played with the rules included in my previous books will encounter no difficulties. For the sake of your convenience, the playing rules themselves have all been grouped together in one chapter instead of dispersed through the book. However, I would like to make very clear that they are 'rules' in name only. In reality, they are playing suggestions. Any reader is free to amend or throw out anything he or she does not like. And I do not want to be bombed, shot or hijacked if you don't like something I say!

For the second time in this series, I would like to propose a special vote of thanks to Mike Spick, an aerial wargamer of many years' experience and the author of a book in his own right (*Air Battles in Miniature*); to Christopher Foss for the loan of photographs; to Otto von Pivka, Bruce Galloway and Paul Sturman for invaluable help and information; to Bob Swan and Vince Driver for the maps and diagrams; and to Linda for her indefatigable patience in putting up with my usual household mess of books, papers and models while writing the book.

CAMBRIDGE   BRUCE QUARRIE
April 1978

Glossary

AA Anti-Aircraft.
AFV Armoured Fighting Vehicle.
AP Armour-Piercing.
APC Armour-Piercing, Capped *or* Armoured Personnel Carrier.
APCBC Armour-Piercing, Capped, Ballistic Cap.
APDS Armour-Piercing, Discarding Sabot.
APHE Armour-Piercing, High Explosive.
ARV Armoured Recovery Vehicle.
AT Anti-Tank.
ATG Anti-Tank Gun.
ATGW Anti-Tank Guided Weapon.
AVLB Armoured Vehicle, Launched Bridge (ie, a bridgelaying tank).
BAR Browning Automatic Rifle.
CEV Combat Engineer Vehicle.
FCS Fire Control System.
GPMG General-Purpose Machine-Gun.
HE High Explosive.
HEAT High Explosive, Anti-Tank.
HMG Heavy Machine-Gun.
HVAP High Velocity, Armour-Piercing.
LMG Light Machine-Gun.
MBT Main Battle Tank.
MG Machine-Gun.
MI Mechanised Infantry.
MICV Mechanised Infantry Combat Vehicle.
NBC Nuclear, Bacteriological, Chemical.
RL Rocket Launcher.
SLR Self-Loading Rifle.
SMG Sub-Machine-Gun.
SPG Self-Propelled Gun.

1

Prelude to conflict

Discussions regarding the establishment of a Jewish national home in Palestine date back to the time of the very first Zionist Conference in Basle in 1897, and during the opening years of the 20th century large numbers of Jews settled in agricultural communities throughout the country, which at that time was under Turkish rule. The Jews had been homeless since the *diaspora* began in AD 70 with the destruction of the Temple in Jerusalem by the Roman ruler, Titus, and their dispersed people have suffered endless persecution throughout the centuries in all but a very few countries (amongst which we can be grateful to count Britain, at least since the time of Cromwell). Russia, in particular, has always treated its Jews harshly, a condition which persists to this day and accounts in part for the widespread military and financial aid the Soviet Union has given to the various Arab nations since the end of World War 2.

At the beginning of World War 1, however, the establishment of a Jewish homeland seemed a mere dream, and it was not until the Balfour Declaration of November 1917 that the idea began to take concrete shape. This declaration stated that 'His Majesty's Government view with favour the establishment in Palestine of a national home for the Jewish people, and will use their best endeavours to facilitate the achievement of this object, it being clearly understood that nothing be done which may prejudice the civil and religious rights of existing non-Jewish communities in Palestine, or the rights and political status enjoyed by Jews in any other country.'

Britain, who had already established a Protectorate in Egypt in 1914, was awarded the Palestine Mandate in 1920, an event which almost immediately provoked the first of a long series of anti-Jewish riots by the local Arab population. These were stimulated by the appointment of a new and rabidly anti-Zionist Mufti of Jerusalem in 1921, and by increasing pressure of Jewish immigration into Palestine after new American immigration laws promulgated in 1924 closed that avenue of escape from persecution to the majority of homeless Jews. Arab fears that they would soon be outnumbered in Palestine led to the establishment of the Jewish Agency for Palestine in 1929 which restricted the annual level of Jewish immigration. However, in 1930 the British Government told the League of Nations that it now considered the establishment of a Jewish national home in Palestine impossible because of the difficulty of reconciling Arab and Jewish interests.

Following the Arab revolt and national strike in 1936, the Peel Commission recommended the partition of Palestine into two separate states, a suggestion which was hardly acceptable to either side in the conflict. The problem was made worse by the increasing number of Jews trying to escape Nazi persecution during the second half of the decade, and in 1939 the Palestine White Paper fixed the level of Jewish immigration into Palestine at a meagre 75,000 over the following five years.

World War 2 brought a hiatus since most Palestine Jews were hostile to the British Government but naturally supported the Allied cause against the Axis powers; the result was that some Jews fought with the British, whilst others began gathering into terrorist groups dedicated to the expulsion of British forces from Palestine. The end result was the *Haganah*, whose *Palmach* (shock troops) were to form the nucleus of the future Israeli armed force, *Zahal*. Terrorist atrocities reached a peak in 1946 with the dynamiting of the King David Hotel in Jerusalem, but tension was maintained during 1947 since Britain had agreed to grant total Egyptian independence in 1949 and began moving military forces from Egypt into Palestine, which was seen as the new British strategic centre in the Middle East. With something of a sense of desperation, the British Government submitted the whole question to the United Nations, whose Special Commission for Palestine endorsed the Peel Commission's idea of partition, and Britain agreed that the Mandate would end on May 15 1948.

Armed encounters between Arab and Jewish terrorist groups grew in intensity during the intervening period, and both sides perpetrated atrocities equally vile as any carried out by the Waffen-SS during the war, including the Jewish massacre of over 250 men, women and children in one village and the Arab reprisal in which 77 Jewish doctors and nurses travelling under Red Cross auspices were slaughtered. The increasing violence and obvious Jewish determination to gain control of Palestine once British forces withdrew caused hundreds of thousands of Arabs to flee from the affected area, and by May 1948 it was estimated that the Arab population of Palestine had dropped from 700,000 to a mere 170,000.

The 1948 war might actually be said to have begun before the British withdrawal, since four brigades of the so-called Arab Liberation Army commanded by Fawzi Kaukji, totalling some 5,000 men, had infiltrated Palestine from Syria in March of that year. For the most part, however, these forces contented themselves with guerrilla tactics by disrupting supply convoys to the many small and isolated Jewish settlements. Prior to independence, military engagements between the ALA and the *Haganah* were largely restricted to struggles for control of particular roads. The largest such operation, involving around 1,500 men on each side, was over the Tel Aviv-Jerusalem road, and lasted over a fortnight before the ALA, their field commander killed, lost heart.

A major battle then developed for control of the vital port of Haifa. The resident British troops retired into the harbour area itself on April 21 and four Israeli columns immediately attacked the Arab defenders. There was fierce fighting throughout the night but on the following day the local Arab commander deserted and, again, the ALA lost heart. The cease-fire thus left the Jews with the upper hand. A similar operation a few days later also put Jaffa into Jewish hands.

The formal Arab invasion of Palestine began on May 15 when the Arab Legion crossed the Allenby Bridge and seized various towns around Jerusalem, while two Egyptian columns simultaneously struck north for Jerusalem and Tel Aviv. A British resolution for a four-week truce was eventually accepted and went into effect on June 11. This gave both sides time to regroup but proved more advantageous to the infant Israeli Defence Force (IDF).

When the truce expired on July 9 it was followed by an immediate Israeli offensive in three different areas. The first, under Colonel Alon, succeeded in capturing Lydda, with its airport, plus Ramallah, Latrun and other Arab Legion strongholds, although it must be noted that the AL troops fought with great courage and determination. The second operation, aimed at recovering the Jewish settlement of

Mishmar Hayarden from the Syrians, was poorly co-ordinated and well and truly repulsed. The third offensive, designed to consolidate Israeli control of the Haifa and Acre sector, was more successful and Nazareth was recaptured.

A second truce was imposed on the belligerents by world opinion after ten days of this fighting, and the period from July 18 until October 15 saw no major military engagements although there was sporadic fighting on a small scale. What infuriated world opinion even more, though, was the murder of the UN's Swedish negotiator, Count Bernadotte, by members of the extremist Jewish Stern Gang in September. The Jews had never liked Bernadotte as he was widely suspected of having been a Nazi sympathiser during World War 2, but nevertheless his assassination was tactless to say the very least.

During the period of the second truce the Israeli forces were strengthened from the thousands of immigrants who had begun pouring into the country since independence, while the Arab nations were split by dissension and hampered by the economic burden of the Palestinian Arab refugees.

The main Israeli objective during the next phase of operations, which lasted from October 15 to 21, was to relieve their settlements in the Negev which had been surrounded by Egyptian forces and were in some danger of being starved to death. The first attack was unsuccessful but on the following day one of the two important hills which dominated the access road was taken. The Egyptians counter-attacked on the 17th but were thrown back, and further Israeli pressure during the 18th, followed by an attack during the night of October 19/20, succeeded in breaking the Egyptian encirclement. Now it was the turn of the Egyptians to be surrounded, as the Israelis captured Beersheba and cut off Egyptian forces in the Hebron area.

While this was happening, the ALA had been reorganising in Lebanon and on October 28 the Israelis launched a new offensive to nip this threat in the bud. Although Kaukji was ready for them, the IDF proved stronger. Meirun and Sasa both fell and the ALA ran.

The Israelis now turned their attention back to the encircled Egyptian forces in the Hebron area. During November the Egyptians made two attempts to break the stranglehold, both unsuccessful, and in December Colonel Alon struck with 15,000 men. A diversionary attack pinned Egyptian attention in the west while the main attack force struck in the direction of Asluj and El Auja. Both towns fell on December 27 and Israeli forces now penetrated into Egypt itself, surprising and scattering an Egyptian brigade during the night of the 28th-29th and racing for El Arish, where they captured several Egyptian aircraft. However, the town itself did not fall because intense international pressure forced the Israelis to evacuate Egyptian territory at the beginning of January 1949. Egypt sued for peace and Britain, recognising a *fait accompli*, finally acknowledged Israel's independence. The other Arab nations, with the exception of Iraq, also agreed to armistices during January.

And so the stage was set for the next three decades of internecine warfare—internecine because both the Arabs and the Jews acknowledge the common ancestry of Abraham.

2

What it was *really* like!

The main Arab-Israeli Wars of 1967 and 1973 are still so comparatively recent that relatively few first-hand accounts of the fighting as seen by the troops at the 'sharp end' have so far been published. Security consciousness also plays a large part in the lack of published material, together with a degree of Israeli reticence about their victories and Arab reluctance to publicise their defeats.

In many respects there has been little difference in the quality of the fighting from that encountered by the 8th Army and Afrika Korps in the 1940-1943 campaigns previously related by Don Featherstone in the first and fourth books in this series. The tanks themselves are somewhat more sophisticated, better armed and better armoured (though not always so), and the impressions of heat, dust, noise and confusion are identical.

Arab tank crews, and Israelis using captured Soviet-made equipment, are at a disadvantage, since their crew positions are very cramped. The Russians have concentrated on a low silhouette and well-sloped armour plate in most of their tanks, with the result that headroom is virtually non-existent. Moreover, their vehicles do not adapt to desert conditions as well as American or British designs, and the Arab tendency to go into action closed down must make the atmosphere inside their tanks intolerable.

One extremely readable account of the 1967 conflict does exist and, since its author travelled with the armoured spearhead of General Israel Tal's forces on the north flank, it makes very convincing reading. This is *The Tanks of Tammuz*, by Shabtai Teveth, published in hardback by Weidenfield & Nicolson and in paperback by Sphere. Even General Moshe Dayan described it as '. . . an outstanding book, the best I have read . . . about our wars'. Indeed, for anyone wargaming the battles of this period, it is a 'must', and the following extracts, designed to show a little of 'what it was *really* like', can only give a taste of its content.

The first extract concerns part of the attack on the Rafa Junction. 'Three Centurions stormed through and were on their way, but the fourth, one of Shamai's company, was hit by anti-tank fire and burst into flames. In a second the crew had jumped out and were rolling themselves in the sand to smother their burning clothing. They then turned to their tank and tried to put out the fire with extinguishers, but to no avail; the tank was a mass of flames. Another Centurion from Shamai's company thrust forward, its commander, Lior, standing upright in the cupola, and almost drove into the burning Centurion. "Reverse!" Lior ordered the driver, meaning to bypass it, but at that moment a bullet struck him in the head. The driver, who had received no further orders, continued in reverse, and there was almost a collision, but the gunner took over command of the tank and ordered the

What it was *really* like!

driver forward.'
   A little later Israeli tanks were west of Sheik Zuweid and halted, taking up hull-down positions to block any Egyptian counter-attack.
   ' "Cut motors," ordered Captain Aharon, to save fuel, and there was suddenly deep silence. The tank crews were not used to it. The drivers, gunners and loaders had been close to vomiting from the gases of the ammunition and the motors, and after placing lookouts, Captain Aharon permitted them to take a breath of fresh air. Together with his second-in-command he inspected the condition of the tanks. Every single tank had been hit, and the two officers were amazed at the strength of the steel. In some of the tanks it was actually possible to see straight through the holes made by Egyptian armour-piercing shells.'
   Despite their superior armour and firepower, even the heavy IS-III tanks used by the Egyptians were often at a disadvantage against the well-trained Israeli tank crews. At one point eight Pattons managed to knock out no less than ten of these monsters in a single engagement. But a little later Captain Danny was less fortunate. With a company of nine Pattons he engaged an Egyptian force of two T-34s, an SU-100 self-propelled gun and two anti-tank guns. One T-34, the SU-100 and the anti-tank guns were despatched promptly, but then another SU-100 appeared and more Egyptian tanks became visible in the distance. Captain Danny's tank chose this moment to stall.
   ' "Driver, start up!" said Captain Danny to his driver.
   ' "It won't start, Sir."
   'There was a fiery flash above his head, coming from behind. The shell fell and exploded in front of him. Danny gritted his teeth. Still the engine would not start . . .
   'Danny turned his head round and saw two tanks burning; one tank commander was lying on the turret. A third tank seemed to be out of action though not burning, and in that one too he could see the tank commander lying on the turret.'
   At first he thought that the tanks were knocked-out Egyptian vehicles, then it suddenly dawned on him that they were his own. The Egyptians had got behind his force and were attempting to encircle his remaining six Pattons. To his relief, his driver now managed to get the tank engine started again using the auxiliary generator. The tank reversed and Danny led his remaining force into the shelter of a small valley, where they took up firing positions.
   'Danny placed two Pattons in firing positions to the front, in the direction of the anti-tank guns, and four Pattons facing the rear. The range in front was between 900 to 1,200 metres and in the rear from 1,200 to 1,500 metres. His four Pattons facing the rear had already located five Stalins [IS-IIIs]. Rapidity and accuracy in firing was here decisive. Danny himself hit the far right Stalin, which was exposed; it burst into flames, emitting thick yellow-coloured smoke. . . . Within a few minutes five Stalins were blazing.'
   But Egyptian reinforcements were moving up, supported by mortars, and a fourth of the Pattons was soon disabled. A fifth had to be abandoned when its engine spontaneously caught fire. And then . . . but we'll leave them there—you'll have to read the book to discover the eventual outcome of the engagement!
   In a later engagement a force of Egyptian tanks established themselves in an excellent ambush situation flanking the road to Ismailia. 'The Egyptian tanks [T-55s] had been hidden in very good firing positions, at short range. The first shell had struck Shamai's Centurion, destroying the 0.5 Browning machine-gun and striking the top of the cupola. A larger splinter cut through Major Shamai, killing him instantly. Shamai's tank crew did not lose their presence of mind and withdrew immediately. The second shell struck the third tank in the column. Its commander,

Tank Battles in Miniature

Sergeant Giora Shklarchik, was about to give a fire correction to his gunner when he felt a heavy blow and saw black smoke rising from his tank. At first he did not realise what had happened, but understood when he saw that the loader was wounded and heard the gunner yell: "Giora, we've been hit!" The three of them climbed from the tank, their weapons in their hands, then called to the driver to get out of his compartment. There was no reply, and they saw that the tank had received two direct hits, one in the front. The tank continued to circle round and round, then began to slide down the incline, for it had been standing exactly on the crest. When the driver had been hit, his foot had slipped off the brake. The three crew members ran after the Centurion until it came to a stop. They opened the driver's hatch and found him dead.'

The ambushed company continued to fight at unequal odds until reinforcements arrived, then began a counter-attack. While one company advanced directly down the road to draw Egyptian fire, other units breasted the dunes behind which the T-55s were sheltering and fired down into them, while a fourth company moved right out on the flank and commenced engaging the Egyptians from the rear. The Israeli 'steamroller' continued its advance in this leap-frogging way, and at the end of the engagement claimed no fewer than 70 T-55s destroyed.

I hope that these short extracts have given some idea of the quality of the fighting in the Sinai. From a wargamer's viewpoint they illustrate several important factors which should be borne in mind. These include the physiological effect of prolonged action on the crews; the vulnerability of Israeli tank commanders to small-arms fire and shell splinters; the unfortunate tendency of Patton tanks to catch fire; the superior quality of the Centurion's armour; and the degree of mechanical unreliability of tanks engaged in prolonged action. Other factors to be taken into account are the psychological effect of seeing friends killed—especially in burning tanks—and the obvious tactical advantages of flank and rear attacks as well as surprise.

3

Chronology of the Arab-Israeli Wars 1948-1973

'*Shamir* and *Zebra*. This is *Tirah*. *Sunrays* to the mike. Over!'
'*Tirah*, this is *Shamir*. *Sunray* speaking. Over.'
'*Tirah*, this is *Zebra*. *Sunray* speaking. Over.'
'*Shamir* and *Zebra*. This is *Tirah*. Move now and good luck. Over.'
  The time was 0815 hours, June 5 1967. General Israel Tal, alias *Tirah*, had just given the order to advance to his two subordinates, Colonels Shmuel and Raphoul. The Israeli 'blitzkrieg' was about to break on unsuspecting Egyptian heads, and its armoured spearhead was General Tal's division in the north. Tal, the founder of modern Israeli tank forces, was then 43 years old. He had fought with the Jewish Brigade in North Africa during World War 2 and had risen rapidly through *Zahal*'s ranks after independence in 1948, becoming General Officer Commanding [Israeli] Armoured Corps (GOCAC) in 1964. His formation was now charged with the task of creating the initial Israeli breakthrough, its objective the strategically important rail centre of El Arish with its accompanying airfield. His basic force comprised three brigades equipped with approximately 250 to 300 Centurions and Pattons, facing which was the Egyptian 7th Infantry Division reinforced by an artillery brigade and accompanied by an estimated 100 tanks holding strong defensive positions protected by deep minefields.
  Tal's force was the strongest of the three Israeli spearheads in 1967, the others being the divisions under Generals Abraham Yoffe and Ariel Sharon, operating in the centre and south respectively on a front stretching from Rafa to Kuntilla. Its component forces were 'S' armoured brigade, under Shmuel, 'Z' parachute brigade under Raphoul, and 'M' reserve brigade, under Colonel Men. But before examining their operations in detail, it is worth taking a brief look at the intervening years between the successful War of Independence in 1948 and the events which finally led up to an Israeli pre-emptive strike in 1967.
  Zahal—an abbreviation for *Zwa Haganah Le'Israel*—had its origins, as we have seen, in the various terrorist groups which existed before independence: the *Haganah* and the Begin and Stern gangs. In 1948 the *Haganah* was an estimated 3,100-men strong. It was an organisation which stressed personal initiative and equality, traits very dear to the Jewish character but which caused General Tal considerable problems when he became GOCAC, as we shall see. Prior to independence the *Haganah* had been organised into 'regional commands', three urban and three rural. The *kibbutzim* were strongly manned by trained paramilitary personnel as a safeguard against Arab terrorism, but in the first four weeks of the War of Independence the lack of a proper military command structure made itself abundantly felt. The Jews fought fiercely, but with little co-ordination. The supply situation was usually in a state of chaos. There was no standardisation in

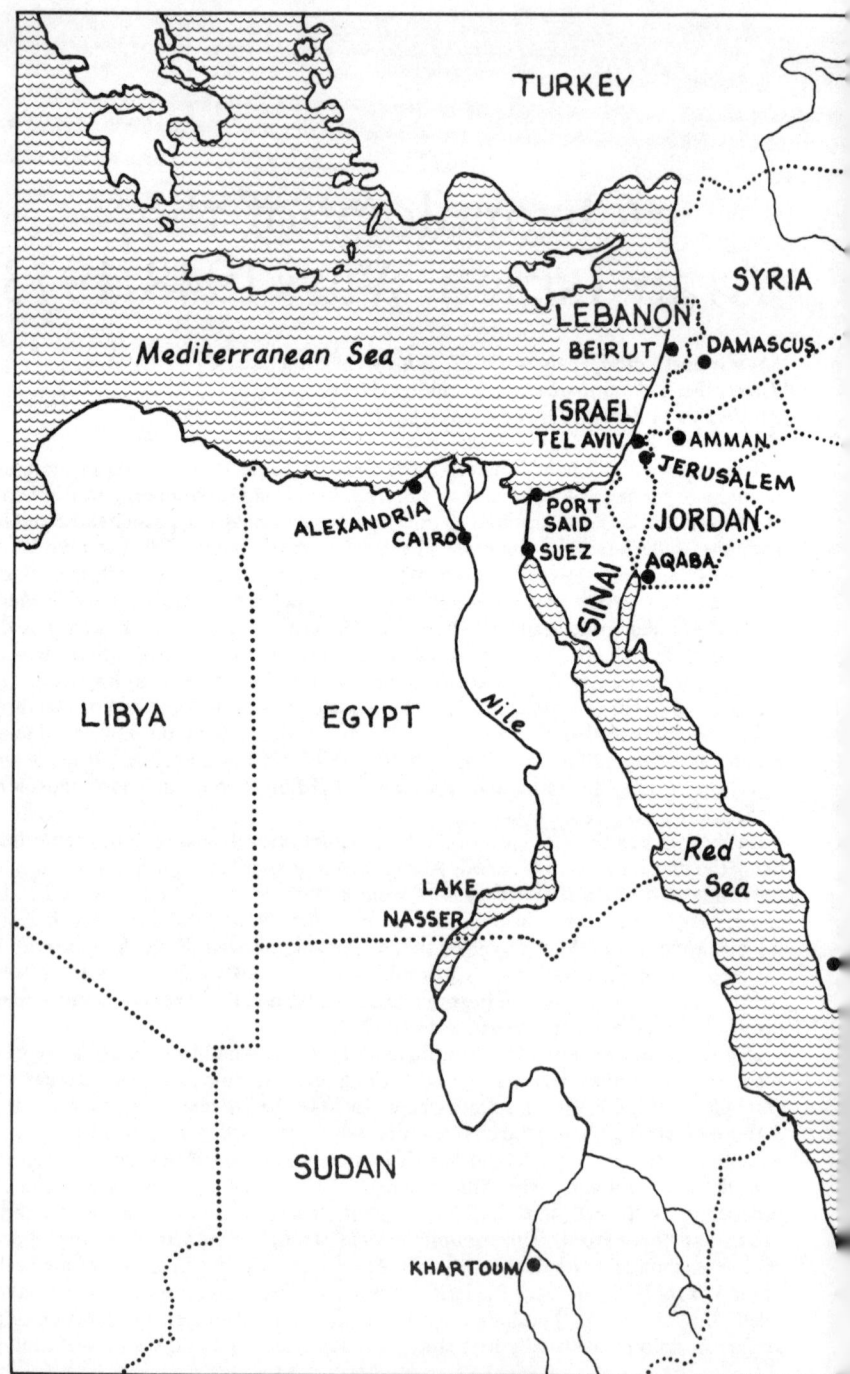

Chronology of the Arab-Israeli Wars 1948-1973

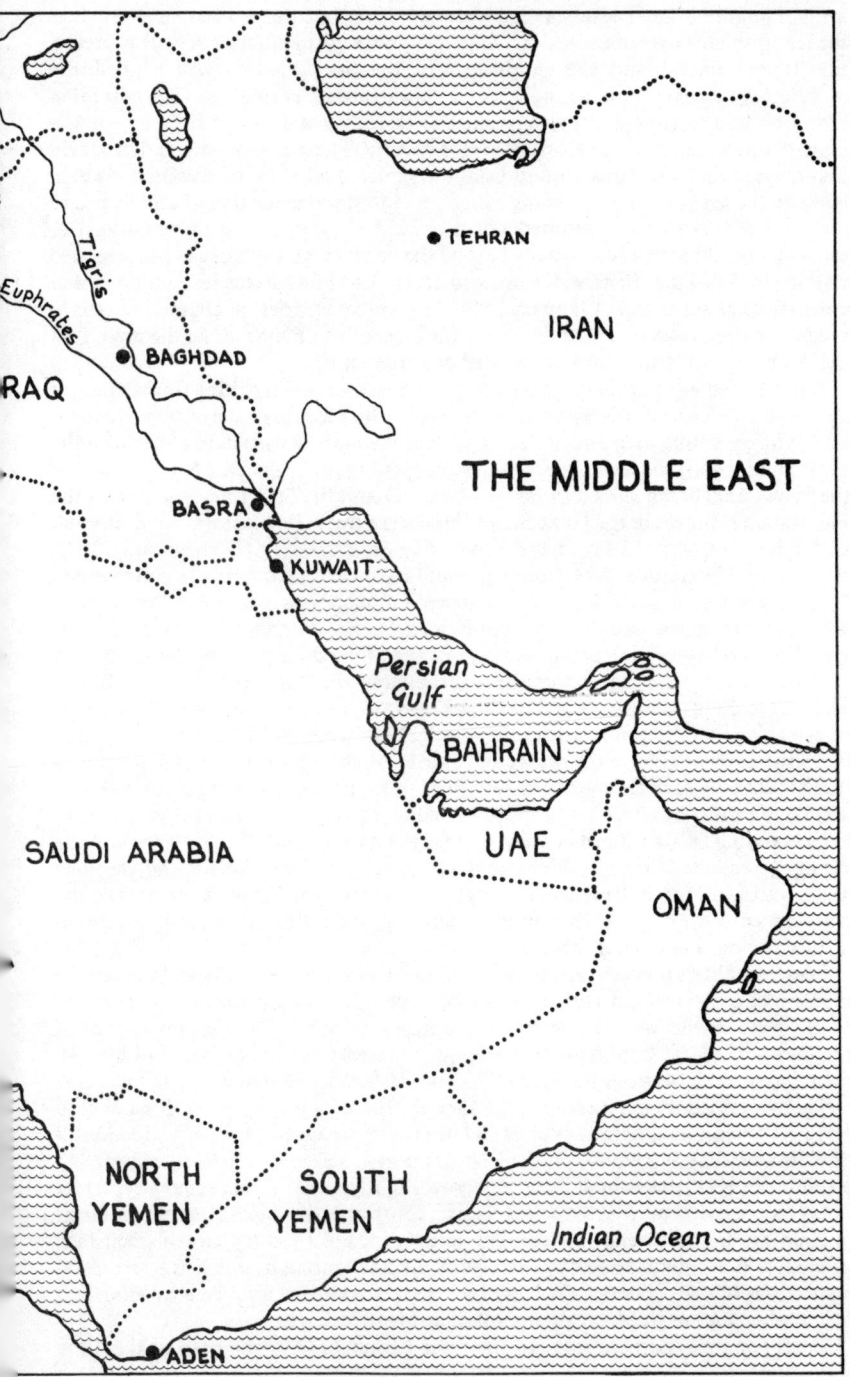

arms or ammunition. There were few heavy weapons, and those there were—such as the few obsolete tanks discussed in Chapter 4—were mishandled. Tactical appreciation lacked finesse and the enthusiasm of the troops led to vast expenditure of priceless ammunition as well as to unwarranted casualties. The situation obviously had to change if the new state of Israel—so far only recognised by the United States, Canada and Russia—was to survive. The answers provided by David Ben-Gurion included conscription from the ranks of eligible immigrants, all men between the ages of 18 and 55 being called up, and standardisation of uniforms and pay. Aided by large arms shipments from abroad, these measures proved effective, the Arab invaders were forced back beyond the borders, and an uneasy peace settled over the Middle East. Britain, France and other abstaining states recognised Israeli independence at the end of January 1949. The Arab countries, of course, refused to accept the *status quo* and have persisted until recently in maintaining the myth that the country with which they are at war does not exist!

But this was only part of the problem. The Israeli borders resulting from the end of the 1948 war carried the inevitable seeds of future conflict: Jerusalem divided, Syrian forces sitting high and dry in the Golan, the narrow strip of land between the coast and Jordan, the lack of an Israeli port opening on to the Red Sea (passage of the Suez Canal being denied to Israeli shipping) and the ludicrous situation of the Palestinian refugees in the Gaza Strip; these were the major factors. As Randolph and Winston Churchill say in their book *The Six Day War* (Heinemann, 1967), 'Surrounded by friends, such frontiers would have been inconvenient. Surrounded by enemies who preached war and extermination it was not likely that such a situation could be indefinitely maintained.' The 'horrible example' of the Palestinian refugees in their squalid camps, maintained for years by the Arabs as a rallying cry for left-wing sympathisers throughout the world (when they could so easily have given their professed 'brothers' the aid they so urgently needed rather than leaving them to rot) is still a sore point. These refugees fled the former state of Palestine in their thousands, as we have seen, to escape *Arab* terrorism; Israel's fragile economy at that time could not afford to support them, although those who wished to return have always been welcomed. Meanwhile, the camps served as an ideal breeding ground for discontent and for the recruitment of volunteers into the various so-called 'Palestinian liberation' organisations. Liberation for who, one may ask? Arabs working in Israel enjoy a higher standard of living on average than the populaces of Egypt, Syria, Iraq or any other Arab state with the possible exception of Jordan and a couple of others.

Leaving politics behind, an immediate military reorganisation began in Israel the moment peace gave them a breathing space. A new defence service law was passed in 1949 whose objects were the creation of a professional but small standing army of regulars and a large but highly trained force of reservists from all walks of life. All men and women between the ages of 18 and 26 had to serve for 2½ or two years respectively in *Zahal*, men between the ages of 27 and 29 for two years. Men were to serve in the reserve until the age of 49 and women to the age of 34; both had, and still have, to spend a day a month plus one 30-day period a year in refresher training. As a result of these laws, which have only been slightly modified subsequently, Israel today has perhaps the most efficient 'citizen army' the world has ever seen in terms of training, initiative and morale. The latter is aided by every Israeli's constant awareness that they are beset by enemies on all sides and that, due to the territorial restrictions of their country, the loss of a campaign which would be a token defeat for another nation would spell annihilation for themselves.

Israel's main enemy throughout the period from 1948 to the present day (one should perhaps view President Sadat's current overtures with caution) has been Egypt, although Syria has perhaps been the most vociferous and implacable. In the early 1950s Egypt underwent two rapid changes of government. First, King Farouk was forced to abdicate and his place taken by General Neguib in 1952; then two years later Neguib was himself overthrown and placed under arrest by Nasser. During this period Egypt's main concern was the eviction of British Protectorate forces from the Suez Canal zone rather than the extermination of the state of Israel. Arab labour strikes and increasing anti-British terrorist activities finally led to the UK signing an agreement with Nasser to evacuate the zone in 1956.

Western hopes that President Nasser might prove a 'moderate' in Middle Eastern politics were shattered by his arms deal with Russia in 1955. The following year, after British forces had evacuated the Canal zone, Britain and America announced that they would no longer continue to finance the Aswan Dam project. Nasser retaliated by nationalising the Suez Canal Company, 7/16 of which was owned by Britain, although its administration was predominantly French. You might say, 'we were not amused.' In the interim, Israel had also become increasingly intolerant of Egyptian terrorist incursions, and the end result was the Sinai Campaign in October 1956.

For the 1956 campaign, the Israelis set themselves three objectives: the destruction of terrorist bases in the Gaza Strip, the destruction of Egyptian bases and airfields in the Sinai, and the opening of the Straits of Tiran to Israeli shipping. The first phase of operations in the south managed to capture the Mitla Pass through a daring paratroop landing supported on the ground by fast-moving armoured and infantry forces. This succeeded in turning the Egyptian flank and cutting off many of their forces. The following day (October 30) Nakhl fell, and on October 31 the British and French began landing invasion forces in the Canal Zone. Simultaneously, an Egyptian armoured force was destroyed by the Israeli Air Force in the south at Bir Salim and on the night of October 31/November 1 Rafa was stormed and captured, cutting off Arab forces in the Gaza Strip. The following evening El Arish fell and the Egyptians ordered the evacuation of the Sinai, being more concerned with handling the Anglo-French invasion. Israeli forces finally succeeded in breaking through the Mitla Pass and the Sinai was theirs, although an Anglo-French ultimatum forced them to halt 16 miles (25 kilometres) east of the Suez Canal. The Israelis, having achieved their main objectives in a brilliant campaign, accordingly turned to mopping up the pockets of terrorist resistance in the Gaza Strip.

However, the UN now intervened and severely censured all three participants in the 1956 campaign. Britain and France were ordered to withdraw their forces by December 22, at great loss to national prestige. Israel was also ordered to withdraw from the Sinai by March 8 1957 and, although forced to give up Sharm el Sheikh, passage of Israeli shipping through the Straits of Tiran was guaranteed by a UN peacekeeping force.

Although the 1956 campaign was thus a diplomatic and strategic blunder by all participants, it had valuable lessons for the Israelis: in the context of this book, the most significant was the daring and original (though unauthorised) handling of Israel's 'S' brigade by Colonel Uri Ben-Ali, which provided the first 'home-grown' example of the disruptive capability of armoured units driving through and operating behind the enemy's lines. Thus, one might say, were the seeds of the 1967 campaign sown. Shabtai Teveth, in what is probably the most dramatic and immediate book ever written on tank warfare since World War 2, *The Tanks of Tammuz* (Weidenfeld & Nicolson, 1969), says: 'Colonel Uri Ben-Ali conceived the idea that it would be possible to bypass the [Abu Agheila] region by using the Deika road... At that part of the route the wadi forms a narrow canyon and at both ends the Egyptians had built fortifications manned by guards. Thus they were safeguarded against surprise attacks from the rear of the Abu Agheila region. As soon as the brigade went into action, Colonel Ben-Ari dispatched a reconnaissance party to see if the way to Deika was negotiable. They discovered that the Egyptians who should have been stationed at Kusseima had fled to the Egyptian rear through the Deika and that their panic-stricken flight had infected the guards...' As a result, Ben-Ari charged his tanks through the pass before the Egyptians could re-man it and brought his brigade squarely across the Egyptian axis of operations, where it proceeded to wreak havoc.

Up to this point the armoured force had been very much *Zahal*'s 'Cinderella' but now, suddenly, everything changed. Successive commanders, notably Generals Haim Bar-Lev (1957-1960), David Elazar (1960-1964) and Israel Tal, gradually began building up an efficient and modern force. New tactics were devised for breaking through the type of defensive positions which Russian advisors were teaching the Egyptians, and urgent attention paid to obtaining more modern equipment (see Chapter 4).

But Nasser was not sitting still. From 1957 he accelerated the purchase of Soviet equipment and welcomed Russian technicians and advisors, while at the same time planning his abortive United Arab Republic, a supposed union of all Arab nations against the 'common enemy'. Created in February 1958, this short-lived coalition soon foundered through internal dissension and distrust; although Syria joined and Iraqi insurgents killed King Feisal, American and British troops safeguarded the Lebanon and Jordan from revolution. Shortly after the UAR fell apart with Syria's withdrawal in 1961, Egypt became involved in a war with Yemen, which turned the heat off Israel for a short space.

The Syrians were still in the running, however, and the next stage in the escalation of hostilities was the so-called 'Tractor War', when Syrian guns and tanks began shooting up Israeli agricultural workers and equipment on the border *kibbutzim*. The Israelis retaliated by placing tank units in the threatened areas, and two years of intermittent tank duels across the border followed until the Six Day War intervened.

This was a significant period for the development of both Israeli and Arab armoured forces. The latter were acquiring more and more modern Soviet equipment, together with the usual complement of advisors, and were becoming increasingly dependent on Russian technology and tactics—neither of which, as it turned out, were to prove really suited to the Middle East situation. For their part, the Israelis were concentrating on improving their standards of gunnery and maintenance, both of which had been shown up in a very bad light during the early stages of the 'Tractor War'. The basic problem, as analysed by General Tal, was the traditional Israeli personal independence. Every tank crew had its own methods, training was often inadequate, and every junior officer with a bright idea immediately began promulgating his (often erroneous) concept. General Tal clamped down. Dress, drill and training were standardised, gunnery practice was systematised, and proper maintenance rigidly enforced. There were outcries about the infringement of personal liberties, but Tal pointed out that the maintenance of an effective mechanised army, with all its sophisticated equipment, demanded teamwork, almost to the point of unquestioning conformity, rather than individualism. Despite initial resentment, his ideas began to justify themselves in the border clashes. Tanks no longer stalled or shed their tracks as a result of faulty maintenance, and gunners no longer wasted dozens of rounds of expensive armour-piercing ammunition as a result of incorrectly adjusted sights. The Syrians ceased encroaching too closely on the Israeli border, and the Israeli tank crews had to practice their skills on targets five miles or more away.

So we approach the critical year of 1967. Border incidents had been hotting up, and in November 1966 Israel launched a massive reprisal raid against Jordan, whom she accused of harbouring *El Fatah* terrorists. Then in April Israel launched an air strike against Syrian artillery which had been bombarding *kibbutzim* workers, and in the mêlée shot down six Syrian MiGs (see Chapter 15). In the spring of 1967 Egypt, who had earlier signed a new defence agreement with Syria, ordered the removal of the UN peace-keeping force from the Canal zone. Without waiting for U Thant's reaction, Egyptian forces began taking over UN posts, and on May 19 the Secretary-General acceded to this *fait accompli* and ordered the immediate withdrawal of the Brazilian, Canadian, Danish, Indian, Norwegian, Swedish and Yugoslavian troops who had so long suffered the heat of the desert for such a forlorn task.

The next step was the closure of the Straits of Tiran to Israeli shipping on the pretence that these waters—guaranteed, like the Dardanelles and the Bosporus under the 1958 Geneva Convention, open under international law to all shipping—fell within Egypt's 12-mile zone. Israeli attempts to acquire effective international repudiation of Egypt's claims were met by Arab threats of oil embargoes, and it rapidly became clear that, regardless of public sympathy, this was a problem Israel would have to solve on her own. Nasser had already ordered the full mobilisation of the Egyptian army and, on May 22, had stated publicly that if Israel wanted war, then *ahalan we-sahalan* ('welcome').

Events came to a head at the end of May when King Hussein of Jordan flew unannounced to Cairo and signed an unprecedented defence agreement with Nasser (there being little love lost between the two men or their countries), and the following day Iraq agreed to provide military support in the event of a war between Jordan and Israel. With her four major enemies mobilising on to a war footing and obviously anxious to provoke a showdown, Israel could prevaricate no longer, nor could she afford to wait for her enemies' preparations to be completed: she had to strike first.

This is where we came in. The balance of power in the Middle East at this time was approximately as follows: Israel 264,000 troops (20 per cent regulars and 80 per cent reservists) with around 800 tanks and 300 combat aircraft of various types; Egypt 240,000 troops, 1,200 tanks and 450 aircraft; Syria 50,000 troops, 400 tanks and 120 aircraft; Jordan 50,000 troops, 200 tanks and 40 aircraft; and Iraq 70,000 troops, 400 tanks and 200 aircraft. Standing on the sidelines were the Lebanon, with 12,000 troops, 80 tanks and 18 aircraft; Saudi Arabia with 50,000 troops, 100 tanks and 20 aircraft; Kuwait with 5,000 troops, 24 tanks and nine aircraft; and Algeria with 60,000 troops, 100 tanks and 100 aircraft. Surrounded, with indefensible borders, Israel had no option but to launch a pre-emptive strike. But Israeli leadership was divided: Prime Minister Levi Eshkol was a man of peace and wished to avoid war at all costs, while David Ben-Gurion's followers were 'hawks'. One of the hawks was Moshe Dayan, whose exploits had made him a popular Israeli hero. Gaoled at the age of 24 for his activities in the *Haganah*, he had later served with the British during World War 2 and lost an eye during a commando raid, but was chiefly revered for the role he had played as Chief of Staff (the excutive head of *Zahal*) during the 1956 Sinai Campaign. Now, in 1967, the public demanded his reinstatement to deal with the new emergency and, on June 1, Eshkol reluctantly agreed to Dayan's appointment as Minister of Defence.

The remarkable efficiency of Israel's 'citizen army' was to be proved time and again over the next few days, but in many ways its most dramatic expression came in the speed of the call-up. Brigade commanders summoned battalion commanders who telephoned or raced round to see company commanders who organised their sergeants to notify the men—and women. Shopkeepers, accountants, typists, journalists, schoolteachers, mechanics, salesmen—they all responded to the call, went home to change into their uniforms, and presented themselves ready for action. Issued with arms and ammunition, they then proceeded to wait. Gradually the tension mounted. Shabtai Teveth visited the 14th Battalion of General Tal's 'S' Brigade at the end of May:

'The crew had finished greasing the tank. The 0.5 mm [sic] Browning machine-gun had been cleaned; the crew's packs were attached to the turret. Two of the crew were playing draughts, another couple were reading newspapers. A corner of the netting was used as a kitchen and coffee was boiling in a tin on a spirit stove. I asked the men how they felt.

' "Fed up waiting," was the sergeant's comment. "Time's come to fight."

' "And you?" I asked the others.

' "Same," they said. "Fed up waiting."

'There was no doubt in their minds as to the outcome. They could not lose.'

The Israeli Cabinet finally took the decision to attack first during the long night of June 3/4, and the time of waiting was over. The air strike, described separately in this book by Mike Spick, went in at 0745 hours on June 5 1967, and half an hour later the tanks and armoured half-tracks began to roll. It would not be a piece of cake, and there would be casualties; but it was to prove far easier than anyone had dared predict.

This is not the place to discuss the naval side of the conflict, although brief details are given in Chapter 17 for those of you who wish to introduce this side of things into your campaigning. In June 1967 there were only two events of significance. One was an Israeli naval raid on Port Said which had the effect of inducing the Egyptians to withdraw their 18 missile-carrying warships (capable of reaching Tel Aviv) to the comparative safety of Alexandria; and the second was the embarrassing Israeli attack on the American electronic spy ship USS *Liberty*, a simple case of mistaken identity, understandable in a tense situation, but nonetheless tragic. The Egyptians, so far as I know, only ventured on the naval offensive once, with three submarines which were rapidly detected, depth-charged and sent packing, although none were sunk.

So one returns to the Sinai, a harsh and barren wasteland broken only by the occasional clump of scrub grass, scoured clean by a constant burning wind and inhabited solely by the odd nomadic bedouin. Like all desert landscapes, it appears virtually flat to the uneducated eye, but the successful tank commander is the one who can spot the shallow depressions and low ridges which will enable him to enter into a hull-down position, and who can recognise from afar the deceptively smooth areas of soft sand which will hinder his vehicle's advance. Israeli tank commanders, like their earlier counterparts in the Afrika Korps and 8th Army—and unlike Arab tank commanders, who go into action 'buttoned down'—have the slow-moving, distant gaze of men accustomed to 'the blue'. Like the sea, the desert is a friend to be treated with respect.

On June 5 1967, however, the Sinai was crowded. By this time the Egyptians had concentrated no fewer than seven divisions in the arena: 4th Armoured, 2nd, 3rd, 6th and 7th Infantry, 20th PLA and a special armoured *kampfgruppe* of divisional strength without a number. Against these, the Israelis had precisely three divisions, one armoured, one mechanised and the third reserve (Yoffe's). For organisational details please refer to Chapter 10. Total Egyptian forces were approximately 100,000

Chronology of the Arab-Israeli Wars 1948-1973

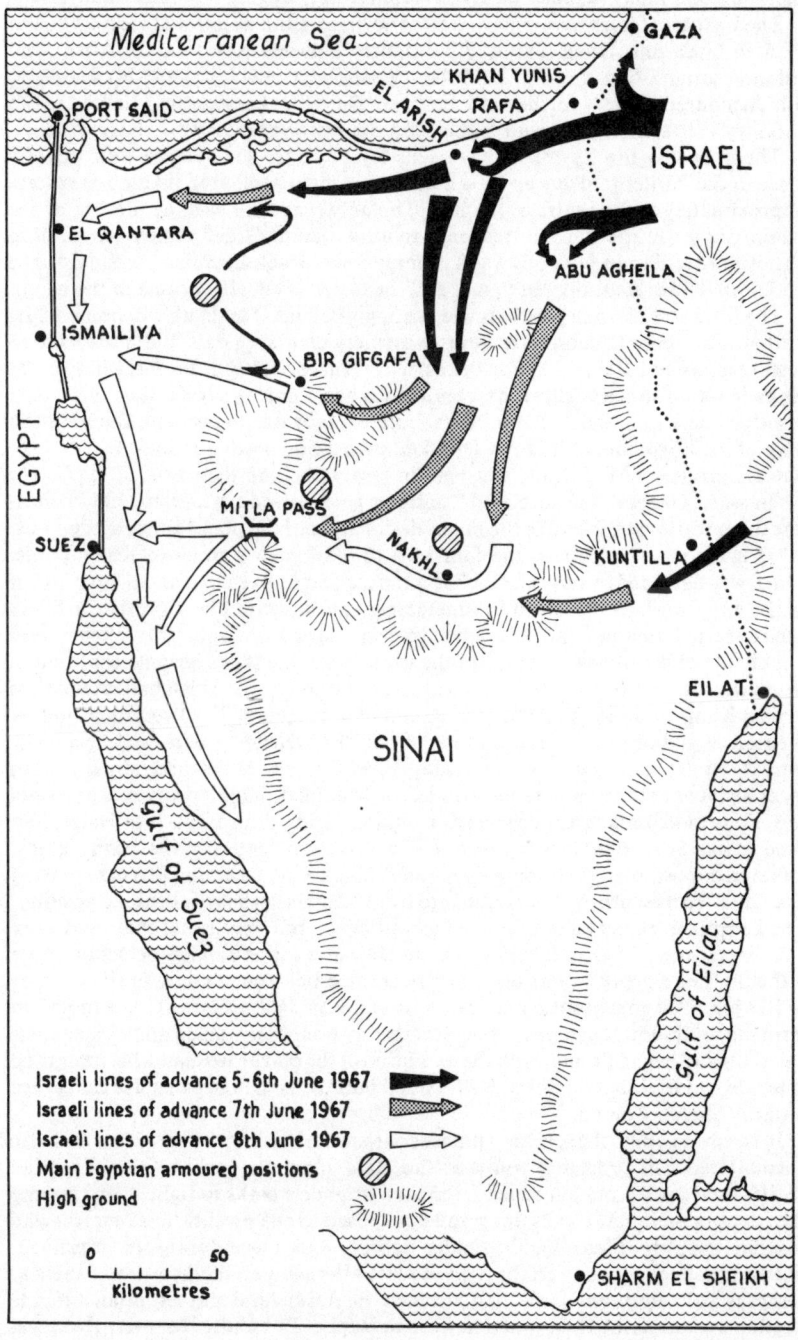

men and 950 tanks, against an Israeli strength of roughly one third that total.

The Egyptian forces were deployed from north to south as follows (see map): 20th PLA in Gaza and Khan Yunis, 7th Infantry between Rafa and El Arish, 2nd Infantry around Abu Agheila, 3rd Infantry between Gebel Libni and Bir Hassneh, 4th Armoured slightly to the west between Bir Gifgafa and Bir Thamada, 6th Infantry between Kuntilla and Nakhl and the *kampfgruppe* west of Kuntilla.

Theoretically, the Egyptians were sensibly deployed for defence with infantry close to the border to delay an attack and their main armoured division in reserve approximately at the centre of the line. The only real error was the placing of the *kampfgruppe* in the south in response to an apparent Israeli armoured build-up opposite Kuntilla. In fact, this was a dummy force which Egyptian reconnaissance had been deliberately allowed to see, and the main Israeli effort came in the north.

The Rafa and El Arish positions were strongly defended in depth with minefields, barbed wire, infantry positions, reserve artillery emplacements and an armoured reserve of around 100 tanks. For the attack, General Tal split his force in two: 'S' Brigade was to attack northwards, capturing Khan Yunis and Rafa, then move west towards Sheikh Zuweid; while 'Z' Parachute Brigade was to outflank the southern edge of the Egyptian 7th Infantry Division, then swing north into their rear to take out the artillery. 'M' Brigade was held in reserve behind the paras.

'In war,' General Tal once said, 'nothing goes according to plan, but there is one thing you must stick to: to the major designation of the plan.' How right he was. 'S' Brigade struck north on the four-mile (6.5-kilometre) route to Khan Yunis, which was defended by several PLA battalions, a 25 pdr battalion and a battalion of tanks and anti-tank guns, and immediately ran into trouble. Egyptian artillery shells started falling, and the advance was slowed by anti-tank ditches and minefields while, when they reached the town itself, the tanks became confused in the narrow streets. S/14 Battalion ran into trouble and S/10, which had intended to bypass Khan Yunis to the south, was summoned to its aid. The two groups met at the railway station, by which time most of the PLA defenders were beating a hasty retreat, and pushed on towards Rafa. However, six tanks had already been incapacitated and 35 commanders killed or wounded, mainly from machine-gun fire. Four more tanks were damaged by mines during the approach to Rafa. This time it was S/10 Battalion which had the easy task, entering the town against minimal opposition to find some Egyptian soldiers actually sitting in a cafe playing draughts! To its south, S/14 had run into trouble against a heavily fortified position. The Egyptians were well dug-in and camouflaged, and were firing their anti-tank guns in salvoes of five to increase the chances of a hit and make detection more difficult. The Egyptians put up a stiff resistance but were rapidly outflanked by S/10 while S/14 engaged their attention frontally and a third Israeli force moved in from the south. Finding tanks in the rear, the Egyptians once again abandoned their positions and began fleeing, with the exception of the odd brave man who attempted to tackle a tank with a bazooka. Both Israeli battalions then began a headlong race towards Sheikh Zuweid.

In the meanwhile, the southern pincer consisting of 'Z' and 'M' Brigades had also encountered stiff resistance south of the Rafa Junction, including an Egyptian IS-III heavy tank battalion which forced the Brigade's tanks to fight them, leaving the paras in their half-tracks dangerously exposed to enemy anti-tank, mortar and machine-gun fire. Fierce hand-to-hand fighting took place during the afternoon, but eventually the paras won through. By late afternoon on the first day of the war General Tal's northern force had reached El Arish, and the Egyptian brigade positions south of the Rafa junction were in Raphoul's hands. However, there was an unpleasant surprise in store for, although they did not know it at the time, the Israeli attack had completely missed the southernmost of the Egyptian brigades. The first inkling of this came when helicopters, brought in to evacuate Israeli wounded, came under intense fire from the ground. An attack was launched immediately and fighting for this position lasted until well after dark.

Further south, General Yoffe had had a much easier day. Advancing through an area of deep sand dunes which the Egyptians had thought impassable, his division covered some 60 miles, reaching the vicinity of Bir Lahfan at around 1800 hours without a single casualty. Here, however, they encountered Egyptian reinforcements being sent north towards El Arish. Fighting between the two groups continued throughout the night of the 5th/6th, but several Egyptian tanks were destroyed and in the morning an Israeli air raid sent the remainder packing, hotly pursued by a group of Yoffe's tanks.

General Sharon's command had been split into two, one force advancing parallel to Yoffe towards Abu Agheila in the centre, the other in the south opposite Kuntilla. Abu Agheila was a vital communications centre which had to be captured before the Israeli advance could proceed further, and naturally was heavily defended by the Egyptian 2nd Infantry Division reinforced with 80 to 90 tanks and six artillery regiments. General Sharon's plan of attack involved a complex interleaving of all arms: artillery to pin the Egyptians frontally, four attack columns composed alternately of armour and infantry, one to the north, two in the centre and one to the south, followed by a helicopter assault on the rear Egyptian artillery positions. It was a bold plan and would make an ideal wargame.

By 1500 hours on the 5th, Sharon's forces were in position about five miles (eight kilometres) from the Abu Agheila defences. The northern column ran into Egyptian tanks which forced them to fall back, but a renewed assault broke through and by late afternoon had reached the Abu Agheila-El Arish road. After dark they pushed further forward, ready to strike southwards to support the main attack on Abu Agheila itself. In the meanwhile, the southern prong of Sharon's force had advanced to the Kusseima-Abu Agheila road so that, by nightfall, the Egyptians were cut off from all their lines of communication. At dusk the helicopters landed a battalion of paras behind the Egyptian positions, whose attention had been engaged during the afternoon by the Israeli artillery and the two frontal columns. Shortly before 2300 hours the main attack began: tanks from the front and down from the north, paras against the rear of the artillery positions and mechanised infantry from the south. There was heavy hand-to-hand fighting in the trenches, but in five hours most of the Egyptian positions were in Israeli hands. The tanks had actually achieved little up to this point, being unable to fire accurately at night, but as dawn broke they moved forward to engage the Egyptian armour and a fierce two-hour battle ensued. By 0600 Sharon was able to order a further advance towards Kusseima.

In the north, General Tal had run into problems outside El Arish in the heavily defended Jiradi area. A small unit of tanks had succeeded in breaking through due to their speed and the element of surprise, but the Egyptians regrouped behind them and a fierce battle took place during which Major Elad, commander of S/14 Battalion, was killed. Even then, after the battalion finally broke through, the Egyptians once again fell in behind them and closed the gap. 'M' Brigade was unable to come to the aid of 'S' Brigade, having run out of fuel for its tanks, so Tal ordered 'S' Brigade's mechanised infantry battalion—which had been engaged in mopping-up operations around Rafa—to press forward. Their task was made doubly difficult by the dozens of wrecked and burned-out vehicles which littered the road, and by heavy traffic jams. Arriving at midnight, they moved straight into the attack, and after four hours of heavy fighting the position was taken for the third time. On this occasion, however, the Israeli forces did not intend to allow the Egyptians to retake it, and dug in.

Unaware of the drama taking place behind them, the tanks of S/10 and S/14 Battalions which had earlier broken through the Jiradi were in El Arish, and by 0400 hours on June 6 had captured the airfield. At daybreak Tal split his division, half being diverted south towards Bir Lahfan to link up with Yoffe's forces, the remainder pressing straight on towards Qantara, on the Suez Canal, which they reached on Tuesday afternoon. Deep sand dunes aided the defenders at Bir Lahfan, and Tal's tanks had a hard fight before they managed to break through and link up with Yoffe's forces around midday. From Bir Lahfan the two forces planned to move south towards Jebel Libni, after which Tal's troops would strike west via Bir Gifgafa towards Ismailia while Yoffe would strike further south first via Bir Hassneh and Bir Thamada before heading for the Mitla Pass and Suez. Simultaneously, Sharon would strike down from Abu Agheila towards Nakhl in the south to link up with his troops pressing west from Kuntilla, then also swing west towards the Mitla Pass.

Wednesday, the third day of the campaign, was decisive. After a short, sharp tank engagement at Jebel Libni, Tal's forces sped west towards Bir Gifgafa. Yoffe pressed on rapidly through Bir Hassneh towards Bir Thamada to block off Egyptian forces retreating west in the southern sector of the front, and reached the entrance to the vital Mitla Pass at around 1800 hours. Half of his tanks had run out of fuel and had to be towed by those which were still mobile, both firing as they went. Tal established a blocking position at Bir Gifgafa. There was no escape for the Egyptian tanks being pursued by Sharon: they would have to fight.

After a pause during Wednesday night to allow the troops—most of whom had been on the go since early Monday morning—to sleep, Sharon continued his long southward trek towards Nakhl. En route he came across an amazing sight: an entire brigade of Egyptian IS-III tanks abandoned in the middle of the desert. Their commander had heard of the Israeli successes and, deciding discretion was the better part of valour, had fled with his men in the brigade's half-tracks!

At Nakhl, Sharon laid a trap for the Egyptian forces retreating from Kuntilla. Leaving the bulk of his tanks deployed on the eastern outskirts of the town, he took the remainder in a long loop to the north-east. The Egyptians ran into the blocking force at Nakhl and were then taken in the rear by Sharon's own group.

At Bir Gifgafa Tal's blocking force of two battalions had a more difficult task against an Egyptian armoured brigade, whose assault was actually supported by Egyptian ground-attack aircraft. The situation here became critical during the night when a new force of Egyptian T-54s arrived and blundered into the Israeli positions. The light Israeli AMX-13 tanks were no match for the heavier T-54s, and after a couple of hours the battalion received orders to withdraw slightly, until it could be reinforced by heavier armour. The arrival of a medium tank company redressed the balance, allowing the Israelis to re-occupy their original positions, and Tal then sent a further armoured brigade southwards to attack the Egyptians in the rear. Outnumbered, and having already lost several tanks, the Egyptian brigade was soon overwhelmed.

Yoffe's force at the Mitla Pass, a solitary brigade under Colonel Iska, also found itself in difficulties as thousands of Egyptian troops tried to pour through the 15-mile (23-kilometre) gap towards Suez, and by 2200 hours on Wednesday evening was surrounded and in grave danger of being overrun. A second brigade was ordered to make a night march to relieve Iska. Advancing through the darkness it suddenly found itself accompanied by a large force of Egyptian tanks moving in the same direction. The Egyptians took the Israelis for friendly forces in the darkness, but the Israelis, of course, knew that they had no other tanks in the vicinity and began shooting up the thoroughly confused Egyptians.

The arrival of the fresh brigade was a godsend to Iska's men, who had been fighting almost continuously now for 72 hours and were running very low on ammunition. Relieving them in the middle of a pitched battle was not easy, but was finally accomplished on Thursday morning. Unable to break through the stubborn Israeli positions, and unable to retreat because of Sharon's approach, several Egyptian tanks actually tried to climb the steep walls of the pass, where they became stuck 'like flies on a wall', in General Yoffe's words.

During the afternoon Yoffe's new brigade battled its way through to the western end of the pass (the canal side) where they encountered strongly defended Egyptian positions blocking their further advance. Yoffe ordered a daring night attack, his tanks charging forwards with headlights blazing, and the petrified Egyptians abandoned their positions and fled. By 0200 hours on Friday morning, June 9, Yoffe's troops had reached the canal. One armoured brigade was sent north towards Ismailia, but ran into heavy opposition from Egyptian tanks occupying hull-down positions behind the crests of dunes. The Israelis countered by splitting their force, two companies moving through the dunes and the remainder of the tanks advancing along the road to draw the Egyptians into revealing their positions. By this method the small Israeli force succeeded in destroying some 70 Egyptian tanks for the loss of only ten to themselves by the time they reached the canal facing Ismailia.

On Thursday night Egypt asked for a cease-fire. In one of the fastest and most decisive military operations of all time, Israeli forces had succeeded in breaking the proud Egyptian army, capturing over 700 tanks and 5,000 officers (other ranks, after being given food, water and medical attention and disarmed, were allowed to swim home across the canal, where a large number were actually machine-gunned by their own troops).

Earlier, Jordanian forces in Jerusalem and on the West Bank had opened fire on Israeli positions shortly after they received news of the Israeli offensive in Sinai, and Jordanian forces moved forward to occupy Mount Scopus shortly after midday on the 5th, followed by Government House in the early afternoon. Israeli tanks and paratroopers began moving forward, and by 1600 hours had retaken Government House. The heavily defended Police School was a different story. Occupied by around 200 fanatical members of the Arab Legion, it took 500 Israeli paras several hours to capture, and did not fall until nearly 0400 hours on Tuesday morning, after the Arabs had lost more than half their men.

By 1000 hours on Tuesday morning most of the fighting in the demilitarised zone was over, and the Israelis now turned their attention to the Old City. This proved more difficult as neither side wished to use heavy weapons which could damage the historic and religious sites, and in the ensuing small-arms fire-fight the Israelis were at a disadvantage, having to move through the open whilst the Arabs were well dug-in. To the north-east of the Old City, however, Mount Scopus finally fell to the Israelis after the collapse of the Police School.

On Wednesday morning the Israelis attacked again, the regiment on Mount Scopus advancing uphill to Augusta Victoria, while infantry attacked the Old City again. This time heavy weapons were employed, although great care was taken to miss the Holy Places, and by 1000 hours the Temple Mount and the Wailing Wall were in Israeli hands. Defence Minister Dayan visited the latter in the afternoon and left a prayer for 'peace in Israel'.

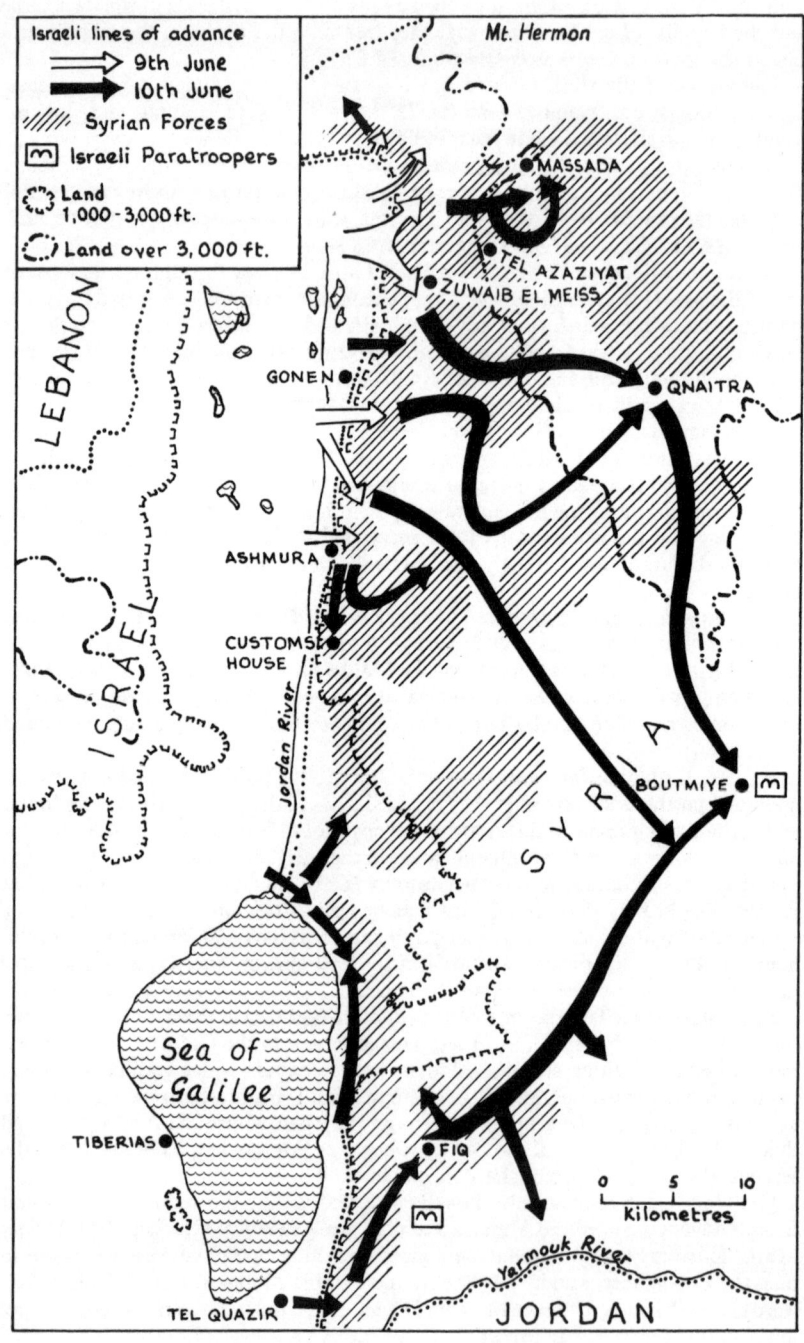

With Jerusalem securely in Israeli hands, the IDF was ready to complete operations on the West Bank. There had only been minor action here on the 5th, Israeli forces moving down from the north in the direction of Jenin. On the 6th a further attack in the north from Sandala had reached Jenin and Qabatiya, a third force had advanced eastward from Kalkilya, and a fourth had reached Ramallah, just north of Jerusalem, and taken it in a night attack.

In the north around Jenin the Jordanians had a strong force of old M47 Patton tanks, but were left in a difficult situation because the Israeli Air Force made repeated attacks on their supply columns. In the end nearly half the tanks had to be abandoned when they ran out of fuel, ammunition or both.

Now, on the Wednesday, the road seemed clear for the projected Israeli pincer movement, General Elazar's forces moving down from the north, Colonel Uri Ben-Ali's moving east and north from Ramallah. Ben-Ali pressed on to Jericho, which fell after a short battle—trumpets were not needed—while south of Jerusalem Colonel Amitai broke through the Jordanian positions and advanced on Bethlehem and Hebron, both of which fell after token fights during the afternoon. General Elazar's forces in the north moved down through Tubas to Nablus, where they met up with part of Ben-Ali's command and swung east and west to finish mopping up Jordanian troops still on the West Bank. By dusk on June 7 this phase of operations was completed. Jerusalem and the whole of the West Bank were in Israeli hands while their armoured forces in the Sinai had reached the Suez Canal.

In the north the Syrians remained strangely quiet, seemingly content to shell Israeli positions from the security of the Golan Heights and make no more than tentative thrusts with small units at isolated Israeli *kibbutzim*. It was not until Thursday of the war that the Israelis turned their attention to this sector. The key to the Syrian positions was the Golan Heights, defended by complex fortifications some ten miles (16 kilometres) in depth with dug-in tank, artillery and Katyusha rocket batteries. The Israeli answer was the Air Force. For two solid days they pounded the Syrian bunkers. Anything in the open was totally demolished, but the bunkers themselves had been well-designed and were impervious to both bombs and napalm. In the end it was the defenders' morale which cracked under the merciless hammering—one raid every ten minutes—and by Saturday morning the Syrian troops were abandoning their bunkers in droves. Meanwhile, on Friday morning the first Israeli ground attack had been launched against the steep slopes above Kefar Szold, bulldozers leading to clear a path for the following tanks and half-tracks. The engineers suffered heavy casualties, especially from well dug-in tanks, which eventually had to be destroyed by infantry armed with hand grenades. But after three hours' vicious hand-to-hand fighting in the trenches and bunkers, the Israelis proved victorious.

Two subsidiary attacks further south, in the Gonen and Ashmura vicinities, were also successful, and by nightfall the Israelis had two footholds on the Heights. On the following morning both forces struck out towards Qnaitra through the difficult rocky terrain, reaching it by 1300 hours and capturing it in an hour's fighting. Meanwhile, in the south, a further attack by infantry and tanks up the Yarmouk Valley succeeded in pinning the Syrians while a paratroop force was dropped by helicopter in their rear. By Saturday evening the vital Heights were in Israeli hands, and both sides accepted the cease-fire which the UN Security Council had been calling for since Friday morning.

The war left Israel in a stronger position than at any time since her declaration of independence in 1948. She had possession of Jerusalem and the West Bank of the Jordan; she had thrown the Syrians out of their dominating position on the Golan

Heights, safeguarding her *kibbutzim* from further shelling; she had practically destroyed the Egyptian army and established a vital buffer zone against future aggression in the Sinai; and she had captured Sharm El-Sheik, giving her access to the Red Sea.

The campaign showed up a number of important military factors, not all of them new. First, the vital aspects of surprise, maintaining the initiative, keeping your opponent off balance, and achieving local superiority in order to achieve breakthroughs. Second, it reinforced the Israeli philosophy that wars must be short, since a small country with a population of only 2½ million cannot sustain a long campaign or heavy casualties; and that they must be carried into the enemy's territory. Third, it showed up the battlefield superiority of the individual Israeli soldier, a superiority created by training, discipline and a determination to win through the knowledge that the alternative would mean the total annihilation of his country. Fourth, the superiority of Israeli armoured fighting vehicles, even against more modern Soviet equipment. Fifth, the importance of achieving aerial supremacy as rapidly as possible. Sixth, the need to maintain objectives and avoid being sidetracked. Seventh, the importance of co-operation between the various arms—tanks, infantry and artillery, supported by the Air Force. And eighth, that a motivated 'citizen army' can prevail against highly trained regulars. For the various Arab troops were well-trained, beyond a shadow of doubt. Unfortunately, they had been trained predominantly in Russian defensive tactics and, when these failed due to the speed of the Israeli operations and the sudden appearance of enemy forces in their rear, the average Arab reaction was to run. Part of this was due to poor leadership. Except in the Jordanian forces, officers kept very much to themselves and scorned the 'peasants' they commanded. The campaign produced many examples of Arab officers deserting their men and leaving them to fend for themselves. Under such circumstances courage alone cannot prevail—and it must be stressed that many individual Arab soldiers did fight with guts and determination.

But if the territory gained by Israel in the Six Day War gave her, for the first time, a genuine strategic option and a euphoric sense of confidence in *Zahal*, the lessons of the conflict were not lost on the Arabs. Thus, the 1973 *Yom Kippur* or *Ramadan* War needs really to be seen as a continuation of the events of 1967 after both sides had paused to reorganise and re-equip. With the territorial advantages she had gained, Israel could afford to let an enemy strike first (as actually happened), making the Arab state concerned the aggressor and giving Israel increased bargaining power in the UN; or she could strike first from a position of strength. The situation was not unlike that faced by Napoleon in 1809 after the creation of the Confederation of the Rhine. On the other hand, the fact that the Sinai was now Israeli rather than Egyptian-controlled meant that the 'early warning' period of an attack was considerably diminished, forcing Israel to maintain a stronger border force than in the past.

The intervening years between 1968 and 1970 are generally known as the 'War of Attrition', a period during which terrorist raids into Israel were maintained while troops on the borders, especially along the Suez Canal, were kept on a constant, wearying, state of alert by intermittent Egyptian artillery fire.

The basic threat which the Israelis had to face was that of a strong Egyptian amphibious operation across the canal which would give them a bridge-head in the Sinai. As usual, there were two schools of thought regarding the best way of countering this menace, one arguing for a continuously manned line along the whole length of the canal, the other for light early warning observation posts supported from the rear by strong mobile reserves. Generals Tal and Sharon supported the latter option, Generals Gavish and Bar-Lev the former. The 'Maginot Line' mentality won and General Bar-Lev began constructing his positions—heavily fortified posts some seven miles (11 kilometres) apart along the whole length of the canal, interspersed with lighter observation bunkers, interconnected with numerous roads and communication trenches and supported with tanks and artillery. The basic fault in this 'Bar-Lev Line' was that the Israeli defence posts were only lightly manned and generally incapable of withstanding a concerted assault. Also, the two armoured brigades permanently stationed along the canal were too thinly spread to exercise a decisive counter-attack and the third brigade held in reserve had too far to move and was insufficiently strong.

The War of Attrition began escalating when the Egyptians began sending commando groups across the canal to attack individual Israeli outposts in 1969, to which the Israelis retaliated in kind with their own commandos and paras. The artillery duel hotted up, the opposing air forces began to come into play, and Nasser accelerated the deployment of SAM anti-aircraft missile sites behind the canal.

In August 1970 both sides agreed to a cease-fire, but the Egyptians had an ulterior motive. Freed from the harassment of Israeli artillery bombardment and commando raids, they were able to establish SAM sites very close to the canal, with the result that Israeli aircraft approaching within 12 miles (19 kilometres) of their own frontier were in jeopardy.

At the end of 1970 two events which were to have far-reaching results occurred: President Nasser died on September 28, and King Hussein of Jordan quashed an internal Palestinian revolt, which restored tranquility to the West Bank.

The new Egyptian leader, Anwar Sadat, projected a totally different international image to that of Nasser; in his public statements, and in his extensive negotiations with the Nixon régime, he gave the impression of really wanting to find a solution to the Middle East problem, and even of being prepared to recognise the state of Israel. But during the first two years of his rule President Sadat succeeded in playing off the Americans and the Russians against each other, signing a new arms treaty with the latter while promising the former that Soviet advisors would be expelled once agreement had been reached on an Israeli withdrawal from the Suez Canal. However, the two super-powers were approaching a new situation of détente in the spring of 1972, and the arms which Sadat had asked for at the end of 1971 had been diverted to India to aid in their own war with Pakistan. In July of the same year Sadat asked the Soviet Union to remove its forces and advisors from Egyptian soil, to the satisfaction of Egyptian army commanders who had become tired of the Russian technicians' overbearing superciliousness. However, this was short-lived; in October President Assad of Syria flew to Moscow and negotiated a *rapprochement*. The Soviet advisors were re-admitted and Soviet warships allowed free access to Egyptian ports. A new arms deal was signed under which the Soviet Union agreed to supply Egypt with *Scud* tactical missiles capable of reaching Israeli population centres from Egypt itself.

By April 1973 a new war seemed imminent: Sadat told a newspaper reporter in an interview that 'the time has come for a decision . . . the time has come for a shock . . . everything in this country is now being mobilised in earnest for the resumption of the battle, which is now inevitable . . .' World opinion considered Sadat's statement an extreme form of brinkmanship, and even the highly efficient Israeli secret service did not believe that Egypt was yet ready for another war. They gave 1975 as the most probable date.

The man in charge of Egyptian military preparations for the coming conflict was

General Ahmed Ismail, a clear-thinking leader who has assimilated the lessons of the Six Day War as well as any Israeli commander. He realised that, in order to be successful, the Egyptians had to achieve surprise, aerial supremacy and concentration in great force in a very short space of time.

In May 1973 Israeli intelligence noticed a strong Egyptian build-up of forces behind the canal and General Elazar, by this time Chief of Staff, ordered a partial Israeli mobilisation. Nothing happened, however, and the Israeli forces stood down, but the alert had cost several million unnecessary pounds and would be remembered in October when a similar situation appeared to be brewing.

The careful preparations continued throughout that summer. Joint plans for the war were discussed by Egyptian and Syrian leaders; King Hussein, who had been somewhat ostracised by the other Arab leaders after his quashing of the Palestinian revolt, was brought back into the fold—though only as a silent partner; and talks took place between Egypt and the oil-producing Gulf states, including Saudi Arabia, regarding the introduction of embargoes aimed at Western powers friendly to Israel.

Despite the vast strides in training, morale and equipment which had been made in the Egyptian army since 1967, their task in 1973 was not an easy one, thanks to the high ramparts on the Israeli side of the canal which made a tank crossing impossible. The initial assault had thus to be made by infantry, equipped with scaling ladders and sufficient supplies and ammunition to hold their own for at least 24 hours. Breaches were to be blown in the Israeli ramparts not by explosives, but by high-pressure water hoses, no fewer than 80 special units being created and trained for this task. After consolidating the bridgeheads, Egyptian units were supposed to head for the Mitla and other passes into the Sinai, but in fact this second phase never materialised owing to the speed of the Israeli response.

The assault was planned for October 6 for both military and psychological reasons. It was not only a moonlit night, but the tide in the canal was just right for the crossing. Moreover, October is the Moslem fast month of *Ramadan*, during which the IDF was unlikely to expect an attack, and October 6 itself the Jewish feast day of *Yom Kippur*, when defences were expected to be at a low ebb. Secrecy was total. Right up until the last moment the vast majority of Egyptian soldiers thought that they were merely going on another exercise. Indeed, they were not informed until the morning of the attack that this time it was for real, and only five out of 18 officers of Colonel and Lieutenant-Colonel rank were in on the plan before the day itself.

To a large extent the Israeli Defence Forces were lulled into a sense of complacency, partly as a result of their success in the Six Day War, and partly because Sadat had 'cried wolf' so often without anything happening that they no longer believed him. As a consequence *Zahal*'s reserves were on stand-down and only a partial alert was called at the beginning of the Egyptian 'exercise'. The situation is analagous with that of Stalin's Russia in June 1941: all the indications were there to read, but few on the Israeli side—or, indeed, in Britain or America—interpreted them correctly. The Egyptians had three armies mobilised along the canal: in the north, the 2nd Army, comprising the 2nd and 18th Infantry Divisions, the 23rd Mechanised Division, the 21st Armoured Division, an independent armoured brigade and approximately eight artillery brigades; behind this the 1st Army (Reserve), comprising the 3rd and 6th Mechanised Divisions; and in the south the 3rd Army, consisting of the 7th and 19th Infantry Divisions, 4th Armoured Division, 25th Independent Armoured Brigade and a further eight artillery brigades. Facing them were five Israeli 'divisions' commanded by Adan, Gavish,

Magen, Mandler and Sharon.

But the situation in the Sinai was only half the picture. Far more worrying to the Israelis at this time was the concentration of five Syrian divisions, two of them armoured, facing the Golan Heights, and a reprisal action in return for the shooting down of several Syrian MiGs a couple of weeks earlier was feared.

At dawn on the 6th General Eli Zeira, the Director of Israeli Military Intelligence, received a telephone call confirming that an attack was imminent. He immediately notified Dayan and Elazar, who promptly got on to General Benjamin Peled, commander of the Air Force, and General Tal, and an urgent discussion was held at 0550 hours. Unfortunately, Israeli intelligence had got the time of the attack wrong—1800 hours instead of 1400 hours. The traditional times for an attack are dawn and dusk, whichever puts the sun in the defender's eyes, and this time would have been ideal for an Egyptian attack. However, the Syrians had favoured dawn, and the time of 1400 hours was a compromise which the Israelis were hardly likely to expect.

Elazar suggested immediate mobilisation of the reserves but Dayan demurred, suggesting 50,000 troops as a compromise. Elazar's suggestion that the Air Force launch an immediate pre-emptive strike against Syrian airfields was also vetoed by the Minister of Defence. Later in the day Golda Meir supported Dayan on the question of a pre-emptive strike, but agreed to the mobilisation of 100,000 reserves. In the meanwhile, the Israeli field commanders had been instructed to prepare for an attack but not to initiate any hostile moves.

In the Golan the Israelis only maintained relatively weak forces plus a mobile armoured reserve, relying on the natural strength of the position, reinforced by bunkers, to delay an attack until reserves could be mobilised and rushed to the spot. Despite an obvious Syrian build-up in the period since September 13, when the 13 Syrian MiGs were shot down, to over 900 tanks and 140 artillery batteries on October 5, the Israelis could only muster 177 tanks in two armoured brigades, and 11 artillery batteries.

The Syrians struck first at 1345 hours, bombarding the Israeli lookout post on Mount Hermon in the north and overrunning it with helicopter-borne commandos: only 11 out of 55 Israeli soldiers succeeded in escaping. Along the rest of the front the artillery barrage continued for an hour; then the massed Syrian tanks and infantry formations began moving forward. They made excellent targets for the outnumbered Israeli tanks, firing from hull-down positions, and Israeli companies were able to engage entire battalions with a reasonable degree of success. The leading Syrian troops were decimated, but the Soviet 'steamroller' tactic was as effective (though just as costly in lives) in 1973 as it had been during World War 2, and sheer weight of numbers began to tell. In the south, the Israeli 137th Armoured Brigade was cut to pieces and overrun, but in the north the crack 7th Armoured Brigade held manfully on despite being completely surrounded on more than one occasion. The arrival of a fresh armoured brigade helped stabilise the desperate situation on Sunday October 7, although the Israeli forces in the Golan were still heavily outnumbered. By midnight on that day the Syrians had reached as far as they were going to get: the 1st Armoured Division, supported on its left flank by the 5th Infantry Division, had almost reached the River Jordan; the 9th Division in the centre had taken Qnaitra; but in the north, apart from the loss of Mount Hermon, the Israelis were hanging on by the skin of their teeth. The Syrians attacked clumsily, without finesse, and suffered enormous losses in return for their achievements. Tank casualties were often in the ratio of five or even ten for one, and on one occasion three Israeli Centurions succeeded in knocking out 35 Syrian T-55s in a single engagement.

Throughout Monday the beleaguered 7th Brigade in the north continued to fight against overwhelming odds—the Syrian 7th Infantry and 3rd Armoured Divisions plus several independent brigades. The Syrians' new T-62 tanks were fitted with sophisticated night vision devices which gave them an enormous advantage over the Israeli vehicles, and by Tuesday morning the Israeli brigade's tank complement was sorely depleted. The Syrians then unleashed a massive artillery bombardment with guns, rockets and aircraft, under cover of which a strong force of tanks and infantry began to move forward. The Israelis withdrew a few hundred yards to escape the worst of this and prepared for the onslaught. Once the Syrian tanks reached the high ground their artillery barrage ceased, and the surviving 15 Israeli tanks counter-attacked. Surprised, the Syrian tanks fell back, but the odds were still on their side and in a short space of time the Israelis only had seven tanks left in action and, moreover, were rapidly running out of ammunition. Help arrived in the nick of time in the form of a scratch force of 13 fresh tanks. The Syrians had been fought to a standstill and now began to retreat, the tanks in good order, the following columns of soft-skin vehicles in panic.

By Wednesay Israeli mobilisation was really making itself felt. They were still outnumbered on the Golan, but the Syrian attack had lost its impetus and the Israelis went over to the counter-attack. In the south three brigades (14th, 19th and 20th) swept into the flank of the Syrian 1st Armoured and 5th Infantry Divisions, which had achieved the deepest penetration, and pushed them forcibly back. In the centre Laner's Division, comprising two armoured brigades, pushed through to Qnaitra and threw the Syrians out. And in the north the weary but triumphant 7th Brigade also moved forward. This brief statement gives the impression that it was a walkover, but in fact the Syrians fought back with determination and progress was slow, and in the south in particular their anti-tank gun positions were strong and well-sited. However, by midday on the 10th all Syrian forces had been pushed back behind their original start lines and the Golan Heights were again securely in Israeli hands.

Before examining the Israeli advance into Syria itself, we must return to events in the Sinai during these first crucial days of the war. The Egyptian attack began with air strikes by some 240 aircraft against Israeli Hawk missile batteries, radar stations and strongpoints; simultaneously a monstrous artillery barrage by some 2,000 guns was unleashed against the forward Israeli positions, weakly held by a total of just 436 men in fortified positions every seven miles along the whole 110-mile (175-kilometre) front. Following this bombardment, the first assault wave of 8,000 troops pushed across the canal, choosing sites in between the Israeli defence posts. Phase one of the operation was designed to establish a foothold one to two miles (1½ to 3 kilometres) deep along the whole front so that the Israeli mobile reserves would not be able to pinpoint the main thrust. The moment these troops were over, specialist assault teams were sent in to wipe out the Israeli defence posts. With these neutralised, Egyptian engineers then began construction of ten bridges over the canal to allow their tanks and heavy equipment to cross.

The task of the Israeli commander in charge of the armoured brigades east of the canal was not an envious one. General Abraham Mandler knew that the Egyptians were attacking, but did not know where to concentrate his forces for a counter-thrust. Should he try to find and destroy the bridges which the enemy was building, or should he try to join up with surviving forces in the Bar-Lev Line? It was a difficult choice to have to make, and in the confusion the result was that the Israeli tanks were sent in in 'penny packets' to find out what was actually happening as

Chronology of the Arab-Israeli Wars 1948-1973

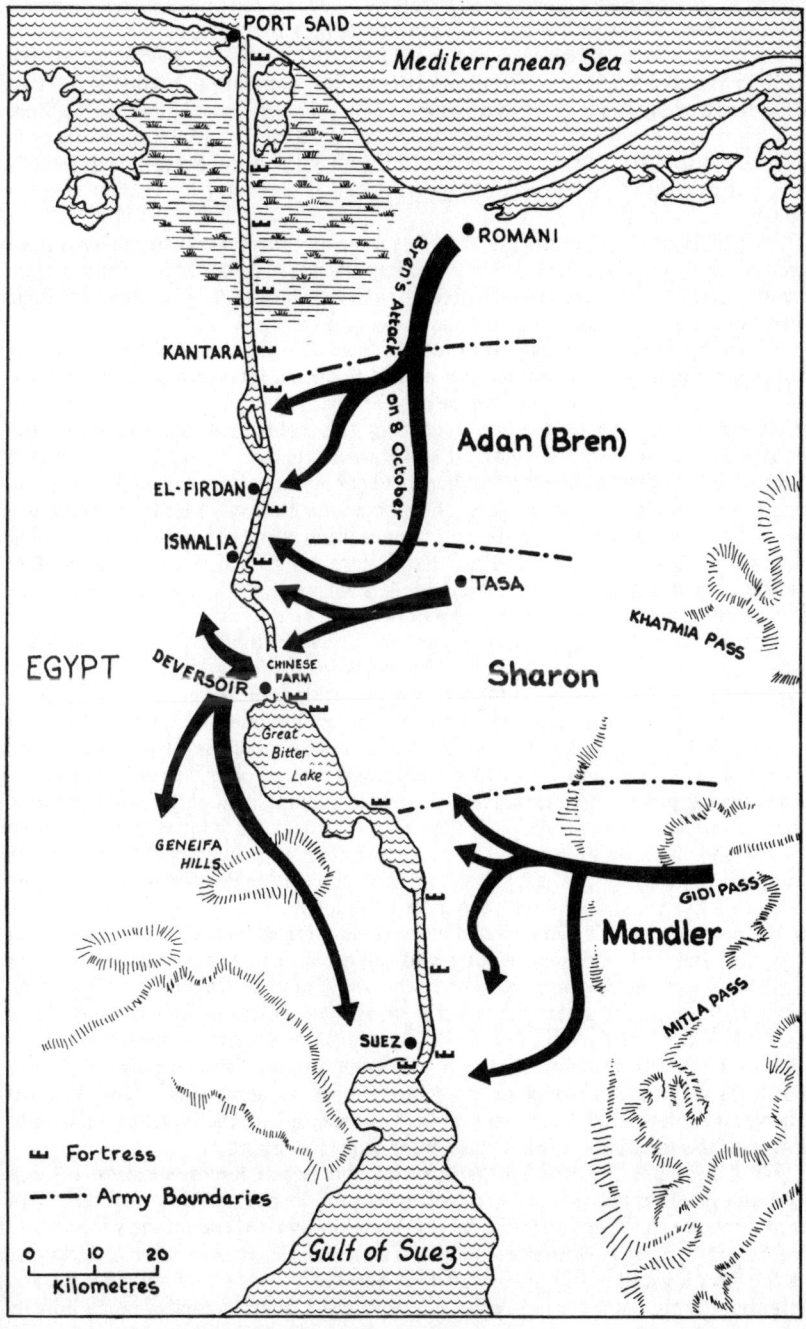

much as anything else. The results were a foregone conclusion. The Egyptian infantry were no longer the terrified individuals they had been in 1967. Endlessly drilled, and equipped with modern *Sagger* and RPG-7 missiles, they hit back hard against Mandler's tanks, and by the end of the first night of the battle his 280 had dwindled to roughly one third that number. Nor could the Israeli forces in the Sinai rely on air support. From a strategic viewpoint, the aircraft were far more urgently needed in the north, against the Syrians, because of the distances involved. Israel's new buffer zone in the Sinai could be sacrificed if necessary; the Golan Heights could not.

At 0900 hours on Sunday the first Egyptian armoured units began swarming across the canal. The plight of the surviving defenders in the Israeli strongpoints was critical, but the mobile Israeli forces in their rear were told to leave them to their own fates and concentrate against the main Arab thrusts.

There are many tales of heroism from this period of the war, of Israeli positions holding out against insuperable odds and of Egyptian infantrymen fighting back against Israeli tanks. Courage has never been restricted to one side in any war, whatever one personally believes regarding the rights and the wrongs of the situation. One of the most outstanding, however, is that of the Israeli southern outpost at Port Tewfik, where 42 soldiers held out for an entire week against a whole army, defying all attempts to enter their positions and only finally surrendering when all their medical supplies and ammunition were exhausted. A gripping account of this epic is included in Chaim Herzog's superb study of the conflict entitled *The War of Atonement* (Weidenfeld & Nicolson, 1975), and the whole book is well worth reading with careful attention.

At 1140 hours on the morning of the 7th, Dayan himself arrived to review the situation in Sinai, and made an immediate decision: withdraw from the canal to the high ground behind it, evacuating wherever possible from the canal fortifications. At a meeting later the same day General Elazar discussed the possibilities of a counter-attack or attacks with the divisional commanders involved, and it was agreed that, if opportunity presented itself, there was no objection to Israeli forces using the Egyptians' own bridges to cross over to the west bank of the canal and take the war into enemy territory. Under the circumstances it is a miracle that such an eventuality was even discussed . . . but remember what happened? The Israelis attacked frontally, under heavy fire from both conventional artillery and the more modern ATGWs, and were repulsed with heavy losses. The reason was simple lack of infantry support. The Israelis had been so mesmerised by their tank successes in 1967 that they believed tanks alone could achieve anything, not realising that the Egyptians had learned the counter to the 1967 tactics. Moreover, the Israelis appeared to have forgotten the cardinal principle of warfare: concentration. The example of Colonel Yagouri is typical. Attacking with a mere two battalions in the vicinity of Firdan, he ran slap into an Egyptian trap with infantry anti-tank positions on all sides. 24 tanks were lost almost instantaneously, and Yagouri himself was blown out of his turret to be captured, before the Israelis managed to extricate the remainder of their task force from the situation.

With the failure of these frontal attacks, the Israeli forces withdrew to high ground east of the canal as ordered by Dayan, and the next few days saw a battle of containment. The Egyptian tactic during this period was to send infantry forward to within 2,000 yards (1,830 metres) or less of the Israeli lines under cover of darkness. In the morning a short but intense artillery barrage would be followed by a massed infantry assault, supported by tanks. These suicidal frontal attacks were uniformly unsuccessful, although one divisional attack on the 9th did manage to break through the Israeli lines before being thrown back by an armoured counter-thrust. By Wednesday, when the Israelis were sweeping forward on the Golan Heights, the situation in the Sinai had been stabilised. The Egyptian troops had worn themselves out in their frontal attacks, and Israeli casualties were levelling off. Confidence was growing and the mobilised reserves were contributing to increased Israeli strength in the Sinai, including large numbers of tanks. It was time for the Israelis to counter-attack.

The basic plan was for a two-division assault across the canal at the junction of the Egyptian 2nd and 3rd Armies, for which a special prefabricated bridge had been prepared. This was a dangerous scheme, because the bulk of the Egyptian armoured reserves were on the west bank of the canal—two armoured and two mechanised divisions plus two independent armoured brigades. At the same time as the Israelis were making their plans, however, the Egyptians were also concentrating for a major push. Coincidentally, both sides chose October 14 as 'D-Day'. The Egyptians attacked in four columns, one in the north from Qantara, one from Ismailia, one towards the Mitla Pass and one in the south along the coast of the Gulf of Suez. The largest armoured battle of all time followed, with some 2,000 tanks locked in mortal combat. However, this time the Israelis were prepared, and had learned the danger of the Egyptian ATGWs. Keeping to the high ground, they used their very accurate long-range 105 mm tank guns to knock out the Egyptian *Sagger* carriers, moving rapidly from one position to another to confuse the missile operators. Egyptian infantry attempting to deploy were met by fierce machine-gun fire from Israeli armoured personnel carriers. And after a struggle the Arab forces began withdrawing.

A revised Israeli plan was presented. Instead of crossing the canal opposite Ismailia, as originally envisaged, the attack would now take place further south at Deversoir, just north of the Great Bitter Lake. The offensive began to roll late in the afternoon of October 15, three armoured columns supported by paras and an artillery bombardment moving rapidly towards the canal while a diversionary attack pinned down Egyptian forces in front of Ismailia. Heavy resistance was encountered in the Chinese Farm area, but Israeli 'watch and dodge' tactics (see Chapter 10) minimised tank casualties from ATGWs. The Israelis were handed a present on a plate when Colonel Amnon's brigade penetrated up the undefended southern flank of the Egyptian 2nd Army, at the boundary between the 2nd and 3rd Armies. Israeli tanks suddenly found themselves in the rear of the Egyptian positions, slap in the middle of the Egyptian 16th and 21st Division administration area. In Chaim Herzog's words the 'force found itself suddenly in the midst of a vast army with as far as they could see concentrations of hundreds of trucks, guns, tanks, missiles, radar units and thousands of troops milling around . . . Pandemonium broke out.' By 9 o'clock that night 'The scene . . . was one of utter confusion . . . units of Egyptian infantry were rushing in all directions, as were Egyptian tanks. The impression was that nobody knew what was happening or what to do. On all sides, ammunition, tanks, surface-to-air missiles on trucks, radar stations were in flames in one huge conflagration which covered the desert.'

Although these descriptions give the impression of a sweeping Israeli victory, in fact the Egyptians rallied promptly and strongly and the Israelis suffered extremely high casualties, some units being reduced to a third of their original strength. However, by the early hours of the morning of the 16th, Colonel Matt's Brigade, which had been entrusted with the actual canal crossing, succeeded after numerous delays in reaching the water. At 0135 hours the first Israeli troops stepped on to the west bank. By 0800 all Matt's infantry were across and tanks were beginning to be ferried over on rafts. Further north, at the Chinese Farm crossroads, the Egyptian forces, which had been holding on against determined Israeli attacks throughout the night, finally broke. However, the Egyptians still clung to the overlooking high ground in strength, and it seemed impossible for the Israelis to bring up their urgently needed pontoons without having them destroyed by enemy artillery fire. The only answer was to get the bridges across the canal under cover of darkness, and they moved slowly forward that night while Amnon's depleted brigade held open the corridor. Because of delays, however, the Israelis did not succeed in getting the bridges to the water until dawn, when it would have been suicidal to have tried to launch them, so a whole day was wasted. There was one major tank battle on the 17th, during which 86 T-62s were destroyed against a loss of only four Israeli AFVs, all to mines. By midnight the pontoon was in place and reinforcements for the men in Matt's beleaguered bridgehead began to pour across. It was the beginning of the end. On the 18th, Israeli forces succeeded finally in getting behind the Egyptian positions at Chinese Farm and broke them. The road to Suez lay open.

Deploying out of the bridgehead with two divisions, the Israeli forces swept south in two columns, down the west side of the Great Bitter Lake and into the rear areas of the Egyptian 3rd Army, while a third force pushed north towards Ismailia. In the north the resistance was stubborn to begin with but soon gave way, and by the 21st Israeli troops were overlooking Ismailia.

In the south resistance from two Egyptian divisions was also fierce, but by the evening of the 18th one brigade had reached the strategically important Geneifa Hills and on the 19th the airport at Fayid was seized, giving the Israelis a badly needed aerial foothold on the west bank. Meanwhile, roving Israeli patrols had been concentrating on destroying Egyptian surface-to-air missile sites behind the lines, and for the first time Israeli aircraft were able to seize virtual control of the air on both sides of the canal.

However, urgent moves were now being initiated to bring about a cease-fire. Soviet Premier Kosygin telephoned President Sadat on the 20th and persuaded him to agree to a cease-fire which would take effect on the 22nd, while American envoy Kissinger talked the Israelis into agreeing.

The cease-fire saw the Egyptians in an unenviable position in the south, where the 3rd Army was completely cut-off, although in the north their forces were still holding up well. As a result, units of the 3rd Army violated the cease-fire and tried to break out, forcing the Israelis to retaliate with an armoured counter-attack which broke right through to Suez itself on the afternoon of the 22nd. Fighting continued during the 23rd and the port of Abadiah was captured. With the remnants of the 3rd Army now besieged in Suez itself, a second cease-fire was agreed and implemented on the 24th.

Equally momentous events had meanwhile been occurring in Syria where, on October 11, Israeli forces began a major counter-attack in the northern sector of the Golan Heights. Facing them were a Syrian infantry brigade and a Moroccan Expeditionary Force. Here terrain favoured the defence, and the Israeli advance, further hampered by determined units armed with ATGWs and by constant Syrian air strikes, could only make slow headway.

In the centre another Israeli division launched an attack straight down the main Damascus road which ran into the same sort of problems. An entire Israeli armoured brigade was surrounded and hacked to pieces before it could be relieved by horrified paratroopers the following morning. But the Syrians were growing desperate and had issued urgent calls for help to their allies. The Egyptian attack in the Sinai on the 14th has sometimes been construed as an attempt to take the

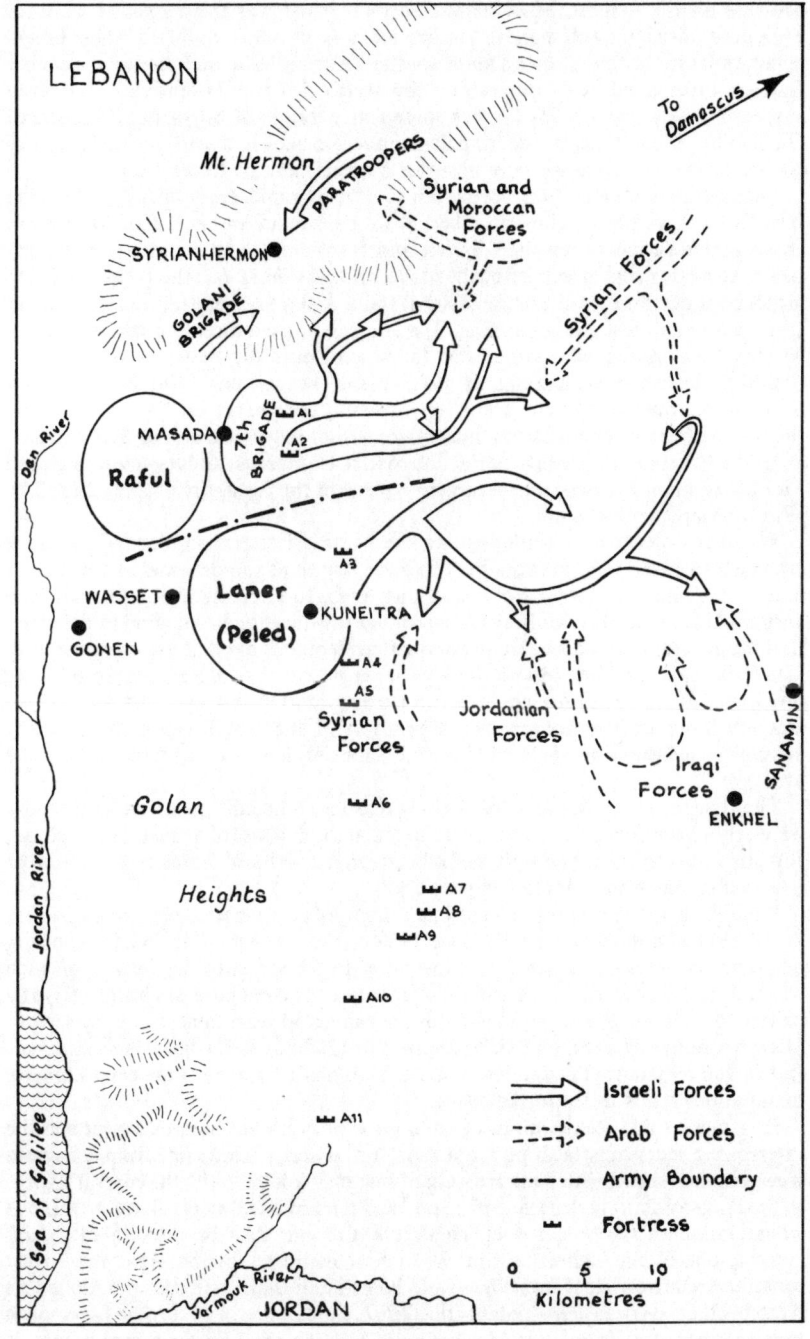

pressure off the Syrians. More helpful to their cause was the arrival of an Iraqi armoured division, although its assistance was of short duration. The Israeli commander in the centre, Dan Laner, spotted their build-up and prepared a classic trap—a three-sided box—into which the Iraqis drove unhesitatingly, not even suspecting its presence. Battle was joined at a range of 80 yards (50 metres)! Outflanked and outfought, the Iraqi division reeled back in disorder with the loss of 80 tanks. Israeli casualties were nil—not a single tank had even been hit.

The next attack came from Jordanian Centurion tanks every bit as good as the Israelis' own vehicles. They attacked with determination but did not receive co-ordinated support from their Syrian and Iraqi allies, and could not make any headway against the Israeli bridgehead. As this was going on, the Iraqis had also attacked against the northern (or eastern) flank of the bridgehead, and once again there was fierce close-range fighting. The Iraqis launched three successive attacks, varying their tactics each time, and for seven hours the battle raged with the opposing forces intermingling at point-blank range, until finally an Israeli outflanking force caught the Iraqis by surprise, over-balanced them and forced them to withdraw. This was the final major armoured battle on the Syrian front. With the Israelis sitting firmly astride the road to Damascus, and having recaptured Mount Hermon, the Syrian government agreed to the cease-fire on the 22nd. The War of Atonement was over.

Whether a permanent settlement to the Middle Eastern problem will ever be resolved is a question open to doubt. The basic issue is as simple—and as complex—as ever: the rights or otherwise of Palestinian Arabs to a homeland of their own. The various Arab nations have always insisted that the question is not open to debate—that the geographical area currently defined as 'Israel' *is* the Palestinian homeland. The fact that Arab inhabitants fled the area in the first place because of Arab terrorism, not Israeli or Jewish, is conveniently forgotten. But even the Americans, staunch though often embarrassed supporters of the Israeli cause, have finally acknowledged that a new State of Palestine is the only key to a long-term peace in the area.

The Israelis themselves are, for obvious reasons, reluctant to surrender territory which they have only gained and consolidated at the expense of a great deal of blood. But any future settlement simply *has* to be arranged with full Israeli co-operation or it is just so much meaningless paperwork.

It has been widely suspected—although no proof is at present forthcoming—that Israel has had a nuclear capacity since 1968 or shortly thereafter. What agonising decisions were taken at Israeli Cabinet level in 1973 regarding the use of such weapons remain currently unanswered—and here the contemporary historian is at a distinct disadvantage compared with his colleagues 50 years hence. The mysterious 'disappearance' of a shipload of plutonium in 1968 has so far not been answered. But Israeli reluctance to admit even one foreign observer to her top-secret *Dimona* installations tends to speak for itself. . .

How much this speculation has had to do with President Sadat's attitude in the intervening years must also be a question for posterity. However, from a current viewpoint he—along with King Hussein of Jordon—appear to be the central figures in the long-continuing debate. Syria and Iraq remain hardliners, along with Libya whose influence has so far been negligible and can thus be discounted. Saudi Arabia, one of the richest, if not *the* richest countries in the area, has so far remained relatively aloof from the whole Palestinian issue, and has even defied its Arab brothers on occasion—notably the OPEC Conference in 1976. The Lebanon is torn by internal strife between Moslem and Christian and, despite recent events, is really a side issue.

In many ways the basic issue is 'super-power' confrontation in the Middle East, and whether either America or Russia is really prepared to go to war over it. At the present time, the indications suggest that they are not. It would profit neither side, and result in disastrous loss of oil resources and revenue. Meanwhile, a healthy state of tension seems to suit both countries admirably well.

Arms manufacture is a strange business. Read Frederick Forsyth's *The Dogs of War*, pages 227 to 231, for a succinct appraisal. The crucial sentence is: 'Arms manufacture simply cannot be kept down to arms consumption except in case of war, and the logical response has to be either to export the surplus or encourage war or both.' What appears to have happened in the Middle East in the past is the latter, although it is a moot point whether the sale of arms itself promotes aggression. If this is the case, then the Soviet and Chinese governments have a large number of lives to answer for. Simply stated, the creation of a sophisticated arms manufacturing industry involves a huge investment in capital and manpower which few countries other than those with an existing business (Israel and South Africa apart) have so far deemed worthwhile.

Where does this leave us? A brief review of events since 1973 would not seem to be amiss. In this one can virtually discount Israel, since successive governments—including Begin's current right-wing 'hawk' administration—have always shown themselves willing to come to terms, with obvious provisos. Terrorist activity is 'out'—hence the recent offensive in Lebanon in support of the persecuted Christian population and against the PLO strongpoints established since Hussein made it clear Jordan would no longer tolerate them. Similarly, the return of strategically important territory—referred to in Arabic journals as 'Israeli land grabbing'—cannot be tolerated. To survive against the hostility ranged against her, Israel has to maintain defensible borders superior to those existing prior to the Six Day War. The country has already made concessions regarding the West Bank and, in particular, the advantages gained along the Suez Canal in 1973. Egypt, under Sadat, has subsequently re-opened the Canal for the first time since 1967, and is currently modernising it.

Sadat is something of an enigma in the Middle East. He is the first Egyptian Premier to have made anything approaching a serious effort to drag Egypt into the 20th century. His economic and educational reforms in his early days of office were unprecedented. However, the ruthlessness with which he quashed the 1975 and 1977 riots against increasing prices, together with his almost fanatical repulsion of Russian influence in the region, indicate that he is no wooly-minded left-winger. He is a pragmatist who realised that the artificial economy created by Nasser could not survive, and that Egypt could not indefinitely sustain the huge expense of a defence budget directed against Israel. His recent overtures should not be seen as idealistic but rather as those of a businessman who is losing money because of a feud. Unlike the hardliners in the Arab world, Sadat is prepared to compromise for the sake of his country rather than continue a war in which the Arabs have already lost four times, and whose furtherance could bring nuclear disaster upon them all.

King Hussein is in an equally anomolous situation. His is the country which has the longest border fronting that of Israel itself, and he and his Hashemite Bedouin followers are probably the Arab people with the least quarrel against the Jews. Hussein's position in the Arab camp has always been precarious. His necessarily ruthless suppression of the Palestinian forces in 1970—'Black September'—produced censure from PLO sympathisers world-wide; he has always maintained close links with the West—in particular Britain (did you know that his own Silver

Jubilee coincided with Queen Elizabeth's in 1977?) and America; and his token engagement in the 1973 war gave a clear indication that, although he wanted to remain part of the Arab world, he was not prepared to provoke full-scale Israeli reprisals. Like Sadat, Hussein has enough problems at home without wishing the further complication of a full-scale war. In many ways King Hussein, who is respected by both East and West, would be the ideal arbitrator for an eventual Arab-Israeli settlement. Indeed, it is strongly rumoured—although not proven—that he has had secret meetings with top representatives of the Israeli government. The problem is that the Arabs themselves do not trust him.

Syria and Iraq also pose problems. For many years the former counted as only a minor power in the Middle East. Involvement in the 1973 war, although unsuccessful and militarily incompetent, brought the country into the limelight as one of the leaders in Arab affairs. President Asad is one of the most respected figures in the Middle East. Having established his country's position and broken its see-saw relations with Egypt and Saudi Arabia, he has continued indefatigably to support the concept of a Palestinian homeland and, as we have seen, has generally been regarded as one of the Arab 'hawks' in the Israeli confrontation. However, even he has apparently come to realise that PLO terrorism, far from advancing the Palestinian cause, has a retrogressive effect, and Syrian intervention in the Lebanese civil war of 1976 *against* the Palestinians, whilst raising quite a few eyebrows, is symptomatic of his realistic outlook.

Iraq, the other 'hardliner', has not played a militarily significant part in the Arab-Israeli Wars. Here, political stability is a long way off since the ruling Baathist party (formed in 1947) is riddled with rival schisms. Since seizing power in 1968, the military-dominated clique headed by Field Marshal Hassan al Bakr has failed to create any form of political unity in its rigidly disciplined and regimented population. The régime is obsessed with security and, although the country is a member of the League of Arab States, is on unfriendly terms with neighbouring Syria, Iran and Kuwait. It also has internal problems due to the continuing war against the Kurds in the north. For these reasons Iraq remains a big question mark when it comes to considering an Arab-Israeli rapprochement, but its comparative geographical isolation from the centre of dispute—Israel—lends hope.

The big question, of course, is: *if* agreement were to be reached on the establishment of a new state called Palestine, where should it be situated? Four wars have proved that the Israelis are not prepared to surrender any of *their* territory and are unlikely to do so in the future. Most of the suggestions which have so far been made have involved Jordanian land, in particular the West Bank. If this is insufficient, then alternative proposals are for a 'divided' state of Palestine, rather like the old Kingdom of Prussia, half on the West Bank and half in the Gaza Strip (*if* the Israelis were agreeable); or a further sacrifice of Jordanian territory to give the new state of Palestine the East Bank as well. The last idea has the merit, from King Hussein's viewpoint, of putting all his 'bad eggs' in one basket.

Whether a solution will be reached in our lifetime remains to be seen. Fortunately, most of the indications are encouraging. The leading Arab nations are beginning to realise that future economic development lies in closer links with the West—particularly America—than with Russia and China; and since America has always more or less openly supported Israel, then an end to the conflict also becomes desirable. The thought of Cairo, Damascus and other major cities being turned into radioactive rubble by Israeli MD-660 *Jericho* IBMs (which have a range of 450 kilometres/280 miles) must also exercise a sobering influence. We can only wait and see.

4
Israeli Armoured Fighting Vehicles

The history of Israel's armoured forces is mainly one of 'making do' and improvising. Although various countries have been prepared to supply Israel with tanks and other armoured fighting vehicles, these have predominantly been of semi-obsolete types which, on paper, have been inferior in fighting power to the more modern designs supplied to the Arab states by Russia. In practice, however, many of these supposed disadvantages have turned out to be quite the opposite because British and American designs have proved more suited to desert warfare. Of course, the machine itself is only half the story in any tank battle; training, discipline and morale account for the balance and, until recently, Israeli tank crews have enjoyed a significant superiority in these qualities.

The infant state of Israel began its existence with a paucity of armoured fighting vehicles but, because its neighbours were no better off, this did not prove too much of a problem. Numerically, the most important tank in 1948 was the old French Hotchkiss H-35/39, of which the IDF possessed a round dozen. A pre-war design, this obsolete vehicle weighed 12 tons and carried a crew of two. It had hull armour 40 mm thick all round, the turret being 45 mm frontal and 40 mm sides and rear. The vehicle was capable of achieving some 22 mph (35 km/h) on hard ground but its average cross-country capability was only 17 mph (27 km/h). Range varied from around 70 to 90 miles (112 to 114 km) depending on the ground and 100 rounds of ammunition were carried for its 37 mm SA 38 main armament.

In addition, the IDF possessed two British Cromwell tanks left behind by the former British Palestine Regiment, and two M4 Shermans of American extraction. The Cromwell had been designed according to the British Cruiser tank concept and foreshadowed the later, more successful, Comet and Centurion tanks. It weighed 28 tons and carried a crew of five at a top speed of 33 mph (53 km/h), although average cross-country speed was in the region of 17-18 mph (28 km/h). The Cromwell had armour of the following thicknesses: hull front 85 mm; hull sides 76 mm; hull rear 33 mm; turret front 101 mm; turret sides 66 mm; and turret rear 61 mm. Its range varied between 96 and 170 miles (155 to 270 km) depending on the going, and it carried 64 rounds for its main 75 mm gun.

The Sherman was to become a decisive vehicle in the development of the IDF's armoured forces and deserves more attention. I do not know which variant the first two such vehicles were, but later acquisitions were predominantly M4A3s (British Sherman IVs). The Sherman had undergone a chequered development and wartime career, for more details of which readers are referred to my earlier book in this series, *Tank Battles in Miniature 3: A wargamers' guide to the North-West European Campaign 1944-45*. The M4A3s supplied by France to Israel were of the older type with vertical spring suspension rather than the more modern and efficient horizontal volute type (HVSS), and carried 76 mm L/52 guns in type T-23 turrets. The vehicles weighed just under 32 tons and carried a crew of five (driver, hull machine-gunner, main gunner, loader and commander). They had a top speed of around 26 mph (42 km/h) and an average cross-country speed of 17-18 mph (28 km/h), giving a range of between 94 and 131 miles (150 to 210 km) depending on speed and terrain. The M4A3's armour thickness was: hull frontal 51 to 65 mm (average 58 mm); hull sides and rear 38 mm; turret front 92 mm; and turret sides and rear 65 mm. 71 rounds were carried for the main 76 mm gun. These vehicles were designated Mark 50 in Israeli service.

France also supplied a large number of CN 75-50 75 mm L/61.5 guns to the IDF, most of which were retrospectively fitted into modified T23 Sherman turrets with a balance weight at the rear and increased mantlet armour. By the time of the Suez crisis in 1956, Israel could field approximately 150 of these modified Shermans (designated Mark 51) and 100 of the unmodified Mark 50 M4A3s.

Further Sherman development continued in the early 1960s, a great number of refinements being introduced to keep it viable as a modern main battle tank (MBT). These included the fitting of HVSS suspension and Cummings 460 bhp engines, but more significantly the French 105 mm L/51 D-1508 gun which used the same ammunition as the weapon fitted to the AMX-30. In order to accommodate the new weapon, the turret was extensively revised, including the fitting of a larger counterweight at the rear and the SAMM CH 23-1 hydraulic aiming system. These modifications were carried out at the French Bourges Arsenal and the new vehicle, popularly dubbed 'Super Sherman', entered IDF service as the Mark 51 HV. As it was one of the most important tanks used during both the 1967 Six Day War and the 1973 Yom Kippur conflict, it deserves special attention.

The basic Super Sherman as described weighed some 38 tons and had a reduced crew of four. It featured two smoke grenade dischargers on either side of the turret and had a top speed in the region of 28 mph (45 km/h), plus a range of up to 160 miles (270 km). Further modified versions driven by the more powerful Pratt & Whitney R-1340-AN-1 engine of 500 bhp are popularly known as 'Ishermans' (Israeli Shermans). These have different steering and transmission arrangements, a revised exhaust system and wider tracks to improve their cross-country performance (which is still not good in comparison with the Centurion or M-60 which we will come on to shortly). Weight of the Isherman is 39.6 tons and, although the top speed remains the same as for the basic Super Sherman, the increased engine capacity has reduced the operating range to 150 miles (240 km) maximum. Ground pressure is 12.66 psi (.89 kg/cm^2), a high factor because of the comparative narrowness of the tank's tracks which contributes to its relatively poor cross-country manoeuvrability. Nor is the power-to-weight ratio of 11.6:1 encouraging. However, the 105 mm gun, firing gyro-stabilised HEAT shells at a muzzle velocity of 3,002 fps (915 m/sec) and a rate of five or six rounds per minute to an effective range of 1,640 yards (1,500 metres) is an excellent anti-tank weapon, and its maximum depression of $-10°$ gives it a great advantage over all modern Soviet tanks when firing from hull-down positions.

After all this, I must confess that I have been totally unsuccessful in my attempts to discover the precise armour thicknesses of the Super Sherman and Isherman; the basis, apart from the improved mantlet, however, must be similar to that of the original M4A3, except that most photographs of Israeli Shermans display additional appliqué armour plates Some of the vehicles supplied appear to have been of the M4A3E2 'Jumbo' version, however, so for the purposes of my playing rules I have taken the following armour thicknesses for these vehicles: hull front

108 mm; hull sides 57 mm; hull rear 38 mm; turret front 100 mm (speculative); turret sides 65 mm (?); turret rear 100 mm (?). If any reader has more accurate figures I would greatly appreciate hearing from him or her.

Once the majority of tanks start becoming obsolete, it has become traditional for them to be converted into self-propelled guns of one type or another, and the Sherman's fate in Israeli hands has been little different. Israel had already received some numbers of French AMX M le 50 SPGs on the AMX 13 light tank chassis (see later), and in addition they acquired some additional French 155 mm L/23 gun/howitzers which they mounted in casemates on Sherman HVSS chassis. These weapons have subsequently been replaced by Israeli licence-manufactured 155 mm guns of greater length. These SPGs, named L-33s after their barrel length, have been in service since 1973. They weigh 41 tons and carry a crew of eight men in addition to 60 rounds of ammunition, have a top speed and range of 22.5 mph and 162.5 miles respectively (36 km/h and 260 km) and maximum armour thickness of 64 mm.

The IDF also fields some M-32 and M-74 recovery tanks on Sherman chassis, bought in the mid-1960s.

Returning to the early days, in 1949 the IDF acquired a few old French Renault R-35 tanks. Like the Hotchkiss, these were veteran pre-war designs armed with the same gun and carrying the same crew of two. However, they were more lightly armoured (15 to 26 mm) and could only manage 11.8 mph (19 km/h) flat out, so were hardly suited to modern armoured warfare! Of far greater significance were the French AMX-13 light tanks which Israel began acquiring in 1954—the country's first 'modern' tanks. Designed by Atelier des Constructions d'Issy-les-Moulineaux (hence the 'AMX') and numbered '13' for their unloaded weight of 13,000 kg (12.8 tons), these vehicles began entering service with the French Army in 1952 armed with a quick-firing 75 mm gun. Israel eventually purchased around 150 of these vehicles, although they were really more suited for the fast reconnaissance role than the major tank battles which were to follow. Carrying a crew of three, the AMX-13 was powered by an 8.25-litre eight-cylinder engine generating 270 bhp at 3,200 rpm giving a top speed of some 37.5 mph (60 km/h). 37 rounds were carried for the main gun in drums of 12, a major drawback being that the weapon had to be reloaded from outside the vehicle. Moreover, the armour plate was only 40 mm thick at best, which hardly inspired confidence in the tank's crew members! Range was a respectable 220 to 250 miles (350 to 400 km). Most AMX-13s in Israeli service were eventually sold off to other countries (eg, Singapore) after the 1967 campaigns proved their ineffectiveness in this type of warfare, but they performed sterling service in 1956. As mentioned earlier, the IDF also acquired some 155 mm guns on AMX-13 chassis (AMX M le 50s).

Most people would agree that the most effective tank seen in any of the Arab-Israeli Wars has been the British-designed Centurion, which the IDF began acquiring in 1959-60. These were early Mark IIIs fitted with 20 pdr (83.4 mm L/77) guns. Weighing 49.5 tons, they had a crew of four (commander, driver, gunner and loader/radio operator) and were powered by Rolls-Royce Meteor IVb 650 bhp petrol engines giving a maximum speed of 12 mph (33.6 km/h) and a range of 65 miles (104 km). Compared with other Israeli vehicles, the Centurion was exceptionally well armoured: hull and turret front 152 mm; hull sides 95 mm; hull rear 51 mm; and turret sides and rear 95 mm. 65 rounds were carried for the main armament.

In the mid-1960s the Israeli Centurions were gradually modified to accept new Vickers 105 mm L/51 L-7 guns and generally uprated to Mark V standards. But this was only the first stage. The Vickers gun soon entered manufacture in Israel under a licence and was not only retrospectively fitted to all Centurions, but also the American M-48s which the IDF had begun acquiring in 1964 (see later). The engine was similarly standardised for both vehicles, that chosen being the 750 bhp Teledyne Continental V-12 air-cooled diesel, which was not only more powerful than the Meteor but more reliable under desert conditions. The increased horsepower available raised the Centurion's maximum speed to 27 mph (43 km/h) and its power-to-weight ratio from 12.7:1 to 14.2:1, giving better acceleration and manoeuvrability. The vehicle's range was also nearly doubled (to 250 miles/ 400 km), and an engine change now only took six hours or so compared with the previous 24—an immensely valuable factor during a fluid armoured campaign. The transmission was also changed, an Allison three-gear box (two forward and one reverse) being introduced in place of the old Merritt-Brown six-gear unit. This further improved the tank's manoeuvrability, in particular reducing its turning circle at full speed from 131 to 43 feet (40 to 13 metres). The modifications introduced totalled more than 2,000 and, although the resulting vehicle is still recognisable as being a Centurion, it has inevitably been nicknamed 'Super Centurion'. Space-saving measures have meant that the number of rounds carried for the main gun has only been reduced by one, from 65 to 64, while the gun itself is capable of sustained accurate fire up to 1,968 yards (1,800 metres), firing HESH or APDS at nine or ten rounds a minute. A ranging machine-gun is used for gunlaying as in the Chieftain. Like the Sherman, a maximum barrel depression of $-10°$ enables the Centurion to fire from hull-down positions more easily than Soviet-designed vehicles.

Despite the fact that the Centurion is now acknowledged as being the best Israeli tank, this was not always the case. When they were first acquired, their crews complained that they were too complicated to maintain, and that the heat inside them was intolerable. Even the Vickers 105 mm gun failed to live up to expectations: in one engagement two Centurions fired no fewer than 89 rounds at two Syrian PzKpfw IVs without immobilising either! In fact, most of these complaints were unjustified, faulty or inadequate maintenance and incorrect zeroing of the gun sights being the real causes for the Centurion's apparent failure, as highlighted by General Tal when he assumed command of Israel's armoured corps in 1964.

A few Centurion ARV Mark 2 recovery vehicles are also known to have reached Israel.

A recent development about which little other than rumour is known is a pure Israeli-designed tank, probably based on the Centurion in most respects but reportedly with a Russian-style 'inverted saucer' type turret, a 120 mm gun and a 1,400 hp engine. Christened *Sabra*, this vehicle is believed to have been under development since before 1973, and it is possible that all the Israelis have done is mount captured Egyptian T-10 heavy tank turrets on modified Centurion hulls. Further information on this vehicle is awaited with interest.

The latest and most exciting Israeli development, about which a little more *is* known, is the *Merkava*. This brand-new design is especially tailored to Middle Eastern requirements and in due course will help reduce the IDF's dependency on Western aid. Weighing some 58 tons and having a low silhouette, the *Merkava* was originally powered by an uprated 900 bhp Teledyne Continental diesel mounted in the hull front alongside the driver's position, but this has reportedly been replaced by twin Boeing 550 turbines. From the one photograph which has so far been published it is difficult to identify the type of suspension used, but one source states hydro-pneumatic. The wheels and tracks are protected by hinged armoured skirts and it is believed that the turret and glacis both feature spaced armour for additional protection against hollow-charge projectiles. The armour used may, in fact, be an Israeli form of 'Chobham armour'. Armament is the faithful 105 mm Vickers, for which a large quantity of ammunition can be carried. The most unusual feature of the *Merkava*, however, is its large rear compartment which can carry a squad of infantry. The tank thus usefully combines the functions of an MBT and an APC. As with the *Sabra*, more details are awaited with interest.

Another development which has also been photographed is a new artillery support tank. A brand-new, rather box-like turret with full 360° traverse has been mounted on some rebuilt Centurion chassis, carrying the Soltam 155 mm gun/howitzer and 60 rounds of ammunition. I do not know whether this vehicle, first announced in 1975, is yet in active service, but it seems probable.

In 1964 Israel purchased 110 M-48A2 tanks from the West German government, which was then phasing in the new Leopard MBT. However, due to political reasons, this source dried up in 1965 and the Americans stepped in to fill the gap with M-48A1s.

The main criticism of the four-man M-48, and its successor, the M-60, is the vehicle's excessive height, making it a large silhouette and consequently an easy target. In other respects, however, it has proved itself a valuable and reliable tank, especially after the usual Israeli modifications. Designed in the first place by Chrysler, the M-48 began entering American service in 1952. The M-48A1 was powered by an 810 bhp Continental engine giving a top speed of 26 mph (42 km/h), the M-48A2 by an 825 bhp version increasing the speed to 30 mph (48 km/h). Fuel injection and increased-capacity fuel tanks raised the vehicle's range from 100 to 162 miles (160 to 260 km), while stowage for the 90 mm main gun was increased from 60 to 64 rounds. In Israeli hands, however, the 90 mm guns have been replaced by the same licence-built Vickers 105 mm weapons as mounted in their Centurions, and ammunition stowage has accordingly dropped back to 60 rounds. In its current guise, and propelled by the Teledyne Continental V-12 diesel engine, the Israeli M-48 weighs 47.6 tons but is still capable of a top speed of 30 mph, while additional fuel storage has further increased its range to 287 miles (460 km). Once again, the gun is capable of $-10°$ depression. Armour thickness on the M-48 varies between 25 and 110 mm.

In 1970 the first M-60A1s began arriving from the United States. This was basically an updated M-48 with the NATO standard Vickers 105 mm gun already fitted in a slightly larger turret with a different mounting and more sophisticated fire control equipment. It has a slower-revving 12-cylinder diesel engine which produces higher torque than that in the M-48 and thus a comparable speed despite lower horsepower (750 compared with 810). The most significant change, however, was in the fuel capacity which was increased from the 279 gallons (1,268 litres) of the M-48 to 312 gallons (1,420 litres) in the M-60, bringing the range up to 312 miles (500 km).

One fault with the M-60 which both the Israelis and the Jordanians encountered was the inflammable fluid used in the vehicle's hydraulic system, which often caused fires to break out after a hit. This has been remedied since 1973 by the introduction of non-flammable liquid.

Rumours that England would or will supply Israel with Chieftain tanks have been circulating for years, but nothing has so far materialised and it looks more probable that, if anything, they may one day get M-60A2s with the Shillelagh 152 mm weapons system. Introducing either or both of these vehicles could easily be justified in a wargames campaign for additional interest and variety.

Turning to the other types of armoured fighting vehicle used over the years by the Israelis, numerically the most significant has been the old American M-3 armoured half-track of World War 2 vintage, which still soldiers on alongside the Shermans. Weighing between 6.8 and 8.3 tons depending on variant, these lightly armoured (7 to 13 mm) vehicles have performed sterling service as armoured personnel carriers and as mobile platforms for a wide variety of weapons. With a range of 200 miles (320 km) and a top speed of 45-46 mph (73 km/h), they had proved themselves in desert conditions long before 1948, in the North African battles against Rommel's Afrika Korps. In Israeli service they are not only used as troop carriers, ambulances, ammunition transporters, command, recce and engineer vehicles, but also in the following specialised variants: as a missile carrier, mounting four French SS-10 or SS-11 wire-guided anti-tank projectiles; in the anti-aircraft role, carrying twin quick-firing 20 mm cannon; in the anti-tank role, armed with either a 106 mm recoilless rifle or 90 mm Mecar smooth-bore gun; and as a mortar carrier, equipped with the Soltam 120 mm weapon and 30 rounds of ammunition.

A larger mortar of 160 mm calibre is frequently mounted on a modified Sherman chassis with folding front and sides to the superstructure.

A more advanced personnel carrier, the American M-113A1, began arriving at the same time as the M-60 tank in 1970. This fully enclosed and fully tracked vehicle, weighing 9.3 tons unladen, can carry its driver and an infantry section of up to 12 men. Its diesel engine gives it a top speed in the region of 43 mph (68 km/h) and a range of 312 miles (500 km). Its light aluminium armour is only proof against low-velocity small-arms fire and shell fragments. Mortar carrier and command post variants (designated M-125 and M-577 respectively) are also used by the Israelis.

American M-110 self-propelled 203 mm (8-inch) howitzers have also been supplied to Israel in small quantities. These are unsatisfactory weapons in many respects as there is no armoured superstructure for the crew, eight (out of a total of 13) of whom have to be carried in a separate vehicle anyway. However, the 203 mm howitzer's heavy 'punch' makes it useful despite the vehicle's drawbacks. Speed is 35 mph (56 km/h) and range 454 miles (725 km).

The Israelis have also used a variety of armoured cars, chief amongst which have been the wartime Anglo-American Staghound and the French Panhard AML 90, ten of which were purchased in about 1965-66. The Staghound was one of the heaviest and largest armoured cars of World War 2, weighing 13.6 tons. It mounted a 37 mm gun with stowage for 103 rounds of ammunition, and carried a crew of five at up to 50 mph (80 km/h). Range was up to 450 miles (720 km) and armour thickness varied from 19 to 46 mm. The Panhard, which originally appeared in 1959 with a 60 mm gun, was rapidly refitted with a larger turret mounting a long-barrelled 90 mm weapon. 20 rounds of ammunition could be carried. This 4.7-ton vehicle had a crew of three and could travel at 62.5 mph (100 km/h) although its range was not as good as that of the Staghound (375 miles/600 km). Armour thickness was also less, varying from eight to 12 mm.

A recent Israeli innovation is the little RBY 1 light reconnaissance vehicle, manufactured by Ramta. This four-wheeled scout car is driven by a Dodge water-cooled petrol engine developing 120 bhp. The wheels are widely spaced and the body high off the ground for extra protection against mines. Armour thickness is 10 mm on the floor and 8 mm around the sides. A crew of up to eight can be carried, armed with a variety of weapons including machine-guns and the 106 mm recoilless rifle. The RBY 1 weighs just over 3.5 tons and can travel at up to 62.5 mph (100 km/h) with a range of 343 miles (550 km).

Observant readers will no doubt make the point that the Israelis have used many

Above *Centurion of the type used by the Israelis with 105 mm gun.* **Below** *M60A1 of the type supplied to Israel, seen here in US Army hands.*

Above *Soviet T-62s on exercise.* **Below** *Egyptian BMP-1 on parade.*

Above *Knocked-out Arab T-34/85.* **Below** *BTR-152s.*

Above *M-110 8˝ SPG of the type used by Israel.* **Below** *French AMX-13 with 75 mm gun.*

Above *Israeli M-3 half-track mortar carrier.* **Below** *PT-76 Model 2 leaving the water.*

Facing page, top *BTR-60s leave a landing ship.* Bottom *M-47 Patton, here actually an Austrian model.* Above *Soviet M-1938 122 mm howitzers.* Below *The unconventional 122 mm D-30.*

Above *M4A3 Sherman.* **Below** *Russian 122 mm 'Katyushas'.* [*All photos courtesy Christopher F. Foss.*]

more vehicles, hydrids and variants than those discussed here, but these are merely the major types for which 1:300 scale models are readily available and which are thus most likely to be required in a wargames campaign. One which ought finally to be mentioned, however, is the Russian T-54 refitted with the Vickers 105 mm gun; several of these, captured in 1967, fought in the Yom Kippur war and provide an interesting variation from other captured types which were, of course, used extensively.

Don Featherstone and I have not, in previous books in this series, entered into the field of vehicle camouflage and marking schemes but, because this is such unknown territory for the majority of modellers and wargamers, a few notes may not come amiss.

Israeli vehicles are normally painted a mid-green shade which, of course, rapidly fades and becomes covered with dust so that the overall appearance is of a sand-coloured machine. Then again, some vehicles do seem actually to be painted a sandy yellow shade. It is difficult to generalise from photographs, but most Shermans, M-48s and M-60s appear to be green, Centurions and half-tracks yellow, and if you are not too fussy this is a good way of helping you to identify the different types on the wargames table: and you need all the help you can get in 1:300 scale! If you wish to add unit identification signs, these normally seem to take the form of a Hebrew letter followed by a single number, a Hebrew letter on its own, or in the form of a 'V', either right way up, inverted or laid on its side. For more details on this subject, I would warmly recommend readers to Otto von Pivka's forthcoming book *Armies of the Middle East*, due to be published during 1979. This will also go into uniform details, etc, for those modellers and wargamers working in larger than 1:300 scales. Hebrew characters can easily be traced or copied from a good dictionary; if you don't possess one, ask your local librarian, but make sure you tell him or her what you are doing or you might be accused of trying to deface the book!

5

Arab Armoured Fighting Vehicles

The Israeli army, despite enormous handicaps and endless supply problems, has tried more or less successfully to standardise its armoured equipment, even to the extent, as we have seen, of re-arming and re-engining totally dissimilar MBTs with the same components. However, the major Arab nations have, until very recently, been so tied to the Soviet Union's apron strings that they have had to accept a wide variety of specialised vehicles, many of them totally unsuited to desert warfare. The main exception, of course, is Jordan, a country which has always preserved close links with Britain and the US, and whose army has gone through much the same evolutionary process as the Israeli Defence Force, currently being equipped with Centurions, M-48s and M-60s.

At the end of World War 2 the Soviet Union had an enormous surplus of AFVs even after rebuilding the armed forces of its satellite states in Europe, and from the mid-1950s large numbers were sold or bartered to the various Middle Eastern states as part of an obvious Soviet ploy to bring them within the communist sphere of influence. As in the case of the Shermans acquired by Israel, these included large numbers of World War 2 vehicles, including T-34s—rightly regarded by most people as the finest tank to see action during that conflict—which are still in service today. Right at the beginning, however, Egypt and Syria even had some old Wehrmacht PzKpfw IVF2s handed over to them after the defeat of the Afrika Korps, and a handful of these are known to have been in the front line as late as 1967. At least one, used by the PLO, was captured in the Lebanon during the Israeli offensive at the beginning of 1978! This was the first version of the PzKpfw IV to have been armed with a long-barrelled 7.5 cm gun. Weighing 23.6 tons, it carried a crew of five and 87 rounds for its KwK 40 L/43 gun at a speed of up to 25 mph (40 km/h), although its average cross-country performance was nearer 10 mph (16 km/h). Range was between 80 and 125 miles (128 and 200 km) depending on the ground, and armour thickness varied from 50 mm frontal to 30 mm on the turret and 20 mm on the hull sides and rear. It has also been widely rumoured that at least one Arab nation acquired a few PzKpfw V Panthers, although where they might have originated is impossible to pin down and photographic 'evidence' is dubious so it is perhaps best to ignore them unless some reader has genuine evidence?

Much better documented and photographed are the T-34 medium tanks which began appearing after Nasser's arms deal with Russia in 1955 and which are still on the active service lists. These seem to have been exclusively (?) of the later T-34/85 pattern with 85 mm guns and proper commanders' cupolas. This vehicle had first appeared in 1944. Weighing 31.5 tons, it carried a crew of five plus 55 rounds for its main armament, and thanks to its Christie suspension and wide tracks could travel at an average cross-country speed of 25 mph (40 km/h), top road speed being

31 mph (50 km/h). Range, depending on the ground, was in the region of 210-220 miles (336-352 km), and armour thickness varied from 45-62 mm on the hull sides and front to 90-110 mm on the turret. T-34/85s in Arab service appear subsequently to have been upgraded with 100 mm guns, resulting in the hybrid so-called T-34/100, and fitted with more sophisticated fire control gear.

Other immediate post-war equipment, some of which appears still to be in use, included Katyushka free-flight missile launchers and BA-64 armoured cars. The latter was a small two-man reconnaissance vehicle, lightly armed (machine-gun only) and armoured (four to 15 mm), but with good range (370 miles/592 km) and cross-country speed (24 mph/38.4 km/h).

The T-34s were supplemented by IS-III heavy tanks, although only Syria seems to have any of these monsters left today. First appearing right at the end of World War 2, this 45.8-ton tank carried a crew of four and mounted the same 122 mm L/43 gun as in the IS-II, together with 28 rounds of ammunition. Neither its speed nor its range were exceptional (up to 23 mph/36.8 km/h and 130 miles/208 km respectively), but its phenomenally thick armour (90 to 230 mm), well-sloped design and low silhouette made it virtually invulnerable at the time. The IS-III is principally interesting, however, in the influence which the latter factors have had on all subsequent Soviet MBT designs. For, while these same factors undeniably produce a sound vehicle in some respects, they have other drawbacks which have become abundantly apparent in the Middle Eastern battles. These include poor visibility and ventilation, and cramped crew conditions which accelerate fatigue and make rapid firing and reloading doubly difficult. The very shallow 'inverted saucer' turret design in all subsequent Soviet MBT designs has also meant that the maximum depression angle of the main armament is limited (no better than $-4°$), meaning that the tanks have to expose more of their superstructures than Israeli vehicles when firing from hull-down positions.

The T-10 heavy tank was a development of the IS-III which is still in service with Egypt and Syria; basically similar in appearance, it features a larger turret, seven instead of six road wheels a side, has a bore evacuator improving the power of its 122 mm gun, and carries 30 instead of 28 rounds of ammunition. Otherwise its armour and performance are virtually identical, although the range is some 25 miles (40 km) better.

The T-54 medium tank was the first significant post-war Soviet design, the interim T-44 being built in only small numbers and rapidly relegated to training duties. It has subsequently been supplied to more than 30 countries and licence-built in four, including Red China. In basic design it is a cross between the wartime T-34 and KV/IS tanks. The T-54 has the same type of Christie suspension as the former, in a slightly longer and wider hull, with an 'inverted saucer' turret mounting a 100 mm D-10T gun having a maximum depression of $-4°$ and rate of fire of three to five rounds (maximum) per minute. Its 520 bhp V-12 engine is capable of driving its 36-ton weight at up to 30 mph (48 km/h), and like most Russian tanks it features relatively wide tracks giving a low ground pressure (80 to 84 kg/cm^2). Range is in the region of 275 miles (440 km) cross-country. It carries a crew of four and 34 rounds for its main gun. This weapon, which is also fitted to the T-55, has unexceptional armour-piercing performance with an effective AP range of a mere 1,100 yards (1,000 metres). Differences between the T-54 and the T-55 are mainly internal, and include a slightly more powerful engine (580 bhp) and increased ammunition stowage (43 rounds). Bridgelaying, mineclearing, bulldozer and ARV versions exist.

The more modern T-62, which first entered service with Syria in 1965, features many improvements although it is basically similar in external appearance. Weighing 37.5 tons, it is powered by a 700 bhp V-12 water-cooled diesel engine and can achieve a top speed in the region of 35 mph (55 km/h). Range is approximately 300 miles (480 km) cross-country. The T-62 has a crew of four as in the T-54/55, but mounts a smooth-bore 115 mm gun firing fin-stabilised shells at up to five rounds per minute. 40 are carried. The main disadvantage of this weapon system is the inherent instability of this form of ammunition over about 1,640 yards' range (1,500 metres) which renders it inaccurate. This is crucial when we come to look at wargames performance, because it is not so much the hitting power of a gun which counts nowadays, as its accuracy. With such a variety of hollow-charge projectiles available, armour thickness is largely irrelevant, and it is usually the first hit which is decisive.

The other tank widely used by Egypt, Iraq and Syria is the light three-man PT-76 amphibious reconnaissance vehicle. Weighing 13.8 tons, the PT-76 is driven by a V-6 diesel producing 240 bhp which gives it a top speed of 27.5 mph (44 km/h) and a range of some 162 miles (260 km). It is equipped with a 76.2 mm gun for which 40 rounds are carried, later models having muzzle brakes and/or bore evacuators and stabilising equipment. In the water, two small jets drive the vehicle at 6 mph (10 km/h).

The basic hull of the PT-76 provides the basis for a wide variety of other Soviet vehicles in Arab service, including the BTR-50 armoured personnel carrier which first appeared in 1957. Performance is identical, the main alteration being the removal of the 76.2 mm gun turret and internal modifications to provide room for 20 infantrymen in addition to the vehicle's commander and driver.

There are other Russian APCs in Arab service. The four-wheeled BTR-40 is an open-topped vehicle similar to the old American White scout car. It is powered by a GAZ six-cylinder, 80 bhp petrol engine producing 50 mph (80 km/h) on the road, and has a range of 178 miles (285 km). It can carry eight infantry in addition to the commander and driver.

The BTR-152 is a similar, six-wheeled vehicle, powered by a ZIL six-cylinder 110 bhp petrol engine giving a lower speed (47 mph/75 km/h) and reduced range (156 miles/250 km). However, it can carry 17 infantrymen.

The BTR-60 is a much more modern design, and features a low-slung and well-sloped fully enclosed hull running on eight wheels. It is powered by twin GAZ six-cylinder, 90 bhp petrol engines, giving a road speed of 50 mph (80 km/h) and a range of 312 miles (500 km), but cross-country performance is reputedly poor. 14 infantrymen can be carried.

The later BMP-1 MICV (Mechanised Infantry Combat Vehicle) combines the features of a fully amphibious light tank armed with a 73 mm gun and a launcher for four *Sagger* anti-tank missiles, with those of a fully enclosed APC capable of carrying eight infantrymen in addition to its crew of three, 30 rounds of 73 mm ammunition and five *Saggers*. Weighing just over 12 tons, the BMP-1 is powered by a 280 bhp V-6 diesel producing 34 mph (55 km/h) on land or 5 mph (8 km/h) in the water. It has a range of 187 miles (300 km). This vehicle did not come into Arab service until after the 1967 war. One drawback with this vehicle is its magnesium alloy armour, which tends to catch fire rather easily.

BRDM-1 and -2 reconnaissance vehicles are also widely used by the Arab nations, the former appearing in the late 1950s and the latter in 1966. The BRDM-1 has four wheels driven by a GAZ six-cylinder petrol engine of 90 bhp, giving it a respectable speed and range of 50 mph (80 km/h) and 312 miles (500 km) respectively thanks to the vehicle's low weight (5.5 tons). It has a crew of five and, in addition to one or two

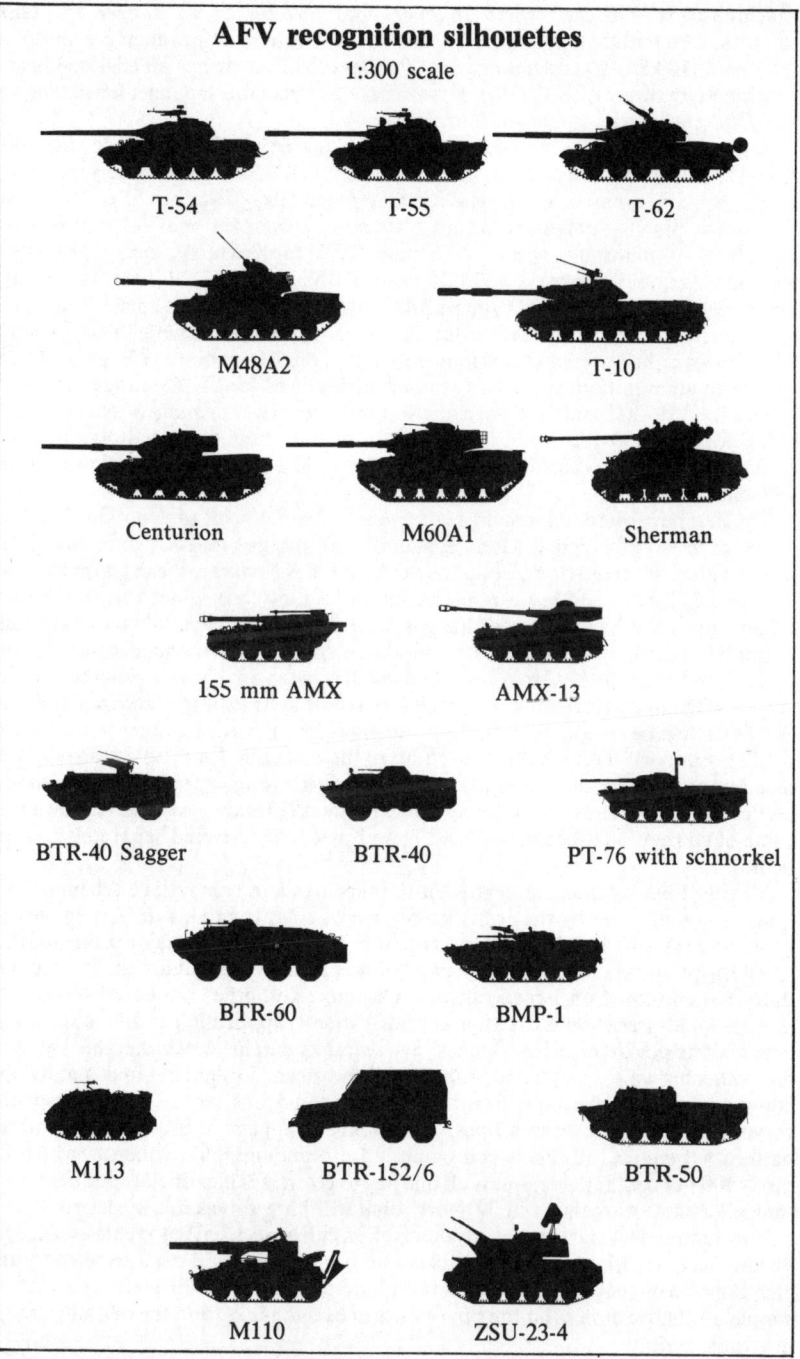

machine-guns, can carry three *Snapper*, four *Swatter* or six *Sagger* anti-tank missiles. The BRDM-2 is similar but has a 140 bhp engine producing a speed of 62.5 mph (100 km/h) and a range of 470 miles (750 km). It has an enclosed heavy machine-gun turret with 360-degree traverse or a retractable launcher for six *Sagger* missiles, and carries a crew of four.

Self-propelled guns in Arab service include the wartime SU-76, SU-85, SU-100, ISU-122 and ISU-152 as well as more modern vehicles. These are described in my earlier book in this series on the Russian Campaign 1941-1945, but brief details are as follows: SU-76—weight 11.5 tons, crew four, armament one 76.2 gun plus 62 rounds of ammunition, speed 14-25 mph (22.5 to 40 km/h), range 210 miles (355 km), armour thickness 16 to 35 mm; SU-85—weight 29.6 tons, crew four, armament one 85 mm M-1943 gun with 48 rounds of ammunition, speed 16-35 mph (25.5 to 56 km/h), range 210 miles (335 km), armour thickness 45 to 75 mm; SU-100—weight 31.6 tons, crew four, armament one 100 mm M-1944 gun with 35 rounds of ammunition, speed and armour thickness as for SU-85, range 185 miles (296 km); ISU-122 and -152—weight 46 tons, crew five, armament one 122 mm D25S or 152 mm M-1937 with 30 or 20 rounds of ammunition respectively, speed 12 to 23 mph (19 to 37 km/h), range 150 miles (240 km), armour thickness 64 to 197 mm.

The first post-war development was the ASU-57 which appeared in 1956. This has a crew of three and weighs 3.3 tons. It mounts a 57 mm gun and carries 30 rounds of ammunition. Powered by a 55 bhp four-cylinder diesel engine, it can travel at up to 28 mph (45 km/h) and has a range of 156 miles (250 km). Since this, the Soviet Union appears to have discarded the self-propelled gun in favour of missile systems (except in terms of low-level anti-aircraft defence) until the appearance of the M-1974 self-propelled 122 mm howitzer, which is not in any case yet believed to be in service with any Arab nations. Their reliance seems to have been placed squarely on the Main Battle Tank, disregarding the traditional Russian reliance on heavy artillery support. This would seem to leave their Middle Eastern customers at a disadvantage unless they go to the extreme of purchasing expensive, 'single-shot', tactical missile systems, for both the 1967 and the 1973 wars have clearly shown the value of conventional heavy artillery. Towed pieces are covered separately in this book.

Moving from mechanical details on to markings and camouflage schemes, the 'plot' is complicated by the fact that the various Arab nations do not employ a consistent system, and the following notes are restricted to the major protagonists.

All Egyptian vehicles seem to be painted in a sandy yellow shade slightly lighter than that employed on Israeli vehicles. On tanks and other armoured vehicles a mottle of mid-green seems to be applied fairly widely; application of this varies from irregular stripes to 'measles' patches. Syrian tanks employ much the same system but with a brownish/grey colour substituted for green. Jordanian tanks and AFVs appear mainly in a chocolate brown shade with sand-pink mottle, sometimes with varying shades of brown in stripes. Iraqi vehicles appear to follow the Egyptian pattern. Of course, all this is going purely from photographic evidence, which is rarely 100 per cent reliable, but is all one has to go on lacking official specifications (modellers and wargamers in 30 years' time will have things much easier!).

Very few tactical markings of any description can be seen on Arab vehicles, except during parades. Most appear to utilise number plates (you'll need to refer to an encyclopedia or good dictionary for Arabic letters) but precious little else apart from simple geometric devices on the turret sides of Syrian tanks, and the odd slogan (?) in Arabic script.

6

Anti-tank missiles and recoilless weapons

A great deal has been written and spoken about the effectiveness of cheap, infantry, wire-guided anti-tank missile systems since the Israelis came a cropper in their initial counter-attack during the Yom Kippur War. Much of what has been said can, fortunately, be ascribed to journalistic heat-of-the-moment extravagance. Looking on the event, the former Israeli head of their Defence Research and Development establishment, Brigadier Uzi Eilam, told a symposium in Tel Aviv that the success of the *Sagger* missile in that war 'was due to its massive employment by infantry, in active defence modes of operation', while the Swedish General Lofgren attributed it to the fact that the 'Israeli tank forces . . . charged right into the jaws of Egyptian anti-tank defences, without artillery and air support and without infantry.' Many other similar comments were made by expert speakers at the same symposium, since the apparent effectiveness of the cheap infantry anti-tank missile deluded many commentators at the time of the 1973 war into believing that the era of the tank was finally ended. But people said the same when air power finally became acknowledged as a crucial battlefield force, and again when cheap, simple systems of the 'bazooka' or 'Panzerfaust' type became available, and the tank is still 'queen of the battlefield' in both Europe and the Middle East.

Precise figures for the effectiveness of the wire-guided anti-tank missile in the 1973 war are impossible to come by; the Egyptians claimed—and foreign observers have subsequently confirmed—that between 70 and 90 per cent of those disabled Israeli tanks captured by the Egyptians after the conflict had been knocked out by missiles of this type. But, according to Israeli sources, these vehicles only account for a small proportion—perhaps ten per cent—of the total casualties, the majority of which they were able to recover. The Israelis attribute most of the casualties to conventional tank and anti-tank gun fire, and consider that, for cost-effectiveness, small disabling anti-tank mines are a better choice in the defence of infantry or static artillery positions.

The facts, as usual when one is writing such a comparatively short time after the event, are difficult to pin down, but certain tentative conclusions can be reached. Firstly, the main reason for the Arab successes with missiles of this type appears to be the fact that Israeli tanks went into the attack without proper preparation or support and that, in the later stages of the conflict, when this support was available, the success rate was far lower. Secondly, it is very obvious that missiles of this type are extremely effective in immobilising or destroying armour given good operator training and the right battlefield circumstances. Thirdly, that ATGWs are extremely cost-effective. And fourthly, that high operator morale is a prerequisite of success. Lieutenant General David Elazar, during the same symposium in Tel Aviv, affirmed that 'the tank was the backbone of the land forces during this [the

Yom Kippur] war, and will remain so in the future. All anti-tank measures, from mines to missiles, were aimed at reducing the efficiency of the tanks in the field and at limiting their success. Indeed, all in all they did succeed in one way or another to inflict casualties and slow down the impetus of the tank, but it is not in their power to defeat the armour; that can only be done by an armoured confrontation.'

The anti-tank missile systems used in the Middle East all follow a common pattern and apart from ranges there is little to distinguish one from another, since any missile of this type is capable of penetrating the maximum armour thickness of any tank in existence. Whether Soviet or American, French or German, they are all propelled by one or two solid-fuel motors; aiming is by optical methods (ie, through a magnifying sight of some description); and they are usually guided to their target by their operators by means of electrical impulses directed down one or two trailing wires.

The earliest such missile, so far as I am aware, to appear on a Middle Eastern battlefield, was the French SS-10/SS-11 supplied to the Israelis in the 1950s. Based on the German wartime X7 project and utilising a joystick control, this two-stage missile had a range of 550 to 3,280 yards (500 to 3,000 metres), a top flying speed of 125 to 207 yards per second (115 to 190 metres per second or an average of 340 mph/ 550 km/h) and an armour penetration capability of up to 600 mm. From 1960 onwards the Israelis also began acquiring the West German BO 810 Cobra, a simpler missile which does not require a launching frame but which takes off from the ground by means of an auxiliary booster. The control system is similar but the weapon has reduced range (437 to 2,187 yards/400 to 2,000 metres), a slower flying speed (187 mph/300 km/h), and reduced AP effectiveness (500 mm). The slower flying speed is both an advantage, in that it gives the operator more time to correct the line of flight, and a disadvantage, in that it gives the enemy longer to bring a machine-gun to bear. However, even with its relatively slow flight speed, the Cobra takes only 24 seconds from launch to impact at maximum range, and in the middle of a battle that is a short space of time in which to spot the tell-tail glow of a missile's exhaust, deduce where you think the operator might be hiding, and fire at him.

More recently, both the Israelis and various Arab nations, including Jordan and the Lebanon, have begun acquiring the American TOW (Tube-launched, Optically tracked, Wire-guided) system. Compared to other systems, this is a sophisticated weapon, despite requiring a launcher similar in appearance to a recoilless gun which is awkward to carry around, and a minimum crew of four men. It can, in common with all weapons described here, also be mounted on a Jeep or other light vehicle. It is officially designated a 'heavy' system and carries a more powerful warhead than others as well as having a shorter minimum and longer maximum range (71 to 4,100 yards/65 to 3,750 metres), but its flight speed of 625 mph (1,000 km/h) must make it extremely difficult to control against anything other than a stationary target. A semi-automatic guidance system, by means of which the operator merely has to keep his target centred in the cross-wires, does help, and a trained crew can get off one shot in approximately every 20 seconds.

Soviet anti-tank guided weapon systems supplied to the Arab nations have for the most part been of similar design, optically aimed, wire-guided devices launched from simple ramps: the *Snapper* and *Sagger*. The ranges are 550 to 2,500 and 3,280 yards respectively (500 to 2,300 and 3,000 metres) and the flying speed for each appears to be comparable to that of the German Cobra, ie, in the vicinity of 200 to 220 mph (320-350 km/h). Armour penetration is just as effective at 400 mm as other more powerful devices, since no tanks deployed in the Middle East exceed much above half that figure. Another missile, the *Swatter*, is a radio-controlled weapon with comparable performance—range 550 to 2,750 yards (500 to 2,500 metres).

Just how accurate are wire-guided ATGWs of this nature? The answer, fortunately or unfortunately, depending on how you look at it, is 'not very'. Pointing a gun at a target and letting fly with a projectile having a velocity measured in thousands of yards or metres a second is vastly different from trying to keep the pinprick of your missile's exhaust centred on the moving, twisting target in your cross-hairs while the projectile apparently dawdles across the battlefield and enemy machine-gun and mortar fire creeps closer. It takes great concentration, practice and strong nerve to discount all the distractions, conquer fear and keep that missile on target. I have no wish at all to disparage the British Army but, during a demonstration of our own Swingfire missile which I attended on Salisbury Plain, the operator only scored one hit out of two against a stationary target at a known range—and nobody was firing back, although doubtless the presence of the television cameras didn't help him! However, this would seem to relate reasonably to the Arab-Israeli experience.

The second question is destructiveness. With such a high armour penetration factor, any ATGW must unquestionably inflict a considerable amount of damage no matter where it actually hits a tank. Both these considerations—accuracy and destructiveness—have to be taken into account in formulating playing rules.

Israel did not acquire TOW until after the start of the 1973 war, so her experience with this type of weapon is limited. The IDF did, however, have some old 1950s period 3.5-inch (89 mm) bazookas, and its modern equivalent, the American single-shot, disposable Light Anti-tank Weapon (LAW). The bazooka, firing a hollow-charge projectile from a simple tube, has an effective range of 110 yards (100 metres) and an armour-piercing capability of 200 to 250 mm. The LAW only has a range of 80 yards (75 metres) and a penetration ability of 150 to 200 mm. Compared with both of these weapons, the Soviet-supplied RPG-7 system used by the Egyptians as close support for their longer-range *Sagger*, etc, is vastly superior. It has a range of around 220 yards (200 metres), is smaller and lighter than a bazooka, and can penetrate up to 250 mm of armour plate.

Both sides made some use of recoilless guns, the Israelis deploying the American 106 mm weapon and the Arabs the Soviet B-10 and B-11 of 82 and 107 mm calibre respectively. The major problem with all recoilless weapons of this nature, unfortunately, is that they are impossible to conceal once fired, because of the huge cloud of smoke and dust they kick up behind them. In terms of effective penetration, they fall in between the bazooka-type weapons and the larger wire-guided or radio-controlled missiles. Ranges are 550 yards (500 metres) for the B-10, 875 yards (800 metres) for the '106 and 1,100 yards (1,000 metres) for the B-11.

7
Towed artillery and anti-tank guns

Despite the preponderance of wheeled and tracked SPGs in use during the Middle East wars, conventional towed artillery has inevitably played its part and cannot be neglected, even if in merely forcing the other chap's infantry to keep their heads down while the tanks roll forward. Anti-tank guns are particularly relevant to this book, but field artillery also had its uses and, though lacking the precision of the AT piece fired over open sights, plays a valuable part in destroying enemy soft-skin vehicles, supply dumps, etc, and in breaking up infantry attacks.

One of the most common pieces in use for many years, and still going strong in the armies of Israel, Egypt, Jordan and possibly other countries involved, is the famous British 25 pdr. Firing a 25 lb (11.34 kg) shell with a calibre of 87.6 mm to a range of 13,400 yards (12,250 metres), this is still a valuable, reliable and serviceable weapon after nearly 40 years' service. It requires a crew of six and can be fired at up to five rounds per minute. Its armour-piercing shell is slightly lighter at 18.9 lb (9.02 kg) than the HE round, but can still pierce up to 72 mm of armour—effective against the sides and rears of most MBTs and all lighter AFVs. Similarly, the American wartime 105 mm M101A1 howitzer is still in service with a few countries, including Israel, Jordan, Libya and others. This weapon, which first entered service in 1939, fires a 105 mm shell weighing 42 lb (19.06 kg) (HE) or 37 lb (16.78 kg) (HEAT) to a range of over 12,000 yards (11,000 metres) (HE) or 1,100 yards (1,000 metres) (HEAT). The HEAT round's armour-piercing capability is some 102 mm at the above range. The gun is, of course, slightly larger than the 25 pdr and requires a crew of eight men, but its rate of fire is also higher, being in the region of eight rounds per minute.

Four Soviet field guns of 122 mm calibre are still in service with Egypt and Syria, etc. The earliest of these is the M-1931/37 firing a 55 lb (25 kg) armour-piercing HE round capable of penetrating 160 mm of armour at 1,100 yards' (1,000 metres') range. It requires a crew of eight and can manage six rounds per minute sustained fire. The M-1938 is a similar weapon requiring the same crew and having the same rate of fire, but firing a slightly lighter HEAT round (29 lb/13.3 kg) which nevertheless is capable of penetrating 200 mm of armour at around 1,100 yards' range (1,000 metres). The M-1931/37 fires an HE shell to a maximum range of 22,750 yards (20,800 metres), while the M-1938 can only achieve 12,900 yards (11,800 metres).

The 122 mm D-74 did not appear until 1955 and is now in service with Egypt. It fires a 60 lb (27.3 kg) HE round to a distance of 26,250 yards (24,000 metres) or a 55 lb (25 kg) APHE projectile with an armour-piercing capability of 185 mm at 1,100 yards (1,000 metres). Crew is ten men and rate of fire six rounds per minute. Finally there is the unconventionally designed 122 mm D-30 howitzer, firing either

Towed artillery and anti-tank guns

an HE round weighing 48 lb (21.8 kg) to a range of 16,750 yards (15,300 metres) or a fin-stabilised HEAT projectile capable of penetrating no less than 460 mm of armour plate at around 1,000 yards (915 metres). This gun requires a crew of seven and has a rate of fire of eight rounds per minute.

Heavier guns in Arab service include both the 130 mm M-46 and the 152 mm M-1937 and M-1943 gun/howitzers. The first of these fires a 73.6 lb (33.4 kg) HE round with a range of 33,900 yards (31,000 metres) or a slightly heavier APHE round with an armour-piercing capability of 230 mm at 1,100 yards (1,000 metres). Crew required is nine men and rate of fire six rounds per minute. The 152 mm M-1937 still in service with Egypt, Iraq and Syria fires a 96 lb (43.6 kg) HE shell to a range of 18,900 yards (17,265 metres), or a 107.6 lb (48.8 kg) APHE shell with an armour-piercing capability of 124 mm at 1,100 yards (1,000 metres). The later M-1943 fires an 88 lb (39.9 kg) HE shell to a range of 13,560 yards (12,400 metres), and can also fire a semi-AP round with a less effective charge capable of penetrating 82 mm of armour at 550 yards' range (500 metres). These guns require crews of nine and seven respectively and have rates of fire of four rounds per minute.

A heavier weapon which is used by both Israel and the Lebanon is the French-designed 155 mm OB 155-50 BF which, as noted previously, is usually fitted in obsolete Sherman chassis as an SPG. This weapon does not currently fire an AP round, but its 95 lb (43 kg) HE shell is quite effective and has a range of 19,250 yards (17,600 metres). The gun needs a crew of 11 and has a rate of fire of three to four rpm. The Israeli Soltam/Tampella weapon fires a marginally heavier shell with a greater range (21,870 to 25,700 yards/20,000 to 23,500 metres), requires a smaller crew of eight and has a rate of fire of four to five rpm.

In common with Jordan, Libya and other countries, Israel also utilises the World War 2-vintage American M114 155 mm howitzer, which fires a 96.6 lb (43.8 kg) HE shell to a range of 18,150 yards (16,600 metres). Crew is 11 and rate of fire four rpm. The M59 'Long Tom', another American wartime gun, is still believed to be in service in Jordan. This fires a 95.7 lb (43.4 kg) HE shell to a range of 24,000 yards (22,000 metres) or an AP projectile capable of penetrating 76 mm of armour at around 1,100 yards (1,000 metres). The crew required for this large weapon is 14 and the rate of fire a meagre two rpm.

Continuing to move up the scale, the large Soviet 180 mm S/23 gun/howitzer has long been in service with Egypt and Syria, large numbers being captured by the Israelis in 1973. This also requires a crew of 14 but has an even slower rate of fire—just one round per minute. Its heavy 300 lb (136 kg) shell, however, has a range of up to 35,000 yards (32,000 metres). Some 203 mm M-1931 tracked howitzers are believed to have reached Egypt, but I have been unable to confirm this.

Turning our attention to pure anti-tank guns, the scene is somewhat less crowded. At the bottom end of the scale the Egyptians are still believed to use a few old Russian M-1943 57 mm weapons. Requiring a crew of seven and having a rate of fire of ten aimed rounds per minute (up to 25 rpm if you don't mind what you hit!), this gun fires either a 6.8 lb (3.1 kg) APHE or a 3.9 lb (1.8 kg) high-velocity armour piercing round with a muzzle velocity of 4,164 feet per second (1,270 m/s). The former can penetrate 106 mm and the latter 140 mm at 550 yards' (500 metres') range. The larger 76.2 mm M-1942 anti-tank gun also requires a crew of seven and has a similar rate of fire, but can fire several different kinds of round including a 13.7 lb (6.2 kg) HE shell to a range of 14,500 yards (13,290 metres). APHE, HEAT and HVAP rounds are also available, the latter having a muzzle velocity of 3,166 feet per second (965 m/s). Armour-piercing characteristics range from 69 mm with

67

APHE to 92 mm with HVAP and 120 mm with HEAT at 550 yards' range (500 metres).

Iraq and Syria both possess a few 85 mm D-44 field guns. This useful weapon can fire both an APHE shell weighing 20.5 lb (9.3 kg) or an HVAP projectile weighing 11 lb (5 kg) and having a muzzle velocity of 3,379 feet per second (1,030 m/s), as well as a 21 lb (9.6 kg) HE round to a distance of 17,110 yards (15,650 metres). Armour-piercing capability is 102 mm with APHE and 130 mm with HVAP, both at 1,100 yards (1,000 metres). Crew is eight and rate of fire up to 15 rpm. In place of this weapon, Egypt possesses the more powerful 100 mm M-1955. Again, this is capable of firing a variety of types of ammunition, including a 34.6 lb (15.7 kg) HE round to 16,840 yards (15,400 metres), APHE and HEAT. The former is capable of penetrating 185 mm of armour, the latter no less than 380 mm. Crew is six men and rate of fire seven rpm. This gun replaces the earlier M-1944 100 mm field gun which had a similar anti-tank performance, the rounds being the same, but a faster rate of fire and longer HE range. The main advantage of the M-1955 is its lighter weight, making it more mobile.

For the most part, therefore, it is obvious that Israel, with a more mobile form of warfare in mind, has neglected the pure towed anti-tank gun in favour of conventional artillery and tanks, whilst, until 1973 at least, the Arab nations have tended to hang on to theirs. It is unlikely that many of these weapons will be used in the anti-tank role at all in the future, since the small, light, infantry anti-tank missiles are so much more cost-effective.

8

Rocket artillery

If one excludes 'heavy' tactical missile of the Lance, *Jericho* or *Scud* types, as one must for wargames purposes, the missile advantage undoubtedly lies with the Arab nations. The Russians, ever since the success of their *Katyusha* during World War 2, have relied fairly heavily on this mass-bombardment type of weapon, and the Egyptians and Syrians have subsequently been lumbered with their cast-offs.

Incredibly inaccurate, and only really suitable for saturation bombing of large areas where pin-point aiming is unnecessary, these weapons are unlikely to be required in any numbers on the wargames tables, so I shall keep this chapter as brief as possible. In any case, there are only a few types to be covered.

The systems employed since the 1950s have included the BM-13-16, a wartime *Katyusha* frame on a post-war ZIL-151 truck; the BM-24 on ZIL-157 chassis; the BM-14-16 on ZIL-151s; the Czech M51 system on Praga V3S chassis; and the BM-21 on Ural-375D chassis.

All of the above weapons fire fin-stabilised free-flight projectiles from rail or tube launchers in multiple salvoes. Like sub-machine-guns, their lack of accuracy is notorious and their effectiveness more terrifying than damaging.

The missiles fired are as follows:

From the BM-13-16, 16 rounds of 132 mm missiles weighing 94 lb each (42.5 kg); from the BM-24, 12 rounds of 240 mm missiles weighing 240 to 247 lb (109 to 112 kg); from the BM-14-16, 16 rounds of 140 mm missiles weighing 87 lb (39.6 kg); from the M51, 32 rounds of 130 mm missiles weighing 53 lb (24.2 kg); and from the BM-21, 40 rounds of 122 mm missiles weighing between 101 and 171 lb (45.8 and 77.5 kg) depending on type selected.

Crews for missile vehicles of these types average six men, and the time taken to reload from two to ten minutes (see playing rules). Similarly, effective ranges vary from 7,190 to 22,420 yards (6,575 to 20,500 metres).

Weapons of this type are really only effective against massed troop concentrations or towns, where a hit anywhere will destroy something. They are of virtually no use against mobile targets.

9
Infantry weapons

At the beginning of the Arab-Israeli Wars, both sides were armed with a mixture of Allied and Axis rifles, machine-guns and mortars, etc, from World War 2, including Mauser Kar 98K and Lee-Enfield .303-inch rifles, Bren guns, Besas, MG 34s and US BARs, Thompson SMGs, .30 and .50-inch machine-guns, etc, etc. Information on all of these is plentifully available in other books in this series and I do not propose to cover the same ground twice. Since 1948, however, several other weapons have come into service which have not been covered previously, paramount amongst which are the Belgian FN FAL, the Soviet AK-47, Israeli *Uzi* and the more recent Israeli *Galil*. The standard rifle used throughout World War 2 and, to a large extent subsequently, was the bolt-action, manually operated weapon, firing selective single shots and using a projectile of fairly heavy calibre and weight. Having long range and being extremely accurate, this type of weapon is mainly reserved for snipers today, having been replaced by weapons based on the 'assault rifle' concept amongst regular infantry formations.

The most successful post-war weapon of this type is probably the Kalashnikov AK-47 of 7.62 mm calibre. This gas-operated rifle carries a 30-round box magazine which can be fired in single rounds, semi-automatic or cyclic with rates of fire of 40, 100 and 600 rounds per minute. Single shot selection means that one round is fired each time you squeeze the trigger; semi-automatic sprays a short, pre-selected burst (normally of three to five rounds), then stops until the trigger is released and squeezed again; and fully automatic, or cyclic, selection means that the magazine empties itself in one fast hosepipe action. Accuracy varies from excellent on single-shot to lousy on fully automatic—in fact, it is so bad except at extremely short ranges that its effectiveness is more moral than physical. Semi-automatic fire in the hands of well-trained troops is far more effective, because it allows them to aim with reasonable accuracy while simultaneously trebling their chances of achieving a hit. It also helps preserve the barrel life of the gun.

The AK-47, which is widely used by all Arab nations, has a folding stock and weighs 11.25 lb (5.1 kg) when loaded. Effective range is 330 yards (300 metres). A modernised version, designated AKM, has also been supplied to Egypt and Syria. This is virtually identical except that production engineering has produced a substantial weight reduction, from 11.25 to 8.8 lb (4 kg).

The conventional Simonov self-loading rifle, also of 7.62 mm calibre, is also in widespread Arab service, although it seems certain that it is now relegated to reserve usage. It has a ten-round box magazine and single shot rate of fire of 20 rounds per minute. Effective range is 440 yards (400 metres).

Purely Arab ventures have been the *Hakim* and *Raschid* rifles. The former is an Egyptian licence-built version of the Swedish AG42 rechambered to accept 7.92 mm ammunition. This self-loading semi-automatic weapon is also now relegated to second-line service. Its rate of fire is 20 rounds per minute from a ten-round box magazine, and effective range is 656 yards (600 metres). The *Raschid* is virtually identical except that it fires 7.62 mm rounds and only has a range of 490 yards (450 metres).

The Egyptians also have some stocks of the Belgian .30-inch Type D automatic rifle, similarly rebored to take 7.92 mm ammunition. This weapon was developed from the American M1918A2 and should almost be classed as a light machine-gun, having a range of some 880 yards (800 metres) and a rate of fire, depending on the position of the selector switch, from 350 to 700 rounds per minute from 20-round magazines.

The famous Belgian FN FAL rifle, which has been adopted by more than 70 countries, has for a long time been the mainstay of the Israeli infantry formations. Firing 7.62 mm ammunition from 20- or 30-round box magazines, the FN weighs roughly the same as the AK-47 but has a higher rate of fire (60 single-shot, 120 semi-automatic, 700 cyclic) and longer range (656 yards or 600 metres). It is available with rigid or folding stock, while a heavy duty barrel and bipod mount can be used to turn it almost instantaneously into a light machine-gun. The Israelis also use the Belgian FN MAG GPMG of 7.62 mm calibre. This gas-operated automatic weapon has a rate of fire of between 250 and 1,000 rounds per minute from disintegrating-link belts or 50-round magazines, and a range of between 880 yards (800 metres) in light machine-gun configuration (on bipod) and 1,530 yards (1,400 metres) in heavy machine-gun configuration (on tripod).

A Czech design, similar in appearance to the AK-47, is the Vz 58 7.62 mm assault rifle used by many PLO units. This has a rate of fire of 40 (single-shot), 90 (semi-automatic) or 800 (cyclic) rounds per minute and a range of 440 yards (400 metres). The German 7.62 mm G3 rifle used by Saudi Arabia has similar characteristics.

Two purely Israeli developments are the *Uzi* 9 mm sub-machine-gun and the *Galil* assault rifle. Although the sub-machine-gun concept has lost favour in recent years, its small size and relatively heavy firepower have always made it an excellent close-quarter weapon, and it is much-favoured by Israeli paratroopers. Designed by Major Uziel Gal, it has a muzzle velocity of 1,312 fps (400 m/s), can take 25-, 32- or 64-round magazines, and has a rate of fire from 64 rpm (single-shot) to 128 rpm (semi-automatic) or 600 rpm (cyclic). As with all sub-machine-guns, the major drawback is the short effective range, around 100 yards (90 metres). A more versatile weapon is the *Galil* assault rifle developed since 1972, which is slowly replacing the *Uzi* in front-line service. In common with weapons being developed in other countries, the *Galil* fires a small (5.56 mm) calibre round at high velocity (3,020 fps or 920 m/s). It has an effective range of up to 660 yards (600 metres) and rates of fire of 40 rpm (single-shot), 105 rpm (semi-automatic) and 650 rpm (cyclic, on bipod LMG mount). 30- or 50-round magazines can be fitted.

Heavier automatic weapons used in the Middle East include the old Goryunov SG 43 machine-gun on wheeled mount with trail. This 7.62 mm weapon fires belts of 250 rounds at between 250 and 650 rpm and has an effective range of 1,100 yards (1,000 metres). It is widely used in a different mounting on Arab AFVs. The PK Series machine-gun is of the same calibre and has identical characteristics.

The venerable Browning .5-inch machine-gun is also widely used, especially on half-tracks and APCs. This fires a heavier ball than the above two Russian guns, but has a comparable range and rate of fire. The M85 is a development of this machine-gun and is fitted in the M-60 tank. Range is the same but the rate of fire goes up to 1,050 rpm.

The heavy Soviet 14.5 mm KPV machine-gun is another useful weapon fitted to a wide variety of AFVs, including the T-10 tank, BTR-152 and BRDM-2. In this form it can be used against ground targets or low-flying aircraft, having an elevation of 80 degrees. Its rate of fire is 600 rpm and range varies from 2,200 yards (2,000 metres) against vehicles to 1,530 yards (1,400 metres) in the AA role. Twin and quadruple mounts are often used.

More recently Israel has begun acquiring the dramatic General Electric six-barrelled 20 mm Vulcan cannon, a truly deadly weapon with a 3,000 rpm rate of fire. Its range is still on the secret list but must be in excess of 3,000 yards/metres.

Mortars, being very simple devices, do not change much over the years, and those in current Arab-Israeli service differ little from World War 2 models except in the use of lighter construction materials. The usual calibres are 60, 90, 120 and 160 mm, with ranges varying from around 500 to 2,000 yards (450 to 1,800 metres) in 500-yard stages.

Now, although I have given some basic statistics for the main infantry weapons used by both sides in the various Middle Eastern wars, they are really only of use if you wish to fight skirmish-type wargames rather than the 'micro-tank' battles with which this book is principally concerned. In the latter context, the basic infantry unit is the section of eight to a dozen men, and each section has a 'firepower factor' representing a composite of the weapon capabilities available to it—but that's all in the playing rules.

10
Organisation and tactics

The basic organisation of Arab and Israeli forces is remarkably similar considering their totally different outlooks, aims, training, doctrine and tactics. In virtually all formations the structure is a pyramid of threes. The major difference occurs at the top of the pyramid, where the largest permanent Israeli ground formation is the brigade of approximately 1,900 men, compared with the Eygptian or Syrian division of around 7,800.

Egyptian and Syrian organisation is closely based on the Soviet model. A division will normally contain three armoured brigades (sometimes called regiments), although divisions with only two brigades have been encountered. An Arab armoured brigade generally consists of three armoured battalions, each battalion comprising an HQ (one tank plus signals and supporting services) plus three tank companies. The company in turn has an HQ (one tank) and three platoons, each of three tanks. The armoured battalion thus has a total of 31 tanks. In addition to this armoured nucleus, each brigade also contains HQ, signals, recce, transport and repair companies, an engineer and an NBC platoon, and an armoured anti-aircraft battery. Fortunately, nuclear, bacteriological and chemical weapons have not, so far, been used in any of the Middle East Wars.

In addition to the three armoured brigades, the armoured division also contains a mechanised infantry brigade. Once again the basic pyramid goes in threes, the brigade containing three mechanised infantry battalions, each of three mechanised infantry companies. The company comprises an HQ (one APC) and three platoons, each of HQ plus three infantry sections, one APC per section. The battalion also contains a heavy weapons company of HQ plus an anti-tank, a mortar and a signals platoon, each of two APCs, the former now almost universally equipped with ATGWs. Finally, the battalion includes a rear services platoon with repair, medical and supply sections.

The mechanised infantry brigade contains, in addition to the MI battalions, an armoured battalion as above, NBC platoon, ATGW company and anti-tank gun company, HQ, signals, recce, engineer, mortar and transport companies, and an anti-aircraft battery.

The artillery regiment attached to each armoured division comprises HQ, transport and repair companies, a medical platoon and three self-propelled howitzer battalions, each battalion of three batteries with six 122 mm SPGs to a battery (thus giving 54 guns per regiment, 18 per battalion).

This is the core of the Arab armoured division, but many more units are attached at divisional level, including signals, engineer, medical, transport, supply and recce battalions, a rocket artillery battalion of four batteries with six *Katyusha*-type launchers per battery, and an air defence battalion of three anti-aircraft batteries currently equipped with ZSU-23/4s. The signals, engineer, medical and recce battalions are each of four companies.

An Arab mechanised infantry division has a very similar basic structure although here the nucleus is reversed, comprising three mechanised infantry brigades and one armoured brigade. The artillery regiment is of slightly different composition, comprising HQ, transport and repair companies, a medical platoon, an anti-tank battery and two howitzer battalions, each of three batteries, plus a rocket battalion of two batteries. At divisional level there are attached air defence, supply, recce, signals, engineer, rocket artillery and medical battalions. The artillery regiment in mechanised infantry divisions deploys 54 guns as in an armoured division, but 18 of these are normally 152 mm calibre weapons.

Reconnaissance battalions are usually of four companies, as stated, each of an HQ (one APC) and four platoons, each with three APCs. Air defence batteries contain three troops of three guns plus an HQ vehicle.

Jordanian and Iraqi organisation is virtually identical at the bottom of the pyramid, working up through company and battalion level in threes. However, the Iraqi armoured divisions have two instead of three armoured brigades plus a mechanised infantry brigade, while their mechanised infantry divisions are of two MI brigades and one armoured brigade, the latter being a rather tank-heavy structure. The Jordanians do not appear to differentiate between armoured and infantry divisions, relying on mixed divisions—one armoured, one mechanised and one artillery brigade per division. These brigades are stronger than their counterparts in other Arab armies, each being of three regiments of three battalions.

In all the above cases the organisation given is only a guide, of course, as units are frequently attached or detached for special tasks. In particular, Egyptian and Syrian armoured divisions often contain an attached heavy tank battalion (T-10s or IS-IIIs) and/or a tank destroyer battalion (SU-100s, etc). Organisation within these battalions is as for regular tank battalions.

Israeli army structure is similar, although the flexibility of independent brigades seems usually to be preferred to the clumsiness of the division (*Ugdah*). At full establishment, however, an armoured division would comprise two or three armoured brigades, with or without the addition of a mechanised infantry brigade. The brigade (*Hativa*) structure itself is also flexible. In an armoured brigade there would usually be three battalions (*Gdud*) comprising an HQ (three tanks and two APCs) and three or four tank companies, a recce platoon and a self-propelled mortar platoon. The tank company has one or two tanks in its HQ plus three platoons of three tanks; the recce platoon four Jeeps, M3 half-tracks or M-113s; and the mortar platoon three self-propelled 120 mm weapons. A mechanised infantry company consisting of three or four platoons, each of three sections with one M-113 per section, plus HQ and three self-propelled 81 mm mortars, may also be attached.

In addition to its armoured battalions, the armoured brigade usually includes a self-propelled artillery battalion with three to four batteries of SP 120 mm mortars (total 18 to 24 vehicles), a recce company with four or five platoons organised as above, and an engineer company.

An SP artillery battalion and recce company are also attached to the mechanised infantry brigades, which comprise three battalions, each of three companies of three to four platoons, as above, and, sometimes, an engineer company also.

Artillery battalions with the heavier 105 or 155 mm self-propelled guns are normally deployed at divisional rather than brigade level. Each such battalion contains 24 vehicles in four batteries of six guns.

Israeli paratroop battalions are also of three companies plus an HQ as in the mechanised infantry units, but the HQ section is so reinforced with heavy weapons that the strength is really that of four companies. An Israeli infantry section is split into two squads of five men, usually armed with three *Uzis* and two FN rifles, although these are now being replaced by the *Galil*. At platoon level a bazooka or LAW will be included, plus a belt-fed machine-gun, while at company level there are normally two or more additional heavy machine-guns and a couple of 52 or 81 mm mortars.

Turning now to tactics, we have already seen to a certain extent how these have evolved to meet changing requirements in the various campaigns from 1948 to 1973, but a little more detail will probably be helpful. In the Six Day War the position is relatively clear—the Israelis were attacking in a *blitzkrieg* manner which would have made Rommel or Patton happy, and the Egyptians and Syrians were predominantly on the defensive. Israeli armoured doctrine at this time had been heavily influenced by the 1956 Sinai campaign, in which their tanks had proved themselves for the first time. It was, indeed, very similar to that of one of the great World War 2 armoured leader's, relying on concentration against a selected point, and a rapid breakthrough into the enemy's rear echelons, leaving the mopping-up process to the following infantry. Outflanking and encircling manoeuvres were also, of course, a firm part of Israeli armoured theory, but they were largely unable to use them in the Sinai in 1967 because of the Egyptian dispositions.

The Egyptians at this time used the Soviet linear system, alternating fortified positions to block the passage of armour with natural obstacles—soft dunes, etc—and artificial ones, ie, minefields. The fact that Yoffe's force succeeded in passing over ground which the Egyptians considered impassable to tanks was a major contributory factor in the Egyptian defeat, just as French complacency regarding the Ardennes virtually sealed their fate in 1940. 'Linear', in Soviet parlance, does not mean a single thin line, it merely indicates a tactical disposition which cannot, theoretically, be outflanked. It is, in fact, a defensive system of great depth, consisting of three main sections: a front line where the majority of the tanks, guns and anti-tank weapons are concentrated; a central tank killing ground; and a rear support line designed to hold if the front line gives way and provide a secure base for counter-attacks. Both the front and rear lines are deeply entrenched and fortified with anti-tank and machine-gun bunkers protected by extensive minefields, providing a formidable challenge to an aggressor, who can only attack frontally. In 1967 a variety of circumstances combined to render these preparations useless: the sheer speed and ferocity of the Israeli assault, which led to the unexpected appearance of Israeli tanks in the Egyptian rear echelons almost before they knew war was upon them; lack of co-ordination between Egyptian forces, in particular between their tanks and their infantry; and poor Egyptian morale due to the low quality of the raw human material and bad leadership. The Egyptian soldier is as brave as any but the majority in 1967 came from peasant backgrounds with little or no education and lacked the sophistication to fight a modern war. By 1973 things were radically different. However, the officer material was, by and large, little better—if at all—and the campaign revealed several instances of Egyptian officers simply abandoning their men in order to save their own skins. Lacking leadership, what could the Egyptian soldiery do except flee or surrender?

The three Israeli armoured commanders, Tal, Yoffe and Sharon, each adopted different tactics for dealing with the Egyptian linear dispositions. Tal, as we have seen, utilised a combination of frontal breakthrough coupled with outflanking tactics; Yoffe succeeded in a hidden manoeuvre through 'impassable' terrain and achieved the same objective; while Sharon used a classic three-pronged tactic—a pinning force to the front, a wide outflanking manoeuvre by armour and mechanised infantry, and a surprise helicopter landing in the Egyptian rear. Wargamers, in my experience, are rarely so sophisticated!

Israeli tactics are, and always have been, firmly grounded in the basic assumption that war must be carried into the enemy's territory, since Israel is too small a country to allow an invader a foothold. Their tactics, in offence and in defence, therefore, are based on high mobility, high firepower concentration and high morale. After the Six Day War, both the Egyptians and the Syrians realised that they would have difficulty in beating the Israelis at their own game—although the Syrians were to try, with disastrous results. In both countries a great deal of thought was devoted to methods of defeating the Israeli tactics; training and education methods were brought up to date, 'political' appointments in the officer corps were weeded out, and especial attention was devoted to ways and means of defeating Israeli armour since it had become so abundantly clear that Soviet AFVs were inferior to the Israeli Centurions and Pattons in a stand-up fight. The Israelis, on their part, were guilty of a degree of complacency following the 1967 war. Its results had been so devastatingly swift and so unexpectedly rewarding that the IDF became blinded to its own shortcomings.

The Egyptian answer to the lessons of the Six Day War relied on a variety of factors. First, they had learned the supreme advantage of surprise and initiative. The next war had, therefore, to be fought at a time and place of their own choosing. Secondly, they acknowledged their own limitations in mobile armoured warfare—a difficult thing for an army to come to terms with, and to their credit that they managed it. Their plan was therefore based on a fast surprise attack on a broad front which would overwhelm the thinly spread Israeli defenders on the east bank of the Suez Canal, followed by consolidation into a strong defensive line against which the Israeli armoured forces would, hopefully, batter in vain, wearing themselves down in a battle of attrition. To counter the Israeli armour, the Egyptians placed heavy reliance on the new generation of anti-tank guided missiles—ATGWs—in the hands of infantry formations, massing their armour in reserve for a later breakthrough when the Israelis had worn themselves out.

These tactics were sound in principle and initially, as we have seen, the campaign went very well for the Egyptians. As they had hoped, Israeli armoured forces threw themselves vainly against the ATGW positions, with heavy casualties.

The Israelis had, of course, been aware for some time of the Arab acquisition of ATGWs but, lacking experience of their effectiveness, had decided on an erroneous and often fatal method of dealing with them—the massed high-speed tank charge to close the range quickly, followed by machine-gun fire to eliminate the infantry. The sensible wargamer will avoid such tactics! After their initial failure, Israeli armoured units evolved a new system, popularly known as 'watch and dodge'. One tank in each platoon is given the sole task of observing for missile launches. Immediately one is sighted, an alert is radioed to the rest of the platoon, who scatter, using the terrain to block the ATGW operator's line of sight and high-speed evasive manoeuvres to throw off his aim. At the same time, the 'watchdog' tank lays down rapid HE fire on the observed ATGW operator's position, to distract if not kill him. Firing at the observed launch site of an ATGW is not always effective, since the operator can be comfortably installed several metres away, but it is difficult for the most highly trained and motivated soldier to concentrate on steering his missile towards an elusive and rapidly jinking target while tons of high explosive are falling all around him.

Organisation and tactics

Laying smoke is another obvious counter-ATGW tactic to further confuse the operator's aim. Salvoes of missiles are, of course, far harder to dodge than a single rocket, and the chances of a hit—deliberate or accidental—are increased, so the Egyptian operators soon adopted this tactic. By this time, unfortunately for them, it was too late, because the Israelis were already across the canal.

Syrian and Iraqi tactics in 1973 were far less sophisticated than those of the Egyptians, relying on the Soviet 'steamroller' to eliminate resistance, using numerical superiority to counter technical superiority. This is, naturally, very wasteful in terms of both men and machines, and the tactic was further rendered impotent because of the difficult terrain and the height advantage which the Israelis enjoyed. Jordanian forces fought more scientifically but their efforts were negated by lack of co-ordination and co-operation from their allies.

What tactics a future conflict will bring to light remain to be seen although, of course, one hopes that such an eventuality will not come to pass. President Sadat's unprecedented speech to the *Knesset* (the Israeli parliament) gives one hope despite the difficulties encountered in subsequent talks, but the Israeli attack on PLO bases in the Lebanon shows that they are not prepared to be pushed around even while negotiating a settlement.

Arab 'hawks' certainly deny the impression that peace will be easy. Military journalist Mahmud Azmi has been widely reported as saying that every future conflict 'will necessarily be a total confrontation. It should be prepared on the assumption that it will be a prolonged and comprehensive war... Our cities, villages, industries, agriculture, communications—all should be ready for a prolonged war.' Similarly, another leading Arab strategist, Haytham al-Ayubi, has stressed the need to force Israel by negotiation to give up strategically important terrain advantages which would 'considerably strengthen the Western [ie, Suez Canal] Front. In order to strengthen the Eastern Front we must organise reinforcements by Iraqi and Saudi troops and open a third front by the incorporation of Jordan.' It hardly sounds promising, does it?

11

Minefields

Mines and minefields have played a crucial part in the 1967 and 1973 Arab-Israeli Wars; indeed, Professor Edward Luttwak actually said at a military symposium in Tel Aviv after the Yom Kippur War that, 'in fact, if I had to allocate money between anti-tank missiles and *these* mine systems . . . I would allocate generously to the mines.' The mines which he was talking about were the small but highly destructive, or at least disabling, type which the Israeli Professor Saadia Amiel had been talking about earlier in the same proceedings, when he said that 'instant barriers can impose prohibitive attrition rates on an armoured or mechanised invader, force him into high density concentrations, slow him down and effectively block penetrations. Becoming quasi-static, he is thus exposed to lethal strikes by precision-guided weapons.' 'Instant mines' are the type which can be dropped in clusters from an aircraft or missile to sow a previously neutral landscape. They are small and light, and they rarely 'kill' a vehicle—but in the 'instant war' situation of the Arab-Israeli conflict, immobilisation of an enemy unit is almost as effective as total destruction. Indeed, in many ways it is more effective, because one thing which these and other wars—such as the Indo-Pakistani conflict—have shown up is the technological and economic inability of small states to sustain a prolonged war. In such a situation, the after-battle retrieval of one's own and the enemy's equipment assumes a new significance. Destroying a tank is not the be-all and end-all: disabling it, so as to take it out of the immediate battle but leaving it recoverable by one's own forces afterwards is even more attractive.

Mining is not new—it was known to the ancient Chinese—but pre-packaged mines only really came into their own during World War 1 and after. They were widely used by the British and Germans during the Western Desert campaigns of 1940-1943, particularly to defend infantry positions and slow an attack or pursuit, whilst the Soviet Union has always relied heavily on them—as reflected by Egypt in 1967. Similarly, during the Yom Kippur War, Israeli forces laid an estimated 750,000 mines in the Canal Zone.

Mines are basically simple devices comprising a firing mechanism, detonator and explosive charge. Firing mechanisms are usually of either the spring or diaphragm type, either of which sets off the detonator when the right pressure is applied, the detonator in turn igniting the main charge. Other mines, particularly of the anti-personnel type, may be set off by trip wires or radio signals. They are usually laid in regular clusters rather than haphazardly, making it simpler to chart routes through them for your own troops and making it easier to find and remove them when required. Today there are a variety of types of mechanical minelayers which automatically dig a hole of the correct depth, insert a mine and cover it up again, while more recent developments not yet seen in the Middle East but promising to

Minefields

have significance in any future conflict are small scatter mines dispersed from an aircraft or missile pod. Anti-tank mines of this type only weigh some 3 lb (1.5 kg) instead of the more conventional 55 to 65 lb (25 to 30 kg), the idea being that it is only necessary to have a small charge in order to strip a tank's track, and thus immobilise it.

Mines are normally constructed of non-ferrous materials to prevent their detection by conventional electric detectors and their firing switches are safeguarded against accidental detonation by enemy radio signals. They can also be set to detonate at a specific pressure so that, for example, if one force knows that its own vehicles exert a signficiantly lower ground pressure than its opponents, the mines can be set for the higher pressure, allowing friendly vehicles to cross minefields with impunity, encouraging an enemy pursuit which will run slap on to them.

In modern war there are various types of minefields: close protective, thickly sown around an infantry position, for example, and covered by small-arms fire; defensive, sown between defended areas to block enemy penetration behind your lines; barrier, to channel the enemy's forces into prepared anti-tank 'killing grounds'; or nuisance, purely designed to hinder an attack and cause a few casualties without stopping it. Phoney minefields, carefully marked on maps which are allowed to fall into the enemy's hands, can also be used to channel his attacks through areas where there are real minefields.

There are various counters to minefields. The mines can be lifted by hand, a laborious process, particularly under fire, and thus usually carried out at night. They can be cleared by mechanical devices, such as flail tanks. Or they can be exploded deliberately by means of explosive charges, linked together in a chain or flexible tube, fired across the field and then detonated.

The perimeters of minefields are normally marked out by low wire barriers. This prevents friendly troops from blundering into them by mistake without affecting their deterrent effect on the enemy's movement. This makes things much easier for wargamers, who do not have to worry about concealment on the table-top but can mark the extent of the fields out with pins and thread. However, the type of minefield needs to be clearly marked on each player's map, and by type I mean density. The density of a minefield is designated by a number—1, 2, 3, etc—denoting the average density per square yard or metre over a 1,000-yard (or 1,000-metre) front. Close protective minefields will normally have the highest density, defensive and barrier a lower density and nuisance fields the lowest of all. Close protective fields will usually include a high proportion of anti-personnel as well as anti-tank mines. These contain small explosive charges which spray a lethal hail of ball bearings or other nasty metal fragments at high velocity over an area of around 25 square yards or metres, and will mow down any unfortunate infantrymen in the vicinity as easily as a machine-gun. They do not have any effect against armoured fighting vehicles.

The way of tackling these minefields in wargames is simple: if a field has a density of '1' each tank entering it stands a ten per cent chance of detonating a mine each move; a density of '2' gives a 20 per cent chance, and so on up to a maximum of '5'. If the field is of the mixed type, including both anti-tank and anti-personnel mines, the proportion of one type to the other should also be noted on the players' maps, and a second dice thrown in each case to decide which type has been set off. Infantry will not set off anti-tank mines, since their weight is insufficient to trigger the detonator, but a tank may set off an anti-personnel mine to the detriment of any supporting infantry in its vicinity—although part of the blast will, of course, be blocked off by the tank itself. Anti-tank mines should be designated 'heavy' or 'crippling' and 'light' or 'incapacitating', the former having the same effect as a hollow-charge projectile in the rules, the latter merely stripping a track and immobilising the tank. Soft-skin vehicles will be destroyed by either type.

12

Helicopters

Mike Spick, the author of the section on aerial combat in this book, discussed the question of helicopters with me when we first began planning it. Were they, he asked, to be treated as aircraft, or low-flying soft-skin vehicles? The latter, after much talk, seemed the logical choice because, while helicopters can fly at more than twice the speed of the average military ground vehicle, their average battle situation speed is lower than their maximum, while either is three times slower than a pure combat aircraft. That is why this chapter falls within my section of this book rather than Mike's and, lacking his specialised aeronautical knowledge, I have decided to treat them in the wargames context exactly as if they move in two rather than three dimensions. This is reasonable, because army co-operation 'choppers automatically hug the ground so as to make themselves difficult targets both for ground-to-air and air-to-air weapons. The former have trouble in tracking such a comparatively fast-moving, low-flying and elusive target, while the latter become confused with ground clutter even if the pilot of a Mach 2 fighter has the guts to come low and slow enough to tackle one.

Helicopters have so far played a minor role in any case in the Arab-Israeli wars, certainly insofar as their anti-tank potential is concerned. Few are fitted with weapons of any sort, the majority being apparently used for fast commando-type troop ferrying or else for simple AOP duties. But the fact remains that several could be, and perhaps are, equipped with ATWGs, so they certainly deserve inclusion. After all, as Mike said in a letter to *Battle* magazine, all wargaming is basically fantasy, and if a wargamer wants to make more use of his available helicopters than the actual protagonists have to date, why should he not have the opportunity?

To specifics: the following are the approximate helicopter strengths of the major countries concerned circa 1971, ie, roughly half-way between the Six Days and Yom Kippur wars: Egypt—an unknown quantity of Mil Mi-1s, 40 Mi-4s, 20 Mi-6s and 80 Mi-8s; Iraq—four Mi-1s, 20 Mi-4s and 12 Mi-8s plus nine Westland Wessex; Israel—five Alouette IIs, between nine and a dozen SA 321s, 25 Bell 205s and ten Sikorsky CH-53Cs; Lebanon—five Alouette IIs and IIIs; Libya—three Alouette IIs and ten IIIs plus eight SA 321s; and Syria—four Mi-1s, eight Mi-4s and 22 Mi-8s. The total helicopter strength in the Middle East can therefore be seen to have been pretty insignificant.

The Egyptian machines were organised into six squadrons of 'light', 'medium' and 'heavy' aircraft; the Iraqi into one Wessex, two Mi-4 and one Mi-8 squadrons; the Israeli into two Bell, one Sikorsky and one Aérospatiale squadrons; the Lebanese into no particular organisation; the Libyans into two squadrons; and the Syrians into one Mi-4 and one Mi-8 squadron. A comparison between the number of squadrons and the number of helicopters gives an indeterminate number of machines per unit in many cases, but a good average is 14.

As the designations 'light', 'medium' and 'heavy' suggest, the characteristics of the various machines vary greatly, and a brief look at these seems to be in order—after all, there aren't many of them.

The Mil Mi-1, first flown in 1948, was the Soviet Union's first production series helicopter. Carrying a crew of up to four, it can achieve a top speed of 118 mph (190 km/h) and a range of 236 miles (380 km). In its military guise it is designated as a light AOP or transport machine, but can also be used as an airborne ambulance with two stretchers and a medic.

The Mi-4, a Russian copy of the Sikorsky S-55, is designated a 'medium' transport and can carry a 12.7 mm machine-gun or two (?) ATGWs as well as up to 14 infantry or a comparable load of freight (ammunition, etc). In its ambulance version it can accommodate eight stretchers. Top speed is 130 mph (210 km/h) and range 124 miles (200 km) fully loaded or 255 miles (410 km) empty.

The Mi-8 is a purely Soviet design intended as a replacement for the Mi-4, is also classed as a 'medium' transport but is larger and faster. First appearing in 1961, it is twin-engined for additional safety, and has a top speed of 155-160 mph (250-260 km/h). It can carry up to 28 troops and has a range of 264 to 590 miles (425 to 950 km) depending on load.

The Mi-6 was the largest helicopter in the world when it first appeared in 1957 and can carry up to 70 troops or 40 stretchers in addition to its crew. It is unusual in having small wings to offset the pull of the rotor, and is again twin-engined for safety. This helicopter has a top speed of 186 mph (300 km/h) and a range of between 385 and 620 miles (620 and 1,000 km).

The Westland Wessex, in service with Iraq only, is a British-designed helicopter in the 'medium' category derived from the Sikorsky HSS-1 with a new engine, and first flew in the same year as the Mi-6. It can carry up to 16 soldiers or seven stretchers, has a top speed of 132 mph (212 km/h) and a range of between 270 and 480 miles (435 to 770 km).

The Aérospatiale Alouette II and III are both light utility helicopters which can be armed with machine-guns or rockets (eg, SS-11). The so-called Alouette IIs in the Middle Eastern service are in fact SE 313Bs powered by 360 instead of the later 523 bhp engines, and the 'III is by far the more potent machine. The Alouette II can carry four, the 'III six troops or two stretchers, the latter also being capable of lifting two heavy machine-guns or 20 mm cannon, or up to four ATGWs. Speeds are up to 115 mph (185 km/h) for the 'II and 131 mph (210 km/h) for the 'III, the former having a range of between 186 and 351 miles (300 to 565 km), the latter between a mere 62 and 341 miles (100 to 550 km) depending on payload.

The Aérospatiale SA 321 'Super Frelon' is an entirely different kettle of fish, being classed as heavy assault helicopter and having no fewer than three engines capable of driving it at up to 155 mph (249 km/h). This machine set up a world helicopter speed record when it first appeared in 1962. In its military transport guise it can carry up to 30 troops or 15 stretchers, and has a range of between 404 and 672 miles (650 to 1,080 km).

The Bell 205 'Iroquois' has been one of the most successful light/medium military helicopters of all time. It went into production in 1959, and was widely used in Vietnam, also providing the basis for the specialised gunship machine known as 'Huey Cobra'. These aircraft are capable of carrying up to 14 troops, six stretchers or a variety of armament including machine-guns and missiles. They can cruise at 111 mph (179 km/h) and have a top speed of 127 mph (204 km/h) with a range of between 318 and 404 miles (511 and 650 km).

Helicopters

The Sikorsky CH-53C is another heavy assault helicopter, developed after combat experience with the CH-54 'Skycrane', and first appeared in 1964. It is a sophisticated, twin-engined machine with a high top speed of 195 mph (315 km/h) and a range of between 257 and 806 miles (413 and 1,297 km). It can carry up to 64 infantry or 24 stretchers in addition to various other loads, including two machine-guns.

In a wargames context only the Mi-4, Alouette III and Iroquois have any anti-tank capability, but it is still useful to know the capacities of the others so that troops can be airlifted into the battlefield, and casualties evacuated if you go that far in your wargames. Use of helicopters should, however, be kept to a minimum, since there have never been enough around for them to be needlessly put at risk, and their major tasks appear to have been second echelon ferrying of freight.

As a footnote, wargamers creating a 'future' scenario should note the fact that, early in 1978, Egypt signed an agreement allowing her to manufacture the Lynx helicopter under licence.

13

Playing rules

Any writer of wargame playing rules invariably comes in for a certain amount of 'stick' from readers who dislike them for various reasons or who disagree with their interpretation of the historical actuality. Having concocted several sets I must have incurred as much criticism as anybody—much of it fully justified, I admit. So to put the record straight as far as the following section is concerned, I would just like to say that these rules are my own personal interpretation and that they work to the satisfaction of myself and the friends with whom I regularly play. I'm not insisting that everybody else has to agree with them, or that they are the 'last word'. Any set of rules benefits from experimentation and modification, and I'd like all my readers to feel free to do both. If a play situation reveals an anomaly—as sooner or later it is bound to, since no set of rules can cover every eventuality—then by all means drop me a line c/o the publishers and I'll give you my interpretation. Alternatively, by applying common sense and your knowledge of modern armoured warfare, resolve the situation for yourself. If there is one type of person whom I do intensely dislike it is the wargamer who argues endlessly over the most minute and insignificant interpretation of the rules in order to secure a minor advantage for himself. So I'd like to make a plea for rationality and friendship in wargames. If you encounter a situation which isn't covered in the rules, don't argue about it, simply spin a coin or roll a dice to decide whose viewpoint should prevail. Discuss the situation after the battle by all means, and try to arrive at perhaps a more logical decision, but don't let it interrupt the game or ruin the amicable atmosphere. Now, on to the rules.

First and foremost, all movement and firing is simultaneous. Players move their pieces at the same time, not alternately, as we are trying to simulate actual warfare, not invent a new form of chess. This involves writing orders, which we shall come on to in a moment. But first, the basic rules of time and space which form the framework within which any set of rules must operate. These are determined by various factors, paramount among which are rates of movement and of fire. Move lengths are different in various historical periods to take account of both. In the 'horse and musket' era it is fashionable to have a move time of 2½ minutes, this allowing a reasonable degree of movement for the rigid infantry formations of the day and a fair degree of effectiveness from massed smooth-bore musket fire. When dealing with modern tanks and weapons, the movement rates and the rates of fire are far faster, so the time scale must be shorter. I toyed for some time with the idea of a 30-second move (you may like to experiment for yourself) but this proved to have drawbacks and in the end I reverted to the one-minute move used in my previous books in this series. This permits a reasonable degree of movement without giving faster-moving vehicles the ability to leap from one side of the table to the other in a single bound, and a satisfactory level of fire effect. The main disadvantage of such a short move time is that it produces unrealistically brief battles of eight to ten minutes' duration which are really no more than skirmishes, so in a *campaign* context the move represents ten minutes, the extra time assumed to be taken up in non-positive activity such as order writing, transmitting and receiving instructions, etc. In the campaign context it also permits the possibility of rushing reserves up from 20 miles or so away, for calling up air strikes, and so forth.

Now for the ground scale, and once again I have settled for the compromise system used in my book on the North-West European Campaign of 1944-1945, whereby for weapon-firing purposes 1 mm on the table equals one metre of real ground (ie, a scale of 1:1,000), while for movement you use one centimetre to represent one km/h of a vehicle's actual speed. This sounds like gibberish, so think of it like this: if a tank has an average speed of 25 km/h, it will be able to move 25 cm on the wargames table per move. The two scales are not strictly related: if 1 mm = 1 m, then 25 km/h should really equal 416 m per minute, ie, 41.6 cm on the wargames table not 25. However, all wargaming involves compromise and a certain amount of 'fudging', and the beauty of this system is that it makes one think and speak of a vehicle's speed in terms of km/h, which *sounds* so much better than mm per minute. Anyone who does not like this system is, of course, perfectly at liberty to alter it so that the range and speed scales are in line, the conversion factor being to multiply vehicle speeds by 16.666 (ie, 1 km/h = 16.666 metres per minute). This has the drawback of producing rather lengthy moves, and if you do adopt this system you would be well advised to go back to a move time of 30 seconds rather than a minute, in which case all rates of fire given in these rules will obviously have to be halved.

Moves and weapon ranges are measured on the table with an expanding steel metric rule or tape measure. Moves are measured from the front of each vehicle, weapon ranges from the centre of the firing tank or gun to the centre of the target.

I have come to the conclusion over the last couple of years that the only really satisfactory way of working wargame rules is through the use of percentage dice throughout the game, and I'm considering revising all my published playing rules on this basis. Consequently, in these rules for the Arab-Israeli conflict, percentage dice are used throughout. These are ten-sided dice, numbered from 0-9, one dice representing the tens and the second the units. They can be obtained cheaply from one of the specialist mail order firms mentioned in the appendix.

Before you begin moving at all, radio 'nets' must be opened and orders given. This is very important because there are many 'dead' radio areas in the Sinai, and a critical factor in several battles was units losing touch with each other for varying lengths of time. To begin with, each vehicle and infantry section must be given a call-sign, a few examples of which have already been given in the text, but they are simple enough to make up. Unit commander vehicles are almost invariably given the traditional designation 'Sunray' in addition to their unit code name. Tank radios normally operate on three frequencies. The unit commander has one frequency which keeps him in communication with his immediate superior at company, battalion, brigade or division level, a second which puts him in touch with his subordinate commanders at squadron level or whatever, and a third which is the intercom through which he speaks to his own tank's crew. In the heat of battle it is all too common for tanker commanders to obtain the wrong radio setting inadvertently, with the result that many a driver has been known to have received a model situation report from his company commander and many a senior officer subjected to a blistering attack on his driving ability and parentage! The chances of an order being received during a battle can thus be seen to be in the region of 1:3, although training and alertness naturally improve the chances. However, due to the areas of dead ground, let us leave it at 1:3 (ie, 33 per cent) for the first occasion (move) on which an order is transmitted, increasing the chances to 2:3 (66 per cent) on the second move and almost 3:3 or 99 per cent on the third. This will provide sufficient delay and confusion to make a game realistic without being too frustrating! For the first move, at the beginning of a battle, it can be assumed that tank commanders are more alert and listening in to their superior's frequency with greater attention; so for the first move only you begin with a 2:3 chance of receiving a message correctly.

How messages are transmitted is simplicity itself. The senior commander on the spot (ie, you, the player) is assumed to have held an Orders Group prior to the battle, during which you will have briefed your immediate subordinates, whilst they in turn will have briefed their own juniors and so on down to individual crew level. Thus everybody has a greater or lesser knowledge of what his immediate task is supposed to be, those at the bottom rung only knowing their own immediate objective in detail. This system precludes 'telepathic' tank commanders suddenly moving on their own initiative to the assistance of a friendly unit on the other side of the wargames table, something one sees far too often in many games. However, this means that general orders for the conduct of a battle can be written down in advance, objectives designated, etc, and the only message which needs to be transmitted at the start of the game is 'Move Now; Over'. To see whether the message has been received and acknowledged, throw a pair of percentage dice for each tank, with a 66 per cent chance of receiving it correctly on the first move and a 99 per cent chance on the second. Invariably, a proportion of your forces will be delayed for a move before starting up for their objectives. Similarly, to change orders, or to transmit a situation report during the course of a game, throw the percentage dice with a 33 per cent chance of success on the first try, 66 per cent on the second, and 99 per cent on the third and subsequent attempts. For simplicity's sake, we allow each tank to receive or transmit two orders per move, or alternatively receive one and transmit one. All orders must be written down if the simultaneous movement system is to operate properly, unless you and your opponent trust each other fully, in which case they can be given verbally. Writing things down is a little bit time-consuming, but does prevent arguments.

The process can be accelerated by devising a system of standing orders coupled with simple symbols and abbreviations which can rapidly be jotted down alongside each unit's name on your order pad.

Electronic counter-measures, ie, jamming, is a complication which can be introduced if desired. The presence of an ECM vehicle must be declared at the beginning of the game and, while it continues to jam, the chances of successful transmissions among the opposing force are halved. Isolated vehicles which may be the cause of the jamming should, unless extremely well camouflaged, be prepared for an immediate artillery bombardment!

Depending on whether you want to take matters to an extreme or not, the Arab player should really be penalised by further reductions in radio communications because Soviet-manufactured instruments (eg, the R 123) have to be pre-set by electronic technicians whereas the American tactical tranceivers (such as the VRC12) can be pre-set by their combatant operators at any time.

Having written and transmitted orders, movement and firing can begin. Now, although all action is simultaneous, it is advantageous to standardise on one sequence of actions in each move, once again to help prevent arguments. The normal sequence is: moving, firing, reaction tests. Reaction tests, or morale, have not been used in any of the previous books in this series, but seemed so vital to me in the context of the Arab-Israeli situation that I have introduced them here. They can readily be adapted for World War 2 scenarios. But first, movement. This is very easy on our basis of 1 cm/minute per km/h of the vehicle's actual speed, but one factor which needs taking into account is that tanks do not charge around at top speed all the time and, if they were to try, the rate of mechanical breakdown would be far higher. For this reason two speeds are given in the following table: a normal cruising speed, and an emergency speed. Vehicles using the emergency speed will incur penalties which we'll come on to in a moment, but first the basic rates.

Movement rates

Vehicle	Cruising speed	Emergency speed	Vehicle	Cruising speed	Emergency speed
H 35/39	27	35	PzKpfw IVF2	16	40
Cromwell	28	53	T-34/85	40	50
Sherman	28	42	T-34/100	40	50
Super Sherman	30	45	IS-III	28	37
Isherman	30	45	T-10	28	37
L/33	25	36	T-54	32	48
AMX-13	40	60	T-55	34	50
AMX M le 50	30	45	T-62	29	55
Centurion III	26	34	PT-76	30	44
Super Centurion	29	43	BTR-50	30	44
Sabra(?)	26	34	BTR-40	60	80
Merkava	30(?)	45(?)	BTR-152	55	75
M-48A1	28	42	BTR-60	50	80
M-48A2	32	48	BMP-1	29	55
M-60A1	32	48	BRDM-1	50	80
M-3	48	73	BRDM-2	70	100
AML 90	70	100	SU-76	22	40
Staghound	50	80	SU-85	25	56
M-113A1	45	68	SU-100	25	56
M-110	32	56	ISU-122/152	19	37
RBY-1	70	100	ASU-57	31	45

Inevitably, some wargamers reading the above list will immediately say 'what about the such-and-such?'. To which the answer must be, there isn't room here, go and look it up for yourself in *Jane's Weapon Systems* or a similar publication and add it in yourself. This book is a *guide* and does not pretend to cover everything!

Be that as it may, we have not quite finished with movement yet, because the type of terrain will impose limitations. Across soft dunes, therefore, or in mountainous countryside such as the Golan Heights, reduce the above cruising speeds by half.

Infantry sections normally move around at a steady 4 km/h (giving them a 4 cm tabletop move) but may 'double' during one move in three. ATGW, heavy machine-gun and mortar sections move at half these rates due to the weight and clumsiness of their weapons. 'Digging in' takes three full moves.

Soft-skin trucks are most simply classified as 'light' (four wheels), 'medium' (six wheels) and 'heavy' (eight or more wheels). Light vehicles have a cruising speed of 50 km/h and an 'emergency' speed of 80 km/h; medium trucks 35 and 50 km/h; and heavy trucks 25 and 40 km/h. These are average cross-country speeds, which should be halved when traversing bad terrain but may be increased by 25 per cent on metalled roads.

One type of vehicle which is not affected by terrain is the helicopter. As Mike Spick says later, they are better treated as fast-moving soft-skin vehicles than as aircraft! The two major roles for which they are likely to be required in wargames are as troop carriers or as gunships, with machine-guns or ATGWs, which we'll come on to in a moment, but first movement—and remember that, since they can hover and do not have a stalling speed, they can move at any speed between zero km/h and their maximum.

Helicopter movement rates*

Type	Cruise	Maximum	Type	Cruise	Maximum
Mil Mi-1	126	190	Wessex	141	212
Mil Mi-4	140	210	Alouette II	123	185
Mil Mi-8	173	260	Alouette III	140	210
Mil Mi-6	200	300	SA 321	166	249
Bell 205	136	204	CH-53C	210	315

*In km/h. The working cruise rate at sea level has been averaged at two-thirds the maximum speed.

Unfortunately, such speeds are impractical to work with on the wargames table for obvious reasons, so we compromise by halving them, giving cruise moves of between 63 and 105 cm. Helicopters coming for a landing will slow down to half this again in the half move preceding landing, and the emergency speed should normally just be used for trying to escape from enemy fire.

To digress for a moment. Many wargamers seem to rely entirely on a points system for building up their armies, and I have been deluged with requests from readers of previous books in this series to provide a points system for building up balanced opposing forces. Why, I don't know. The only time a points system is of any use is in a knock-out competition, and I don't like it even then. So I am not going to provide one here. If you want to fight a 'game' (because that is all it will be) with balanced forces, then work something out for yourself. I fight my battles with unit against unit, regardless of composition, and in my opinion this not only results in more realistic battles, it also produces more interesting ones. If everything is worked out on a points system—and I know WRG (God bless 'em) are very strong on this—it produces a game which is more like chess than a real battle, and I don't want to know. So it's up to you.

Returning to this point about mechanical breakdown, the first observation which must be made is that they were and still are common on both sides, although progressively less so as vehicles become adapted for Middle Eastern conditions. The most common complaint appears to be over-heating, usually due to faulty maintenance, which causes bearings to seize. This can affect engines, transmissions, gun-laying apparatus or virtually any other moving part of a vehicle. My own experience, which, I must admit, is limited to the British Army, indicates that up to 50 per cent of vehicles *may* be unserviceable at any given time during an on-going campaign situation. It is well known that serviceability, particularly of Arab vehicles, has sunk well below this during the various Middle Eastern wars, and in a campaign context this should be your gauge: throw a dice or roll a coin for each vehicle each day to see whether or not it is serviceable. In a one-off battle situation such a system would be boring, because approximately half of your vehicles would be immobilised all the time, so you need to make a compromise.

The following rule is another optional one like radio jamming. It makes games

Playing rules

more realistic but it also makes them more frustrating. The rule assumes that, at the beginning of a game, all vehicles and weapons are fully serviceable but that, as the game progresses, they will become less so, and mechanical breakdowns will become more likely. This also brings us back to the earlier point about 'emergency' or 'charge' moves. The playing rule is empirical, and you may wish to modify it. The way we work it is as follows. All vehicles stand a five per cent chance of being immobilised through mechanical breakdown each move, and must be diced for. If the vehicle has a traversing turret, you should dice twice, to see whether the damage is to the engine/transmission system, or to the turret traverse/gun elevating gear, with a 60:40 probability. The former means the vehicle cannot move until repaired, the latter that it can move but not fire. Field repairs are covered in the next paragraph. If, however, a vehicle is utilising its 'emergency' speed, it stands an additional five per cent per move chance of breaking down (ie, ten per cent at the end of the first move, 15 per cent at the end of the second, and so on until breakdown eventually becomes a certainty). This (a) reflects reality and (b) prevents players, or at least inhibits them, from moving around at full speed all the time. When dicing for a vehicle with traversing turret under *these* circumstances, the probabilities are 75 per cent to the engine/transmission and 25 per cent to the gun.

In order to effect field repairs you must have an engineer vehicle on the table, or else an armoured recovery vehicle or similar AFV to tow the stricken tank back to the safety of the rear echelons. ARVs or AFVs engaged in towing move at a quarter the normal rate for their type. To effect repairs, move the engineer vehicle up to the damaged tank and throw the percentage dice, rounding up to the nearest ten per cent. The result is the number of campaign minutes it will take to effect the repairs (eg, a score of 55, rounded up to 60, means 60 minutes' work, or six game moves). The dice have to be rounded up because a score below ten would otherwise mean that repair would be instantaneous!

We now come to the mechanics of actual combat, and I propose to deal with tank and anti-tank fire first. Percentage dice will be used again, and the entire system is somewhat different to that used in previous books in this series. The reasoning is very simple. Because modern anti-tank projectiles are capable of penetrating the thickest existing armour plate, armoured protection is less important than in the past. Whereas a 1944 Sherman would try to manoeuvre to the side or rear of an opposing Tiger or Panther in order to increase its chances of knocking out the German vehicle, a 1967 Super Sherman wouldn't bother since its firepower is almost as effective against the thick front plates of an enemy tank as against the thinner sides and rear. This means that we do not need elaborate tables giving the armour thickness for turret and hull front, sides and rear, but can utilise a much more simple system whereby vehicles are merely designated 'light', 'medium' or 'heavy'. As we have already seen, it is accuracy which is the critical factor in modern tank battles, the first hit normally being decisive.

Going back to our list of AFVs then, the armour classifications are as follows:

Vehicle	Classification	Vehicle	Classification
H 35/39	Light	PzKpfw IVF2	Light
Cromwell	Medium	T-34/85	Medium
Sherman	Medium	T-34/100	Medium
Super Sherman	Medium	IS-III	Heavy
Isherman	Medium	T-10	Heavy
L/33	Medium	T-54	Heavy
AMX-13	Light	T-55	Heavy

Tank Battles in Miniature

AMX M le 50	Light	T-62	Heavy
Centurion III	Heavy	PT-76	Light
Super Centurion	Heavy	BTR-50	Light
Sabra	Heavy	BTR-40	Light
Merkava	Heavy	BTR-152	Light
M-48A1	Medium	BTR-60	Light
M-48A2	Medium	BMP-1	Light
M-60A1	Heavy	BRDM-1	Light
M-3	Light	BRDM-2	Light
AML 90	Light	SU-76	Light
Staghound	Light	SU-85	Medium
M-113A1	Light	SU-100	Medium
M-110	Light	ISU-122/152	Heavy
RBY-1	Light	ASU-57	Light

Before you can fire at a target you must, of course, be able to see it, so the next step is observation. For this we use the good old clock code, just as in the aerial game (see diagram). For observation purposes it is 'understood' that the commander of a tank normally faces forwards regardless of which way the turret happens to be pointing, unless he is actually engaging a target. When it comes to observation, Israeli

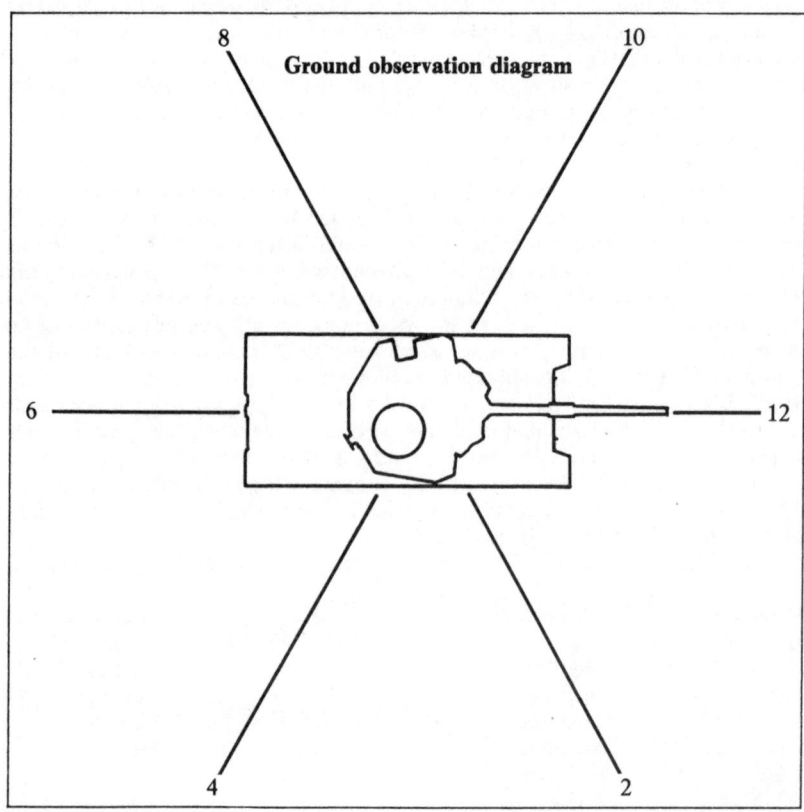

vehicles are at an advantage because their commanders invariably go into the action standing in their turrets, while Arab crews operate buttoned down. (The Israelis suffer a disadvantage in that they incur more casualties among their tank commanders, which we'll get on to in a moment.) Range, movement and cover also affect the chances of spotting a target, and it's out with the percentage dice again.

The basic chances of observation are as follows: **Israeli vehicles**— 12 o'clock to two o'clock and 12 o'clock to ten o'clock, 70 per cent; two o'clock to four o'clock and ten o'clock to eight o'clock, 50 per cent; four o'clock to eight o'clock, 30 per cent; **Arab vehicles**—12 o'clock to two o'clock and 12 o'clock to ten o'clock, 50 per cent; two o'clock to four o'clock and ten o'clock to eight o'clock, 35 per cent; and four o'clock to eight o'clock, 20 per cent.

To these basic probabilities, add ten per cent if the target is moving; deduct five per cent for every 500 metres over 1,000 metres distance (ie, target at 2,500 metres range, deduct 15 per cent); and finally deduct ten per cent if the target is hull-down, 50 per cent if it is turret down with just the commander's head visible. Fully camouflaged vehicles/guns in prepared positions (eg, under nets, dug in) would not normally be spotted until they opened fire, but allow a ten per cent chance of observing them due to extraneous factors such as sunlight glinting off binoculars, etc. 'Dummy' camouflaged positions could worry your opponent!

You may dice for the chances of observing all enemy vehicles in your vicinity each move, but you will engage the first target that you spot and only return to observing when it is destroyed. Helicopters use the aircraft observation system described in Chapter 16.

Having successfully observed a target, you may now try to engage it. Success or failure depends on the accuracy of your gun or missile at the target's range, and to a lesser degree to the state of your crew's training. That's a simple one to get out of the way. If the battle being fought is pre-1964 or post-1967 both Arab and Israeli crews are assumed to be at the same level of training, so there are no penalties. During the period 1964 to 1967, after General Tal took command of the Israeli Armoured Corps, Israeli gunnery training was noticeably higher than that of all Arab nations except Jordan, and they should be allowed plus five per cent on their chances of securing a hit.

Ranges are designated 'effective' and 'long', the chances of a hit at long range being measurably less than at effective range or less, but ranges vary from weapon to weapon so that is the next item we need to examine.

The following list includes the main tank and anti-tank guns which will be encountered, together with muzzle velocity in metres per second (this varies according to the type of projectile, so I have selected the most effective); effective range (ie, the range at which the gun would normally be fired); maximum range (ie, the range beyond which its armour-piercing ability disappears to all wargaming intents and purposes); rate of fire in rounds per minute; and types of ammunition which can be used. There are question marks in several places due to two factors: firstly, the difficulty in obtaining accurate information on modern weapon systems due to security blankets; and secondly difficulties in obtaining information on intermediate (ie, post-war but not modern) weapons because nobody's been interested enough to compile them for public consumption—the *Jane's Weapon Systems* concept is relatively new with the result that precise figures for the 1950s and early 1960s are virtually impossible to obtain. If any reader can eliminate any of the question marks then all modern wargamers, including myself, would be deeply grateful. Definitions of the various types of ammunition can be found in the glossary.

Tank Battles in Miniature

Vehicle	Weapon	Muzzle velocity (m/s)	Effective range (m)	Maximum range (m)	Rate of fire (rpm)	Type(s) of ammunition
H-35/39	37 mm SA 38	700	500	900	8	AP
Cromwell	75 mm QF V	620	640	1,800	10	APC, APCBC
Sherman M4A3	76 mm M1	793	1,000	2,500	18	APDS, APCBC
'French' Sherman	75 mm CN-75	900(?)	1,250(?)	2,750(?)	10(?)	APDS, HESH(?)
Super Sherman	105 mm D-1508	915	1,500	3,000	6	HEAT
Isherman	105 mm	As Above				
AMX-13	75 mm	As for 'French' Sherman				
Centurion III	20 pdr	800(?)	1,000(?)	2,500(?)	8	APDS, HEAT(?)
Super Centurion / Merkava / M-48A1/A2 (mod) / M-60A1	105 mm L-7	1,470	1,800	3,000+	9	APDS, HESH
M-48A1/A2	90 mm M41	1,250	1,500	3,000	9	HVAP, HEAT
AML 90	90 mm	760	1,000(?)	2,000(?)	10(?)	HEAT(?)
Staghound	37 mm	880	500	1,500	20	APC
Sabra	122 mm (?)	As T-10(?)				
PzKpfw IVF2	75 mm L/48	750	825	1,800	10	AP
T-34/85	85 mm L/51.5	792	1,280	2,750	8	AP
T-34/100	100 mm L/56	838	1,460	3,000(?)	8	AP, APC(?)
IS-III	122 mm	620	1,400	3,000(?)	6	APDS, HEAT(?)
T-10	122 mm	620	1,500	3,000+	6	APDS, HEAT(?)
T-54/T-55	100 mm D10T2S	900	1,000(?)	2,500(?)	7	APC, HVAP, HEAT
T-62	115 mm U-5TS	1,600	1,500	3,000(?)	5	APDS, HEAT
PT-76	76.2 mm D-56T	1,000(?)	1,000(?)	2,500(?)	7(?)	APC, HVAP, HEAT
SU-76	76.2 mm L/41.2	620	820	1,500	10	AP
SU-85	85 mm L/51.5	792	1,280	2,750	8	AP
SU-100	100 mm L/56	838	1,460	3,000	8	AP, APDS
ISU-122	122 mm	620	1,400	3,000	6	APDS, HEAT(?)

Playing rules

Vehicle	Weapon	Muzzle velocity (m/s)	Effective range (m)	Maximum range (m)	Rate of fire (rpm)	Type(s) of ammunition
ASU-57	57 mm L/73	1,000	1,000(?)	2,500(?)	10(?)	HVAP
Jeeps, half-tracks, APCs, etc; missiles and recoilless weapons	SS-10/SS-11	190	500*	3,000	NA	HEAT
	Cobra	83	400*	2,000	NA	HEAT
	TOW	277	65*	3,750	3	HEAT
	Snapper	88	500*	2,300	NA	HEAT
	Sagger	93	500*	3,000	NA	HEAT
	Swatter	97	500*	2,500	NA	HEAT
	RPG-7	(?)	50*	200	NA	HEAT
	LAW	(?)	25*	75	NA	HEAT
	Bazooka	83	25*	100	10	HEAT
	106mm recoilless	(?)	50*	800	6(?)	HESH
	B-10 82 mm	(?)	50*	500	6(?)	HEAT
	B-11 107 mm	(?)	50*	1,000	6(?)	HEAT
Towed anti-tank weapons	25 pdr	532	750	1,500	5	AP
	105 mm M101A1	381	750	1,000	8	HEAT
	122 mm M1931/37	800	750	1,500	6	APHE
	122 mm M1938	335	750	1,500	6	HEAT
	122 mm D-74	885	750	1,500	6	APHE
	122 mm D-30	740	500	915	8	HEAT
	130 mm M-46	930	750	1,500	6	APHE
	152 mm M1937	600	750	1,500	4	APHE
	152 mm M1943	432	600	1,200	4	Semi-AP
	57 mm M1943	900+	500	900	10	APHE, HVAP
	76.2 mm	325+	500	1,000	15	APHE, HVAP, HEAT
	85 mm D-44	1,030	750	1,500	15	HVAP
	100 mm M1955	900+	750	1,500	7	APHE, HEAT

*Denotes minimum range at which weapon can be fired. Maximum is the same as effective in these cases. Note that several guns capable of firing different types of armour-piercing ammunition have varying muzzle velocities, depending on the round, of 300 to over 1,000 m/s.

Anyway, having observed a target and decided it is in range (modern range-finding apparatus is sufficiently accurate that the range can be measured before firing in a wargame), all one has to do now is secure a hit. Laser rangefinders, which will probably be used in any future full-scale Middle East war, increase the chances of a first time hit at effective range to 97 per cent! Battle records indicate that a hit will almost invariably be scored at up to 'effective' range within the first three rounds if the target is stationary and within five if it is moving, which gives us a good basis for firing tank and anti-tank guns. Missiles are rather different, the wire-guided type appearing to have a 50:50 chance of a hit against a stationary target and approximately 30 per cent against a moving one. The higher a weapon's rate of fire, therefore, the greater the chances of achieving a hit during a wargames move. Average rates of fire fall into convenient groups of three: 1 - 3, 4 - 6, 7 - 9, 10 - 12 and 13 - 15 (the two exceptions are the M4A3 and Staghound, with 18 and 20, which should be included for wargaming purposes in the latter group). When firing, then, first decide which bracket your gun falls into, and throw the percentage dice one, two, three, four or five times, with a 33 per cent chance of a first round hit against a stationary target, 66 per cent second round and 99 per cent third round, or a 20 per cent first, 40 second, 60 third, 80 fourth and 100 fifth round chance against a moving target. Deduct 20 per cent if the target is hull-down; deduct ten per cent if the firing tank or gun is itself under fire; deduct 25 per cent if the firing vehicle is itself moving; and halve the above percentages when firing at between effective and maximum ranges. The same applies to missiles, which otherwise have a standard 50 per cent chance of a hit against a stationary target or 30 per cent against a moving target. The only missile system with which the chances of a hit increase with the second and subsequent rounds is TOW, which should be given an extra ten per cent chance per move whilst firing at the same target. Helicopters must hover when firing ATGWs but stand a slightly higher chance of achieving a hit, 36 or 60 per cent respectively.

If you hit your target with the first round and have more shots in hand, you can have a go at a second target, but this obviously means traversing your weapon and involves a time penalty of half a move. The second target has, of course, to be observed first.

As we have seen, with modern anti-tank projectiles there is only a very small chance of any vehicle surviving a hit totally unscathed: for unarmoured vehicles the chance is zero; for light AFVs it is five per cent; for medium, ten per cent; and for heavy, 15 per cent. Assuming that the target is damaged, throw the percentage dice again as follows: 0 to 40 equals a hit on turret or superstructure, 41 to 100 equals a hit on hull or chassis (this being a larger target). Hits on hull-down vehicles are automatically on the turret so this dice throw can be waived. Now throw again. Hit on turret—0 to 20 per cent, commander killed if standing in cupola, no other damage; 21 to 40 per cent, commander killed if standing in turret, turret traverse mechanism jammed; 41 to 60 per cent, turret penetrated, all occupants killed, gun put out of action; 61 to 80 per cent, turret penetrated, 50 per cent chance of ammunition exploding and destroying vehicle totally (dice again); 81 per cent or higher, vehicle explodes, all occupants killed. Hit on hull—0 to 20 per cent, tracks broken, vehicle immobilised until they can be repaired; 21 to 40 per cent, transmission damaged, vehicle immobilised and cannot be repaired during course of game but may be salvaged later; 41 to 60 per cent, hit on engine, vehicle immobilised, 50 per cent chance of catching fire, crew bales out regardless; 61 to 80 per cent, hit on engine which brews up automatically, crew bales out; 81 per cent or higher, vehicle explodes, all occupants killed.

Moving on to artillery fire, things become slightly more complicated, so let's get the easy bit out of the way first. Artillery fire may be 'direct', ie, over open sights at a target which is visible to the detachment; or 'indirect' against a target which the detachment cannot see but whose co-ordinates are radioed by an observer. Direct fire with field artillery pieces is tackled in exactly the same way as anti-tank fire, with the same probabilities except that a 'hit' is not assumed to be spot-on, merely within the projectile blast radius.

With indirect fire, you don't actually need to put the model guns on the table, you just need a ground or air observer who radios the co-ordinates of a target which *he* can see. Indirect artillery fire would not normally be used against pin-point targets such as individual vehicles, but more often against large troop concentrations, soft-skin vehicle parks, buildings and fortifications, etc. Indirect fire is also useless against moving targets other than infantry because, by the time an observer has radioed co-ordinates, the guns have been elevated or depressed, and the shell fired, the original co-ordinates will be wrong. It's really up to you to use common sense in selecting targets for indirect artillery fire.

I don't normally like 'gadgets' in wargames—a tape measure and a pair of dice are quite sufficient clutter—but I have been forced to come to the conclusion that 'burst circles' are a good idea. On a piece of transparent plastic or Perspex, mark out five circles with 50 mm diameters as shown in the accompanying diagram. Number the circles 1 to 5 (it doesn't matter in what order). Now, when firing indirect fire, hold the centre of the central circle over the centre of the target, then throw the percentage dice. 0 to 20 equals a hit in circle number 1, 21 to 40 a hit in number 2, 41 to 60 a hit in number three, 61 to 80 a hit in number 4 and 81 to 100 a hit in number five. Any target within the circle indicated is at risk of being destroyed.

If the first attempt misses the precise target required, on the second shot increase the chances of a hit in the central circle to 40 per cent, reducing the chances of a hit in one of the outer circles from 80 to 60 per cent, or 15 per cent each. On the third attempt increase the chances of a hit in the central circle to 60 per cent, giving ten per cent each for the outer circles. If you still haven't got it, your gunners obviously need a refresher course, but in any case a fourth round hit is assumed to be automatic.

Having achieved a hit on something, we now have to apportion damage, and this relies on two factors: the type of target and the weight of the shell. A shell's destructiveness is based on a complex series of formulae resulting in an eventual rule

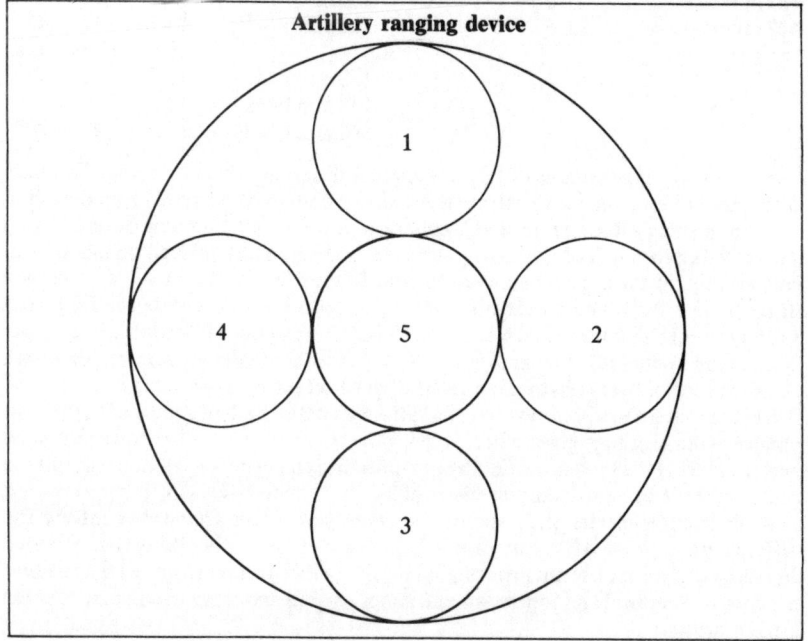

Artillery ranging device

of thumb equation involving two factors: a zone of total destruction based on the equation 100 kg of high explosive to totally destroy anything unarmoured within a 25 metre sphere; and a blast effect radius out to 370 metres with the same weight of explosive. Infantry, soft-skin vehicles, etc, inside the latter zone stand a diminishing chance of being damaged the further away from the centre of the explosion they are. In fact, the residual blast effect from the same 100 kg shell would extend as far as 790 metres, but I do not feel it is necessary to go to these lengths in wargames rules. The following table lists the common artillery weapons deployed in the Middle East over the years, their radius of total destruction in metres, and their blast effect radius, also in metres. As a guide in calculating the latter, the actual warhead in missiles is taken as half its total weight, the remainder being occupied by propellant, etc. This *is* rule of thumb, I admit, but produces a result comparable to that of artillery shells of similar calibre.

Weapon	HE shell weight	Radius of destruction	Blast radius	Weapon	HE shell weight	Radius of destruction	Blast radius
57 mm M-1943	2.8	1	10	130 mm M-46	33.4	8	124
76.2 mm M-1942	6.2	2	23	152 mm M-1937	43.6	11	161
85 mm D-44	9.5	3	35	152 mm M-1943	39.9	10	148
87.6 mm 25 pdr	11.34	3	42	155 mm OB	43	11	159
100 mm M-1955	15.7	4	58	155 mm M114	43.8	11	162
105 mm M101A1	19.06	5	70	155 mm M59	43.4	11	160
122 mm M-1931/37	25.5	6	94	180 mm S/23	136	34	503
122 mm M-1938	21.8	5	81	**Rockets**			
122 mm D-74	27.3	7	101	130 mm M51	24.2	6	45
122 mm D-30	21.8	5	81	122 mm BM21	45.8 or 77.5	11 19	85 143
				132 mm BM13	42.5	11	79
				140 mm BM14	39.6	10	73
				240 mm BM24	112	28	207

Now for the effectiveness of HE fire against different sorts of targets. To begin with, modern medium tanks will not normally be bothered by anything smaller than a 155 mm shell, although there is a chance of a track being damaged, or of radio aerials being torn off, of any crew members exposed being injured or killed and, conceivably, of the engine being set on fire. If a medium or heavy AFV receives a direct hit by a shell of under 155 mm calibre, throw the percentage dice as follows: 0 to 25 per cent, hit on tracks; 26 to 50 per cent, hit on upper hull front; 51 to 75 per cent, hit on upper hull rear; and 76 to 100 per cent, hit on turret. A track hit gives a 50:50 chance of breaking them; a front upper hull hit does no damage unless the driver is exposed, in which case he is killed; a rear upper hull hit stands a ten per cent chance of setting the engine on fire—crew bale out; a turret hit will remove any radio aerials, leaving the tank incommunicado until they can be replaced, and will kill the commander if he is standing in his cupola.

A hit from a heavier shell stands the same percentage chances of hitting the different parts of the AFV, but gives a 75 per cent chance of breaking a track and a 25 per cent chance of setting the engine on fire; other factors identical except that the crew will certainly be concussed and should spend one move inactive to pass the aspirin around.

Light AFVs stand a far higher chance of damage. Treat hits on trackwork as above, other hits as follows: hull front, no damage up to 105 mm, above that a 25 per cent chance of actual penetration with a shell between 106 and 154 mm calibre and a 50 per cent chance of penetration with a really heavy weapon; turret, as hull front; hull rear, no damage with a shell up to 75 mm, 25 per cent chance of penetration up to 105 mm, 50 per cent up to 155 mm and 75 per cent above 155 mm. Exposed crew members will automatically be killed, radio aerials removed from turret. Hits on the hull rear give a 50 per cent chance of brewing up the engine, whereupon the crew will bale out.

AFVs are not affected by near misses, although exposed crewmen may be and should be treated as dug-in infantry, see below.

Any soft-skin vehicle or unfortified building hit by an HE shell is automatically destroyed. Bunkers should be classified 'light', 'medium' and 'heavy', requiring direct hits from shells of up to 105, 106-155 and over 155 mm calibre respectively before any damage is done. Bunkers hit by shells of sufficient weight will be penetrated and their occupants killed. Near misses do not affect them.

Infantry in the open will automatically be killed up to the extent of the radius of destruction. Those further away must be diced for as follows: within radius of destruction × 2, 90 per cent chance of being killed; r of d × 3, 80 per cent; r of d × 4, 70 per cent, and so on. To give an example, a man standing 20 metres away from the centre of a 105 mm shell blast with a radius of destruction of five metres will stand a 70 per cent chance of being killed or incapacitated, one 30 metres away a 50 per cent chance.

Dug-in infantry at the point of impact will be killed, but thereafter their chances of survival increase sharply. At r of d × 2 they have a 75 per cent chance of being injured, at r of d × 3 a 50 per cent chance, at r of d × 4 a 25 per cent chance, and outside that are safe so long as they keep their heads down.

Rockets fired in salvoes 'spread' to a considerable degree. The rule of thumb I applied in *Tank Battles in Miniature 3* has not been torn to shreds by readers as far as I am aware, so it will suffice here: 32 rockets will fall into an area roughly 100 metres square, thus 16 into an area 50 metres on each side, 12 into a 40-metre area and 40 into a 125-metre square. The blast areas will therefore overlap to a considerable degree.

We must now move quickly on to consider infantry fire other than with bazookas or ATGWs. For the purposes of simplicity, each infantry section is treated as a composite unit with a firepower effectiveness commensurate with its weapons. These are small-arms (ie, rifles, sub-machine-guns and assault rifles), machine-guns and mortars, only the latter having to be fired separately. Sections should be identified before the game as ordinary, machine-gun or mortar and organised in the correct proportions as per Chapter 10.

To begin with, depending on the type of target presented, each player should nominate whether he is firing single-shot, semi-automatic or cyclic, the last being something of a panic measure just before you are overrun! Single-shot fire is used at long range, semi-automatic at medium and cyclic at short, the ranges designated being 0 to 100 metres, 100 to 300 metres and 300 metres plus. Infantry sections have a 'firepower factor' of 25 at long range, 50 at medium range and 80 at short range: these represent the percentage chances of scoring hits on their target(s) and also the percentage of casualties which will be inflicted on the target hit. To give an example, an infantry section firing at an enemy section at 200 metres' range stands a 50 per cent chance of hitting it and, having hit it will cause 50 per cent casualties, subject to the following deductions: target unit is running, — ten per cent; target unit is crawling, − 20 per cent; target unit is lying prone, − 30 per cent; target unit is dug-in, − 40 per cent; target unit is firing back, − five per cent. If the section firing is a machine-gun unit the fire can only be semi-automatic or cyclic, and the ranges are longer, so we make short range anything up to 300 metres, medium range up to 600 metres and long range anything above this. Hit chances are 30, 60 and 90 per cent respectively, as are casualties subject to the above deductions for circumstances. Infantry behind stone walls, etc, (ie, in 'hard cover') count as dug-in against small-arms fire, though not, obviously, against artillery or mortar fire.

Mortars are treated in the same way as indirect artillery. Use the hit-point device to determine where the bombs fall, and calculate casualties exactly as with artillery fire. Mortars in the 80 mm bracket have minimum and maximum ranges of 300 to 1,000 metres; in the 120 mm bracket of 400 to 1,200 metres; and in the 160 mm bracket of 600 to 1,800 metres.

Finally, we come to morale, always the most difficult part to write in any set of wargame rules. Morale depends on a variety of factors—training, discipline, education, leadership, availability of supporting units, flank security, comparative strengths, casualties suffered and so on.

The usual method of dealing with morale is to give each type of unit a 'morale factor' and then add or deduct points according to circumstances, and it is relatively easy to adapt the same principle for use with percentage dice. If we say that all units start with a morale factor of 100, representing the soldier's frame of mind when he is reasonably happy, eg, in a secure position, having incurred no casualties and with adequate support, the way to tackle things is to deduct appropriate percentages for changing conditions.

Arab units should really be penalised if you are fighting part of the 1967 campaign, to represent their general low state of morale, training and leadership. This is entering into the thorny area of 'national characteristics' and I leave it entirely optional whether you use the rule or not. If you *do*, then Arab units in this campaign begin with a basic morale factor of 80 instead of 100.

From the basic morale factor deduct one per cent for every one per cent casualties (eg, 20 per cent casualties, deduct 20 from morale factor). Deduct five per cent for every move's distance away the nearest supporting unit happens to be (eg, closest unit three moves' distance away, deduct 15 per cent from morale factor). Deduct ten per cent if the enemy breaks through or suddenly appears on your flank. Deduct 20 per cent for an attack from the rear. Deduct five per cent if the unit is under small-arms fire. Deduct ten per cent if it is under artillery or rocket fire. Deduct 20 per cent from infantry units threatened by tanks unless they have friendly tanks in support *or* they are armed with ATGWs.

To take an exceptional case, a unit beginning with a morale factor of 100 could, say, have suffered 20 per cent casualties, have no supporting units within two moves' distance, be under artillery and small-arms fire, and menaced by tanks in its rear! The total deductions from this lot would be 20 + 10 + 15 + 20 + 20 = 85, in which case it would certainly panic and either attempt to flee or surrender.

Units whose morale falls below 50 will refuse to advance until or unless circumstances alter. Units whose morale falls below 40 per cent will involuntarily retire at their best speed back towards the nearest supporting units and/or cover. Units whose morale falls below 30 will break completely and run, unless surrounded, in which case they will surrender.

14

Skirmish-type games

Does the end justify the means? A rhetorical question, really, because so much inevitably depends on circumstance. When it comes to international terrorism, however, the reaction of all civilised people must surely be 'no'. Holding innocent hostages as pawns for a cause—however worthy—can never be justified. Nevertheless, recent years have seen a diabolical increase in terrorism the world wide, usually perpetrated by supposed left-wing groups whose members hold scant regard for the sanctity of human life—their own or other people's.

I was actually at Frankfurt airport on the occasion that German commandos returned an airliner full of rescued hostages to their families after the Mogadishu raid. Like all of the exultantly cheering spectators, I felt nothing but admiration for the prompt and daring manner in which this rescue had been carried out. But I wish I had been in Uganda at the beginning of July 1976. . .

On June 27 of that year Air France Flight 139 departed from Athens for New York. Unbeknown to the authorities, the passenger list included several terrorists of the Che Guevara and the Gaza Commando groups who commandeered the aircraft en route, forced its crew to detour via a refuelling stop at Benghazi, and finally landed at Entebbe airport in Uganda. Here, the passengers from the highjacked aircraft were housed in the old terminal building under the guns of both the terrorists and Ugandan soldiers.

The terrorists demanded the release of 'political' prisoners in Israeli jails and the return of certain territories to the 'Palestinian' cause. The reasons they had highjacked a French airliner were threefold: first, the plane carried a preponderance of Jewish passengers and people travelling under Israeli passports; secondly because France, as we have seen, has often sided with the Israeli cause; and thirdly because they hoped the highjacking of an airliner belonging to a non-aligned international power would bring extra pressure to bear on the government of Israel.

How naïve can you get? Terrorism is something which faces every civilised nation today, and the governments of the world are only just beginning to face up to the fact that the only way to fight it is by force. The Dutch and the Germans have learned this lesson the hard way; the Soviets have always been ruthless; America, Britain and other Western nations are gradually learning; but the Israelis have always known.

The result was the Entebbe raid, immortalised in several books and at least three films. Whilst the Israeli government played for time, plans were drawn up for the hostages' rescue. Israeli intelligence already possessed the plans of Entebbe airport since it had been constructed largely under the supervision of Israeli engineers during the time when Israel and Uganda had enjoyed good diplomatic relations. The plan called for the use of four C-130 Hercules aircraft filled with Israeli paratroops and the co-operation of neutral governments, especially that of Kenya.

Both were forthcoming and 'Operation Thunderbolt' got under way.

On July 3 the Israeli cabinet gave its seal of approval to the operation and the four aircraft lifted off from desert strips in the south of Israel. The journey was fraught with hazards, from Arab radar stations and Soviet picket ships to severe thunderstorms, but the Israeli aircraft completed the journey uneventfully and touched down at Entebbe only 30 seconds behind schedule after a flight of 2,187 miles.

The paratroopers in one aircraft made for the old terminal building in which the hostages were housed; other groups headed for the control tower and the new terminal building which was occupied by Ugandan troops; and a special task force went for the aircraft dispersal area to destroy the parked MiG-17 fighters on the tarmac. These aircraft had to be eliminated if the getaway was to be successful.

Speed and audacity carried the day. There was token resistance from the Ugandans, but no one really knew what was happening and their efforts were uncoordinated. Two terrorists were shot outside the old terminal, others inside while they were trying to eliminate the hostages. Then, while one group of paratroopers herded the civilians into the waiting aircraft another unit fought off a Ugandan relief column coming from Kampala. Then the C-130s took off for Nairobi and safety.

The result of the raid was seven terrorists killed and all except three of the hostages rescued, for the lives of two Israeli soldiers—militarily, an extremely 'cost effective' operation.

The unit which had accomplished so much was the second battalion of the 202nd Airborne Brigade, an élite formation specially trained for 'troubleshooting' operations. Its composition is somewhat fluid, but organisationally it is built up in the usual Israeli pyramid of threes: three companies, each of three platoons, plus HQ and heavy weapons companies. The platoons each comprise an HQ section of nine men armed with two light machine-guns, a 50 mm mortar and a recoilless rifle, plus three infantry sections of six men armed with three *Uzi* sub-machine-guns, one FN rifle, one FN rifle with telescopic (or infra red) sight and one *Galil* assault rifle. The heavy weapons company, usually mounted in jeeps or Land Rovers, comprises three platoons of eight to 16 men with 106 mm recoilless rifles, 81 mm and 120 mm mortars, and machine-guns.

Arab states (at least until 1973) did not have any comparable task forces, although Egypt is known to have raised some 24 small commando battalions, each of around 250 men, organised in six 'brigades'. These units are known to be heavily armed with anti-tank weapons, especially ATGWs. Syria is believed to have five commando battalions organised along similar lines, and Jordan two.

These small but heavily armed units are ideal raw material for wargames of the 'skirmish' type in which one model soldier represents one man and the combat is between individuals. This type of wargaming has been pioneered by the 'skirmish' trio in Bristol—Mike Blake, Ian Colwill and the late Steve Curtis—who have been particularly successful in popularising Wild West wargaming. The idea was adopted by Don Featherstone in his book *Skirmish Wargaming* (also published by Patrick Stephens) which gives scenarios and playing rules for ten skirmish battles ranging from a Viking raid to street fighting in Cassino in 1944. Let us now come up to date with a 1970s-style skirmish...

When you look at the Middle East situation, you can readily see that the possibilities are virtually endless. Entebbe is a prime example, although you would need special rules to cater for the element of surprise—a good umpire is perhaps the simplest answer. But border and reprisal raids are the simplest to re-enact.

The mechanics of play are simple to master and wargaming of this type has two

Skirmish-type games

big advantages over the normal full-scale battles: the number of figures required is small, so cost is minimal (indeed, a couple of boxes of the cheap Airfix plastic figures is ample—the American Marines and British commandos are ideal); and a game with each player controlling, say, half a dozen figures can be played to a conclusion in an hour or so.

Because one is dealing here with combat on an individual level, the game move must of necessity represent a shorter period of time than in the main 'tank battles' rules, and in fact the scale normally adopted gives a five-second move. Similarly, the ground scale has to be different, and a further attraction of this type of gaming is that it can be directly related to the size of the figures. For example, a 20 mm figure represents a man approximately six feet tall, so 10 mm (one centimetre) represents a yard. Given these two yardsticks, calculating movement is simple. In one move a man may walk four paces (yards), run eight, charge ten or crawl two. In difficult terrain these factors should be reduced by an appropriate amount—usually half.

All other types of activity are, for the sake of simplicity, deemed to take one complete move (five seconds). These can include entering or leaving a vehicle, mounting or dismounting from a horse (or camel), lying down or rising from a prone position, drawing or holstering a sidearm or knife, fixing a bayonet, etc. It is not necessary to go into all the possible permutations. Since each model figure represents a real man he may do anything a real man would be capable of, and all you have to remember is that each form of activity occupies a complete move. This is not to say that a phase can only embrace a single form of activity. For example, a man could easily reload a gun while walking, although he might have difficulty while running.

A few special rules need to be introduced for vehicle movement, so let's take them in order. Entering or leaving a vehicle, as stated above, takes one move. It then takes a move to start the engine and engage first gear. The vehicle then moves off, accelerating (for the sake of simplicity again) at an arbitrary ten kilometres (or miles) per hour per move until the desired speed is achieved. This gives a move of up to 14 cm in the first phase of acceleration, 28 cm in the second, 42 cm in the third, 56 cm in the fourth, 70 cm in the fifth (equals 50 km/h or mph) and so on. Refer to the main rules for actual vehicle top speeds.

Taking one's foot off the accelerator causes a vehicle to lose speed in the same proportions, ie, ten km/h (mph) per move. Braking causes a vehicle to stop at a rate of one yard (or pace, or metre) per km/h of its speed at the time of braking. In other words, a vehicle travelling at 30 km/h (42 cm per move) will come to a standstill after covering 42 cm from the moment the brakes are applied. Switching off the engine, putting the gears in neutral and engaging the handbrake occupy a further move, but vehicle occupants other than the driver may disembark.

If you wish to introduce tanks or armoured cars into skirmish games it can again be done quite simply, although you should allow *two* phases for entering or leaving the vehicle through its hatches. Keeping things simple again, we further legislate that it takes a complete phase to load the tank's main gun, a phase to aim and a phase to fire. Turrets traverse at the rate of 60 degrees per phase (measure with a protractor).

Driving a vehicle using these rules is a simple business without a great deal of record keeping, and it can be quite fun . . . on one memorable occasion I saw a player's jeep crash straight into the wall of a house because he hadn't allowed himself sufficient margin in which to brake!

Still on the subject of record-keeping, you will need a pad of squared paper, one sheet for each figure or vehicle under your control. On the left of the sheet list the figure's name, rank and experience rating (see below). Under this list are details of the weapon(s) carried. Across the top of the page mark the phases—one to ten or however many you can get on the size of paper being used. At the beginning of each phase enter the intended action under the appropriate phase number and opposite the figure's name. Beneath this, opposite the 'weapons' heading, keep track of ammunition expenditure.

Experience ratings. This is a way of introducing a certain degree of individuality into the figures. Each is graded as either a veteran—a soldier of experience, usually a leader, and an expert marksman; an 'average'—the majority; or a 'novice'—an inexperienced recruit, not particularly skilful in weapon handling.

A typical group for a skirmish could comprise something like the following:

The Israelis. Sergeant Levy, a veteran, armed with a *Galil* assault rifle, automatic pistol in holster and combat knife; Corporal Aharon, an average, armed with *Uzi* sub-machine-gun and combat knife; Private Cohen, an average, armed with *Uzi* and knife; Private Goren, a novice, armed with *Uzi* and knife; Private Kalman, an average, armed with FN rifle, bayonet and knife; and Private Segal, a veteran, armed with FN rifle with telescopic sight, bayonet and knife.

The Arabs. Sergeant Hassan, a veteran, armed with an AK-47 assault rifle, bayonet and combat knife; Corporal Nayef, an average, armed with an AK-47, bayonet and knife; Private Hamid, an average, armed with *Hakim* rifle, bayonet and knife; Private Youssef, an average, armed with AK-47, bayonet and knife; Private Kamel, a novice, armed with *Hakim* rifle, bayonet and knife; Private Tarik, a veteran, armed with Type D automatic rifle, bayonet and knife.

In addition to the weapons, you should also list the amount of ammunition carried at the start of the game so that you can keep track of its expenditure. For the *Uzis* a reasonable load would be, say, four 32-round magazines in pouches, one magazine in the gun itself and a sixth magazine taped to the one in the gun for instant reloading. For the *Galil* a similar complement of 30- or 50-round magazines should be carried, 20- or 30-round magazines for the FN rifle, 30-round magazines for the AK-47 and so on. Details of the different types of magazines available are given in the chapter on infantry weapons. Hand grenades may also be carried.

Weapon effectiveness depends on range and rate of fire. For simplicity's sake again I have tabulated these as follows, but you could devise individual ratings for each specific type of weapon if you wish.

Weapon	Range in cm			Time to reload
	Short	Medium	Long	
Revolver	10	25	80	2 phases
Automatic pistol	10	25	80	1 phase
Sub-machine-gun	16	40	100	1 phase
Breech-loading rifle	50	200	500	2 phases
Self-loading rifle	50	200	500	1 phase
Assault rifle	30	120	300	1 phase
Light machine-gun	100	300	800	2 phases
Grenade	8	16	25	Not applicable
Knife	8	16	25	Not applicable

Firing is sub-divided into aimed and 'snap', the chances of a hit being greater with aimed fire. To take up a firing position and aim takes one phase and the man must remain stationary while firing. Snap shots may be fired without aiming or even while on the move.

Skirmish-type games

In order to calculate casualties, use the following table to establish the type of target and the percentage chance of a hit at the appropriate range. Add or subtract percentage variations, then throw a pair of percentage dice to see whether you have achieved a hit.

Type of target	Range		
	Short	Medium	Long
Infantry standing	80%	70%	50%
Infantry walking	70%	60%	40%
Infantry running	60%	50%	30%
Infantry charging	50%	40%	20%
Infantry lying or crawling	20%	10%	1%
Infantry in soft cover	20%	10%	1%
Infantry in hard cover	10%	1%	-10%

Variations

Novice firing	-20%
Veteran firing	+20%
Snap firing medium range	-10%
Snap firing long range	-30%
Firing on the move	-10%
Received light wound	-10%
Received serious wound	-20%
Automatic firing short range	+30%
Automatic firing medium range	+10%
Automatic firing long range	-10%

When firing automatic fire at a group of figures, deduct 5% for every five paces between the figures (eg, four men on a 20-pace front, deduct 4 × 5% = 20%). This rule is introduced to allow for the spread of the bullets between the target figures. Automatic fire may also be cyclic or selective. On cyclic the magazine will empty itself in one frantic burst occupying one phase, giving an additional 10% chance of a hit at short range but deducting an extra 10% at long range because of reduced accuracy. Selective automatic fire is in bursts of five rounds and will normally be used against individual targets rather than groups. Its advantage over cyclic fire is that it gives you four to ten phases of fire before you need to change magazines, depending on the number of rounds in the particular weapon's magazine.

Casualty table

Wound category	1	10	20	30	40	50	60	70	80	90	99%	
A	1	1	1	1	2	2	3	3	4	4	5	A
B	-	3	7	10	14	17	21	24	28	31	35	B
C	-	-	8	12	16	20	24	28	32	36	40	C
D	-	4	9	13	18	22	27	31	36	40	45	D
E	-	5	11	16	22	27	33	38	44	49	55	E
F	-	6	12	18	24	30	36	42	48	54	60	F
G	-	8	16	24	32	40	48	56	64	72	80	G
H	-	-	17	25	34	42	51	59	68	76	85	H
I	-	9	18	27	36	45	54	63	72	81	90	I
J	-	10	20	30	40	50	60	70	80	90	99	J

How to use the casualty chart: first look at the percentage heading in which your final score falls; now, reading downwards from this, take the next highest figure to your score; and finally, read off the wound category. To give an example, firing an SLR at medium range against a moving target gives you a 60% chance of a hit. Ignoring additions and deductions for the purpose of illustration, and assuming you threw exactly 60 on the two dice, means that you have scored a 'J' class wound on your target. Wounds are categorised as follows:

A = dead. B = seriously wounded. Target may not move or do anything for six moves and then may crawl only. May not use weapon(s) except in self defence. C = serious wound to right arm. Target may not move or do anything for four phases, will drop any weapon held in right hand, and may not use that arm again. D = serious wound to left arm. As for C but for left arm. E = serious leg wound. May not move or do anything for four phases, and may then only crawl. May use weapon(s). F = Light head wound. Knocked out for four phases. G = Light body wound. Knocked out for two phases. H = Light right arm wound. No action for one phase, cannot use arm again during game. I = Light left arm wound. As for H but left arm. J = Light leg wound. No action for one phase, then cannot run or charge for rest of game.

To further complicate the above, figures with serious wounds move at all times at half the normal rate.

If firing at a man in a vehicle (soft-skin only) or mounted on a horse/camel/elephant/bicycle, A to F wounds are counted as hits on the rider/driver and you throw a second pair of dice to determine damage; G to H wounds are counted as hits on the mount/vehicle which bring it to a halt in the shortest possible time; while I to J hits count as disabling hits which bring it/them to a halt at normal deceleration rate.

In the case of a G to H hit on a mount/vehicle, it is assumed to have fallen/crashed, and all soldiers affected throw for injury as if for a 50% chance of a hit.

Dice throws under the minimum percentage required count as fluke misses and do no damage. Similarly, if a target figure is partially obscured by cover, hits on parts of his anatomy so covered are counted as misses. And finally, if the target figure is wearing a steel helmet, category F wounds are invalid. (You could, in fact, take this a stage further and introduce plastic body armour (as used in Vietnam), in which case category G wounds are also invalidated, but figures so protected should suffer a 25% movement penalty.)

Grenades, to get them out of the way, explode with a blast diameter of four paces, and anyone in the vicinity must throw for injury as with a 99% chance of a hit. When throwing a grenade, a veteran will automatically hit his target, an average stands an 80% chance and a novice a 60% chance. Every 5% over the probability thrown represents one pace/yard/metre of deviation. If the number thrown is even the throw is 'over', if odd it is 'under' the target. Figures in the vicinity or over or under throws should dice for wounds as if they were the targets.

Coming down to the nitty-gritty, or that phase of action which is best illustrated in the 'Dad's Army' reflection that 'they don't like it up em', one moves on to hand-to-hand combat or mêlée. In the context of the Arab-Israeli conflict the normal weapon categories can be considerably simplified: nobody is going to be using a tomahawk, assegai or cutlass, for example! One is therefore left with the following categories: 1 = unarmed; 2 = clubbed rifle; 3 = knife/hand-held bayonet; and 4 = fixed bayonet. This reduces the normal skirmish mêlée table to more manageable proportions. The vertical columns at either side of the following

Skirmish-type games

table represent your own figure's weapon category, the horizontal columns at top and bottom your opponent's. Where the two meet is the percentage probability of inflicting damage on him.

Own weapon value	1	Opponent weapon value 2	3	4	Own weapon value
1	50%	40%	40%	20%	1
2	60%	50%	40%	20%	2
3	60%	60%	50%	20%	3
4	80%	80%	70%	50%	4
	1	2	3	4	

Now, to this must be added percentage variations again, as follows:

Veteran versus average	+10%	Novice versus veteran	−20%
Veteran versus novice	+20%	Opponent(s) to flank or rear	−20%
Average versus veteran	−10%	Light wound	−10%
Average versus novice	+10%	Serious wound	−20%
Novice versus average	−10%	Opponent in cover	−20%

Throw two dice as for firing and work out damage effect as previously, except that light wounds do not cause your opponent to drop his weapon although he suffers a percentage deduction in the second round of mêlée. If both figures achieve 'hits' they cancel each other out and no damage is inflicted in that phase.

Reaction (or morale) is something inadvertently missed out in Don Featherstone's book mentioned above, but is fairly easy to calculate. After having done all firing and mêlée, throw the percentage dice for all surviving figures. Those scoring 50% and above will stay and fight it out, others will quietly make their apologies and disappear. Veterans add 20% to their dice throw, novices will deduct the same amount. Anyone with a light wound will deduct 10%, with a serious wound 20%. Anyone in a situation where he is outnumbered will deduct 10% for each additional opponent. Those who achieve a minus score have camouflaged trousers...

One of the nice things about skirmish wargaming is the level of player involvement with his own figures. In this it parallels fantasy gaming where each player 'is' a figure. In fantasy games the rewards are gold and 'experience points'. In skirmish games there isn't any gold, but you can certainly acquire experience. The simplest way of doing this is to say that all figures who survive a battle without running away become promoted a grade (eg, novice to average or average to veteran). Those who run away are demoted a grade. Promoted veterans retire to count their medals and write their memoirs...

Going back briefly to AFVs for those readers who wish to introduce them into skirmish games, use the firing rules in the main section for hits and dice for each crew member as with a 50% chance of survival under the skirmish rules whenever a vehicle is penetrated. Or devise something more complicated if you wish. Personally, I feel there is little point, but the principles should be obvious by now. Complicating matters merely slows the game down without materially affecting the outcome.

15

Aerial warfare
by Mike Spick

Four aircraft emerged from the morning sea haze like wraiths. They silently and rapidly grew in size, then as they flashed across the shoreline and eased their noses up over the broken, craggy landscape, the illusion was shattered into a thousand fragments by the screaming thunder of their engines, bouncing and crackling back from the very rocks. In an instant they had vanished again, the only reminder of their passage a distant echoing rumble, gradually fading.

Heading south-west, rising and falling with the contours of the ground, snaking down the shallow desert valleys as though on rails, the leader strained his eyes for the turning point. The sun was already well up in the sky, and the heat had burnt away the early morning mists that sometimes lay in the hollows, even in this waterless part of the world, leaving the air crystal clear. Then . . . in the distance . . . telegraph poles . . . a road. The leader eased into a gentle climbing turn and glanced at his formation for an instant. Three Mystères of the *Heyl Ha'Avir*, the blue six-pointed star shining on their flanks, swayed gently close alongside him. Following the road now, they thundered westward, the sun flinging their shadows erratically across the uneven surface before them. The road twisted and curved, sometimes almost invisible, but always marked by the long hard shadows cast by the telegraph poles. Then at last, the final landmark. A bridge over a shallow ravine. The formation split as the leader pulled up to nearly 1,000 metres, his wingman dropping back and pulling wide, while numbers three and four in the formation swung away to attack from a different direction. Laid out in front of him was an airfield, the main runway clearly defined even though the dust and sand of the desert had become deeply ground into it. There were the taxi-ways, the gun emplacements, aircraft dotted around at dispersal points, and over in the corner, a cluster of buildings and a lazily turning radar aerial. The leader nosed down gently, registering half absent-mindedly that surprise appeared to be total. He had been assured at the briefing that it would be, but the best laid plans had a trick of springing a leak. All his concentration was now focused on the runway, ignoring even the MiG-17 fighter taxiing slowly over to his left. Slung underneath was the secret weapon on which the Israeli Defence Force had pinned its hopes; the runway busting bomb. Levelling out at 328 feet (100 metres), he roared straight down the centre of the runway at 400 knots and dropped. Retro-rockets flared momentarily, slowing the bomb in mid-air. It hung in the sky for an instant, then its nose dropped and a rocket in the tail lit up and hurled it vertically down to penetrate deep beneath the 300 mm-thick concrete. The explosion opened a hole, and rippled the concrete upwards for a considerable distance around. The leader broke hard and was in time to see his wingman release. Another hole in the runway surrounded by damaged concrete. Now three and four were lined up for the attack. A quick glance around and a flicker of light caught his eye. The anti-aircraft gunners seemed to have woken up at last. Once they started shooting you could spot them much more easily. He lined up for a strafing run.

For the next few minutes the four Mystères roamed the airfield at will, shooting up the dispersed aircraft, the gun positions, anything that looked interesting. A check on the time. 0852 hours, time to go home lads, the next wave will be here in three minutes, and mistaken identity is one thing we can't afford. Down on the deck, due north, out to sea, then eastwards and home. The term 'pre-emptive strike' had been coined.

Clashes in the Middle-Eastern sky were, of course, no new thing. They had started back in 1948, when a motley collection of ex-World War 2 aircraft took to the skies. Spitfire IXs were used by both sides supplemented by the Avia C 210, a Czech-built derivative of the Bf 109G for the Israelis and Italian Fiat G 55s for the Egyptians, plus many odds and ends. Neither side had much of an air force, consequently the effect of air power upon the ground war was minimal.

The next major clash came in 1956. At this time the equipment was more modern, but both air forces were relatively tiny. The IAF had about 111 serviceable combat types: 16 Mystères, 22 Ouragans, 15 Meteor jets plus 25 Mustangs, 16 Mosquitoes and 17 Harvard armed trainers. The Mustangs in particular were old and tired having had a chequered career. Originally used in the closing stages of World War 2 by the US 8th and 9th Air Forces, a batch of P-51Ds were bought by Sweden in 1946. Redesignated as the J 26, the Mustangs saw service with the *Flygvapnet* F 4 Wing at Ostersund and F16 Wing at Uppsala. In 1952 they were pensioned off, and a batch of 25 was sold to Israel, to replace Spitfire LF IXes. Their main function in the 1956 war was ground strafing with rockets, but they were also used for disrupting communications by flying through telegraph wires in Sinai. Two of them have subsequently reached this country for restoration, and I am assured that at least one has a notched propeller!

The EAF was stronger on paper, but had an appalling serviceability rate, less than 40 per cent. The fighters serviceable were 30 MiG-15s, 12 Meteor F 8s and 15 Vampire PB 52s, and the bombers were Il 28s with only 12 serviceable out of 24 with the rest in store.

The dice, however, were loaded. Before the Israelis launched their attack on October 29, no less than 36 F-84 F Thunderstreaks and 36 Mystère IVAs of *L'Armée de l'Air* were installed on Israeli airfields, initially to provide air defence, but soon to join the attack. During the first two days, the IAF claimed eight victories over Sinai, four MiG-15s, three Vampires and a Meteor. Then, on the night of October 31/November 1, the blow fell. The Royal Air Force joined the scrum with Canberra B2s from Cyprus, B2s and B5s from Malta, and no less than four squadrons of Valiant four-jet bombers from Luqa. The attack was taken up next day with RAF Venom FB 4s and Hunter F5s from Cyprus, assisted by *Armée de l'Air* Thunderstreaks from Cyprus and Israel. And to cap it all the Fleet Air Arm waded in from carriers with Sea Venoms and Sea Hawks, together with the *Aeronavale* with Corsairs. A total of 260 EAF aircraft were destroyed on the ground for an Anglo-French loss of ten, all to ground fire. Sporadic resistance was encountered, for instance a MiG-15 being shot down by Sea Venoms as late as November 5. A total of 11 EAF aircraft were lost over Sinai compared to 18 from the IAF of which nine were the elderly Mustangs. Two lone raids by solitary Il 28s were made over Israel, both were totally ineffective.

Nine years passed before the next, small-scale, air clash occurred, although from then on, the pace gradually increased, reaching a peak on April 7 1967 when six Syrian MiG-21s were claimed by Mirages. The intervening years had been used by both sides to re-equip. And so the scene was inexorably set for 0845 hours, June 5 1967, which is where we came in.

The situation had been hotting up for some time. Gamal Abdul Nasser, the Eygptian President, had announced to the world that he intended to administer a pill to the camel. He inserted the pill into a tube, and inserted one end of the tube into the camel's mouth. He then prepared to blow down the tube so that the camel would swallow the pill. But the camel blew first!

Before we return to the events of that momentous day, it would be as well to compare the respective air forces, together with any factors which may have influenced the Israeli plans. Orders of battle given in various sources are contradictory, so I have inserted notes where it seems relevant. Transport aircraft and helicopters have been omitted as these are really only a form of fast, soft-skinned vehicle with good cross-country capability, and are thus covered elsewhere.

The *Heyl Ha'Avir*, deployed in four squadrons of interceptors and five squadrons of fighter-bombers (note that interceptors had bomb-carrying capability), would be approximately: 72 Mirage IIICJs in three squadrons of 24 aircraft; 18 Super Mystères (IVB) in one squadron; 40 Mystère IVAs in two squadrons of 20 aircraft and 25 Vautours in one squadron; 40 Ouragans (obsolescent, but used) in two squadrons of 20 aircraft; 60 Magister armed trainers, in three squadrons of 20 aircraft; and two battalions of Hawk surface-to-air missiles. These were deployed around Haifa and Tel Aviv, which between them contain two-thirds of Israel's industrial capacity. Total 36 launchers. One source states 48 Skyhawks which, although on order at this time, were not delivered until the following April.

The immediate opposition was the Egyptian Air Force, which was by far the largest of the Arab forces. Its approximate composition, in squadrons of about 18-20 aircraft grouped in Air Brigades, was: 100-120 MiG-21Cs and Ds in three regiments (six squadrons); 80 MiG-19s in one regiment of four squadrons; 200 MiG-15s, MiG-17s and Su7s. The MiG-15 was by this time obsolescent, also there were insufficient trained pilots to be able to use anywhere near this number. Five squadrons were operational—say 100 aircraft; 30 Tu 16 jet bombers in two regiments; 40 Il 28s in two regiments; 120 assorted trainers, some of which could be armed, although the previous note on pilot shortage applies; and 25 batteries of *Guideline* SAM 2 missiles (150 launchers).

The training of Egyptian personnel was not of a high standard. This showed both in poor combat quality and high unserviceability rates. The other disadvantage was in having to provide defensive cover to a large area.

The Syrian Air Force is next in order of importance but was small in comparison with the EAF, although a certain perspective can be gained when it is realised that the Syrian/Israeli border is less than 45 miles (70 kilometers) long. They had 40 MiG-21Cs in two squadrons; 60 MiG-15s and -17s in three squadrons; six Il 28s; and ten batteries of *Guideline* SAM 2 missiles (60 launchers) covering Damascus. Remarks on standards of training apply to the SAF equally.

The Royal Jordanian Air Force was better trained than most Arab nations but, with a much longer frontier to defend than anyone else, it was totally inadequate. Sources again differ widely, but I would settle for a strength of: 24 Hunters (various marks) in two squadrons; and 16 Vampires (serviceability uncertain) in reserve.

Finally of the countries bordering Israel comes Lebanon. The Lebanese Christian and Muslim factions are usually to busy hammering the daylights out of each other that they would not bother about the Jews. However, the Israeli High Command had no means of guaranteeing that they would stay on the sidelines (they did), and had to plan against their potential. There was, in fact, a slight brush on the first day, but nothing serious, except for the Lebanese Hunter pilot who was clobbered. The Lebanese had 12 Hunters in one squadron.

Iraq does not border Israel, but they decided to join in the fun, much to their detriment, with: 60 MiG-21Cs in three squadrons; 30 MiG-19s and -15s in two squadrons; 50 Hunter 59s in four squadrons plus a recce flight; ten Il 28s; six Tu 16s; 20 Jet Provost armed trainers, and five batteries of *Guideline* SAM 2s (30 launchers).

Israel then had about 250 fighting aircraft counting the bulk of the Magisters, of which barely half could be considered modern combat types. Against these were ranged, discounting the Lebanese, approximately 750 jet combat aircraft, over one third of which were modern fighter or attack types, and 90-plus were jet bombers capable of doing untold harm to Israel's economy, bearing in mind that Tel Aviv, containing more than half of the country's industrial capacity, is just ten minutes' flying time away from the borders of more than one hostile nation, an impossibly short time for effective interception. On paper, the IAF was badly overmatched, but other factors were working to redress the balance. The first of these was serviceability. IAF serviceability on the morning of June 5 1967 was 99 per cent. An optimistic assessment of overall serviceability of the aircraft of the Arab nations would be 75 per cent, which alone would be enough to reduce the numerical odds from 1:3 down to 1:2.25. The next factor was combat training, which among the Arab nations was indifferent, as was to be highlighted by the course of events. It would almost certainly be no exaggeration to say that this was enough to tilt the odds sharply in favour of the IAF. And finally, the master plan.

The Egyptians, believe it or not, were alert to the possibility of a surprise attack. The traditional time for a surprise air strike is dawn, with the attackers coming low out of the east with the rising sun at their backs. Consequently airfield defence was at its most alert at dawn. Fighter patrols were up and the radar operators were on their toes. The High Command might be snoring in bed, but they were instantly contactable by telephone.

Four hours later, when the strike came in, everything had changed. The sun was still in the east, about 45° up in the sky, and was hot enough to have burnt away the morning mists which may well have shielded some airfields from attack, or at very least obscured navigational pinpoints from the low-flying raiders, thus causing delays, errors and confusion. The dawn patrols would be back on the ground, the High Command should be in their cars travelling to work and unable to respond quickly, and the radar operators yawning sleepily in the air-conditioning after their early reveille.

The surprise factor was exploited to the limit by the IAF who left a mere 12 aircraft behind on home defence. Mirages and Super Mystères attacked airfields in the Canal Zone, Mystères and Ouragans hit airfields in Sinai, while Vautours made deep penetration raids on southern airfields. The Magisters were used for ground-strafing the Egyptian army positions in Sinai. Ten airfields were hit in the initial strike by sections of four aircraft, 7½ minutes being allowed over the target in which to plough up the runway and expend rockets and cannon shells on other worthwhile targets. The second wave was due in precisely 2½ minutes after the first had left. Back at base, the IAF was accomplishing near miracles in turn-round, some aircraft being back over the target within an hour. In all, 19 airfields were raided in under three hours and 300 EAF aircraft were destroyed, nearly all on the ground. One airfield was left with its runway intact. El Arish was earmarked for use by the IAF as soon as it could be captured. After the initial surprise a handful of MiGs got into the air, and a few interceptions were made, generally to the detriment of the EAF. Two Mystères were lost to interceptors in exchange for several MiGs, more MiGs being lost when they tried to land back at their cratered airfields. By 1035 hours the EAF had ceased to exist as an effective force, and the IDF ground forces, supported by Magisters, swept into Sinai.

As the *Heyl Ha'Avir* paused to recover its breath, the northern and eastern skies were invaded, the Syrians attacking an oil refinery at Haifa, the Jordanians an airfield at Kfar Sirkin. Neither raid was particularly damaging. By noon the IAF was once more in full cry, hammering airfields outside Damascus in Syria, Ajlun radar station, Amman and Mafraq airfields in Jordan. Exit the Syrian and Jordanian Air Forces. Later that afternoon, the attack switched westward again, 23 Egyptian radar stations being attacked, plus several *Guideline* batteries. The positions of the *Guidelines* were known well in advance, having been reported by photo-reconnaissance since the previous October. Several *Guidelines* were fired, but achieved nothing. The IAF flew nearly 1,000 sorties on this first day, some pilots doing as many as eight trips. It is probable that, quite apart from battle damage, serviceability was considerably reduced.

On the morning of June 6, the Iraqi Air Force took a hand, attacking Netanya with one Tu 16. Big deal! The *Heyl Ha'Avir* riposted, and nothing more was seen of the Iraqis. Fighting had flared on the West Bank by this time, and interdiction sorties were flown. During the night, air strikes had been made on the Police School and other Jordanian strongpoints in Jerusalem. The targets were illuminated by two searchlights on the roof of the Histadrut building. On the West Bank, Jordanian lines of communication were the prime target. They were repeatedly attacked to such good effect that over 40 tanks were captured undamaged, having run out of fuel. Airfields and radar installations in Sinai continued to be attacked, and the Mitla Pass was blocked at the western end by air strikes. Meanwhile the Syrian ground forces started to make threatening noises. At the end of this, the second day of the war, Israeli losses were 26 aircraft, six of them Magisters. Ten per cent may seem severe, but let us have a look at the state of the opposition.

The EAF, being the largest force, had sustained the most casualties. 95 MiG-21s, 20 MiG-19s, 82 MiG-15s and -17s, ten Su 7s, all the Tu 16s and 27 Il 28s, plus 32 transports and 13 helicopters were out of action, and hardly any airfields left in a usable state. Quite a lot of the remaining MiGs were in store or unserviceable. Many of the survivors were marooned on their airfields by cratered runways, which is why the airfield attacks were resumed on the second day. The Syrians had lost 32 MiG-21s, 23 MiG-15s and -17s, two Il 28s and two helicopters. Jordan had lost nearly all its Hunters on the ground, plus some older aircraft. Iraq's losses were relatively light, but were proportionate to their involvement. They lost nine MiG-21s, one Tu 16, five Hunters and one transport. Lebanon, nominally a non-combatant, contrived to lose a Hunter in the general mix-up.

June 7 saw the IAF, now effectively reduced by casualties, battle damage, unserviceability and pilot fatigue to what might be reasonably assessed as half strength, hammering supply lines and ground units on the West Bank and in Sinai. Algerian MiGs arrived in Egypt to supply local air defence.

June 8 saw the EAF remnants in the air again over Sinai. They carried out a few small air strikes in support of the retreating ground forces but with little effect. Having almost run out of worthwhile targets to the east and west the IAF turned its full force against the Syrian ground positions on the Golan Heights, also Syrian lines of communication.

By the morning of June 9 Egypt and Jordan were out of the war, and the IAF launched heavy attacks on Syrian bunkers and gun positions on the Golan, commencing at 0320 hours, nearly an hour and a half before dawn. Losses were caused by the 200-odd AA guns deployed by the Syrians, but continuous attacks were kept up.

June 10. Attacks on Golan were kept up and retreating Syrian ground forces were hammered. At 1930 hours a ceasefire took effect. During the final four days, the IAF had lost a further five aircraft, all to ground fire, their total losses being 31. Thus ended the Six Day War. A total of 50 Arab aircraft were claimed in air-to-air combat, 30 of them during the first day and nearly all the rest on the second day. IAF air-to-air losses were minimal, reflecting to a fair degree the relative standards of training of either side.

Peace in the sky did not last long. There now started the fourth war, the War of Attrition, with little activity on the ground apart from commando raids and artillery barrages.

After the Six Day War, 20 Egyptian airfields were left, two-thirds of these within reach of Israeli strikes. Construction commenced on a further 15, mainly in the Delta and the Nile Valley. The lesson of June 5 had been well learnt; aircraft were to be dispersed in reinforced concrete shelters, well camouflaged and ringed around with flak and missiles. Egypt was not the only country to learn this lesson; East German airfields sprouted similar structures with startling rapidity. Apart from being difficult to spot and well defended, these shelters were proof against anything less than a direct hit with a 500 lb bomb. And to compound the problem, any would-be raider had no means of telling whether the shelter was occupied or not. By July 1968 an estimated 80 per cent of EAF losses had been made good by the Soviet Union, although during the rebuilding period the policy was to avoid contact and concentrate on training.

The IAF had not been idle. In addition to their original 20 airfields, they commissioned a further five in Sinai, and also constructed six desert landing strips. Some Hawk batteries were deployed along the Bir Gifgafa ridge in Sinai.

As early as July 8 1967, the two sides were at it again, the IAF strafing Egyptian artillery positions, while four MiG-17s were intercepted by Mirages and one shot down nine miles east of the Canal. From this point on, desultory fighting took place, with conflicting claims being made. On October 24, Egyptian Navy missile boats in Alexandria and Port Said were attacked. From then on, Russian ships were deployed in Egyptian harbours, effectively inhibiting further air strikes.

1968 was a quiet year, marked only by the courts martial of the four EAF commanders, and not until the middle of 1969 did the pot start boiling again. The reconstituted EAF was now approximately: 100 MiG-21s, in six squadrons; 80 MiG-19s in four squadrons; 40 MiG-17s in two squadrons; 85 Su 7s in five squadrons; 15 Tu 16s in one squadron; 30 Il 28s in two squadrons; 25 batteries of *Guidelines*, plus a few *Goas*.

Against this were ranged some 60 Mirages, 40 Mystères, a dozen or so Vautours, and eight batteries of Hawks. In May, against the judgement of their Russian advisers, the EAF started to rattle their cage, and limited sorties were allowed. Prior to this, *Guidelines* had had their first success on March 9, bringing down a Piper Cub artillery spotter. After several inconclusive engagements during which conflicting claims were made, the IAF strafed artillery positions on the west bank of the Canal during the afternoon of July 20, killing six Russians. The EAF reacted strongly, and at dusk 30 Su 7s and MiG-17s, escorted by ten MiG-21s, penetrated 60 miles into Sinai. Mirages intercepted and claimed one MiG-21, two Su 7s and two

MiG-17s shot down, for two losses. EAF claims were 19 for two losses. It is possibly significant that General Mustapha al-Hennawi, the EAF Commander, and General Mohammed Ali Fahmi, the Air Defence Commander, were both dismissed on the 24th, being replaced by Major-Generals Ali Baghdadi and Hassan Kemal.

In 1967, what little air fighting there was had been with guns. Both sides were now equipped with air-to-air missiles, with infra-red homing guidance. A new aircraft entered the scene, the American-built A4D Skyhawk, becoming operational on August 9. The first of these to be lost was shot down by ground fire over Port Tewfik on the 19th. September opened with strikes on missile sites by the IAF. On the 11th, the Egyptians hit back in strength, over 100 aircraft penetrating Sinai air space. The raid lasted an hour, the Israelis claiming eight shot down by interceptors, two by Hawks and one by flak, for the loss of one Mirage. The EAF admitted two losses, but claimed three shot down by fighters and one by flak. Also in September, the first Phantoms started to arrive in Israel. More hammering continued until the end of the year, summarised by Moshe Dayan as 61 EAF planes shot down and 24 *Guideline* sites destroyed. Egypt had made 13 air attacks since April.

The start of 1970 saw the IAF Phantoms and Skyhawks equipped with ECM (electronic countermeasures) pods. Deep penetration raids were instituted, Inshas, Dahsur and Tel-El-Kebir all being hit. During February, claims made by both sides since the June War could be summarised as follows: Israel 68 claims for 19 losses, Egypt 140 claims.

Phantom delivery was now running at four per month, the original order of 50 to be completed during June. On March 18 the United States announced the arrival of lots of *Goas* in Egypt, plus more *Guidelines*. A 'SAM' box was formed between 19 and 30 miles (30 and 50 kilometres) behind the Canal, approximately 50 miles (80 kilometres) long and 15 miles (25 kilometres) deep with *Guideline* batteries spaced at six mile (10 kilometre) intervals.

In early April, Russian-flown MiG-21Js started to arrive, about 150 in all, and assumed responsibility for the defence of the Nile Valley and the Delta. In the face of the possible political repercussions the IAF ceased their deep-penetration raids on April 17. The Soviets were deployed on four airfields near Cairo and one at Beni Suef, over 60 miles (100 kilometres) south. By this time, *Goa* missile batteries were deployed, but due to calibration difficulties, they were not operational. It is interesting to note that during this period of fighting that both sides left each other's oil wells alone.

June 30 saw a change in the pattern. Four MiG-21s, believed piloted by Russians, were brought down, all in air-to-air combat. Two Phantoms and a Skyhawk were lost, two to missiles, one to flak. All of a sudden the ECM pods were not working. The *Guidelines*' radar systems had been improved, also they were being fired in six-missile ripples for greater effect. The IAF ordered bigger and better ECM pods, with Boeing C97 Stratocruiser ECM aircraft as backup. At least one C97 was shot down. The War of Attrition ended with a ceasefire on August 7. This war has, of course, nothing to do with tank battles, but it does illustrate the changes in the air arms of both sides more or less as they happened, and sets the air power scene for the next round.

A more serious attempt to give the camel a pill came with the Yom Kippur War, or the War of Ramadan, depending on which side you were on, which opened on Saturday, October 6 1973, with the Egyptian Army crossing the canal and a massed Syrian tank attack on the Golan, both of which are described elsewhere.

The composition of the combatants was as follows:

Israel—128 F4E and RF 4E Phantoms; 162 A4E and A4F Skyhawks; 70 Mirage

IIICJs and Kfirs; 24 Super Mystères. In reserve but not used were 23 Mystére IVAs, 30-plus Ouragans, 80-plus Magisters and ten tired Vautours. In addition there were six Boeing C97 Stratocruisers in the ECM role. Ground defences consisted of ten batteries of Hawk missiles and about 300 AA guns of different types, mainly Bofors 40 mm.

Egypt—300 MiG-21s; 200 MiG-17s; 120 Su 7s; 25 Tu 16s. Possibly as many as 100 MiG-21s were in reserve due to lack of trained pilots, and about 50 MiG-17s. *Flight International* of July 26 that year gave a figure of nine MiG-21 squadrons. Assuming that no more than two extra squadrons could have become operational in the following three months at an establishment of 18 aircraft per squadron, this gives a maximum operational strength of 198 MiG-21s. The four squadrons of MiG-19s reported in mid-1969 appear to have vanished. This is typical of the Middle East, where almost every source of information is conflicting. Of the Tu 16s, 15 were reconnaissance aircraft, ten were bombers equipped with *Kennel* air-to-ground missiles. The ground-to-air defence consisted of 168 batteries of *Guidelines* and *Goas*, comprising 1,174 weapons ready for launch, most of which were in the SAM box on the west bank of the Canal, backed up by a new fly in the ointment, the SA 6 *Gainful*. In addition, the ground forces were equipped with the highly mobile radar-directed ZSU 23-4 gun, and the man-portable SA 7 *Grail*, in considerable quantities.

Syria—200 MiG-21s; 80 MiG-17s; 50 Su 7s. Of these, again due to a pilot shortage, it seems unlikely that more than 120 MiG-21s were operational. Ten Il 28s were also on strength but not used. It seems likely that they were unserviceable. Ground-to-air defence consisted of about 20 *Guideline* and *Goa* batteries, mainly deployed around Damascus, 96 weapons for launch, with ten *Gainful* batteries with a total of 60 launchers up front in Golan. Like Egypt, Syria also possessed considerable numbers of ZSU 23-4 guns and *Grails*.

Iraq—85 MiG-21s; 15 MiG-17s; 50 Su 7s; 36 Hunter FGA 9s and FR 10s; nine Tu 16s. In the event, the Iraqi Air Force took little part in the proceedings. Spare aircraft from Russia had not been shipped in as they had in Egypt and Syria; it seems likely that the above is a fair assessment of operational strength. Ten Il 28s, aged and almost certainly decrepit, were on strength but not used. A few *Guidelines* were deployed in airfield defence.

Jordan—18 F-104A Starfighters; 45 Hunters (various marks). It has been stated in at least one source that the RJAF took no part in the war. Be that as it may, and it does seem unlikely that the Starfighters did anything other than defensive patrolling, a few Hunters were lost, and two Pakistani pilots captured by the Israelis.

At 1400 hours in the afternoon of October 6 1973, the EAF and SAF launched a concerted offensive, the EAF launching about 100 aircraft across Sinai against main airfields, the communications centres of Bir Gifgafa and Bir el Thamada and the IDF forward HQ at Tasa. The HQ deep underground escaped untouched, but runways on the airfields were damaged, thus forcing the Israelis to launch counterstrikes from airfields in Israel itself. Synchronised with the Egyptian raid came a Syrian attack also by about 100 aircraft in waves of 15-20, against airfields, Israeli army establishments, and targets in and around Haifa.

The IAF riposted first with attacks on the Canal bridges, which were fairly ineffectual, then the full Israeli air strength was deployed to stop the Syrian attack through the Golan Heights. At the same time raids were launched on Egyptian and Syrian airfields. Losses were very heavy, with 30 Skyhawks and ten Mirages being lost, mainly over Golan. The Arabs had a couple of jokers up their sleeve in the form of the fully mobile *Gainful* missiles, the ZSU 23/4 radar controlled ack-ack gun, and the man-portable *Grail*, all of which were in considerable numbers right up front covering the land battle. The IAF losses were bad enough, but add to this the aircraft which suffered major damage, probably a further 50-60, and it can be seen why air strikes were called off after two hours, being resumed on the northern front at dusk in a much more circumspect manner, raiders going eastwards over Jordan, or westwards over Lebanon, round Mount Hermon, and in through the back door, concentrating on airfields and *Gainful* batteries.

During the 7th and 8th, IAF attacks were concentrated against airfields to keep the Egyptian and Syrian heads down, while ground strikes were mainly against the dangerous Syrian penetration in the north, and its lines of supply. Cumulative damage to the *Gainful* batteries was by now having some effect, and losses were not quite so bad as on the first day. As soon as the main Syrian armoured thrust had been stopped, attacks were once more switched to the Canal bridges, but these broke down on the triple obstacle of massed missile defences, heavy smoke screens, and the speed at which the bridges could be repaired. Somewhere about this time, Egyptian Tu 16s attempted to stretch the already thin IAF by stooging around over the sea and launching their *Kennel* air-to-surface missiles at Israeli cities. At least one was intercepted and brought down; no details of damage done by this means are available.

By Tuesday, October 9, the remnants of the Syrian *Gainfuls* were being withdrawn to cover Damascus, and the nature of the air war changed. Israel was going to need six years to recover from this war; long-term damage had therefore to be inflicted on the opposition. At just past noon, the Syrian Air Force HQ and the Ministry of Defence buildings in Damascus were attacked with rockets by six Phantoms. Further attacks were carried out on heavy industrial plants. At the same time, the Lebanese radar station at Jebel el Baroukh, believed to have been aiding the Syrians, was bombed. During the next few days, attacks were successfully carried out on power stations at Damascus and Homs, and oil targets at Homs, Adra, Latakia, Tartous and Banias.

By October 10 the Eygptians were running short of *Gainfuls*, although *Guidlines* and *Goas* remained in reasonable supply. The depleted IAF was by this time contriving to be everywhere at once, although the main concentration was now over Sinai. Sometime in the next couple of days, Libyan Mirages arrived in Egypt, reportedly flown by Pakistanis. Several were shot down, some possibly by friendly forces as mistaken identity would be all too easy.

Jordan entered the war on Saturday October 13 by reinforcing Syria, thus avoiding a direct confrontation, but by this time the IAF, although badly battered, had a fair degree of air superiority. The SAF was shattered, but the EAF was still an active force, although I am forced to the conclusion that the colossal amount of missiles loosed off by the Arab forces had to a certain degree proved counter productive, in that heat seekers particularly tend to lack discrimination and reportedly a large number of Arab aircraft were lost to friendly fire. This would be likely to inhibit operations in a missile-intensive zone. That the EAF was by no means finished was shown on Sunday October 21, when intensive attacks were launched on Israeli land forces on the west bank of the Canal, though 17 Egyptian aircraft were claimed shot down on this day alone.

Losses during the period of the war, which lasted three weeks, were approximately as follows:

Israel—33 Phantoms (35 replacements received during the war); 53 Skyhawks (46 replacements received during the war); 11 Mirages (two replacements received during the war); six Super Mystères (nil replacements received during the war). Of these, 20 were lost in air-to-air combat, 40 to SAMs, 30 to flak, two supposedly to friendly fire and the rest were either destroyed in accidents or on the ground. The *Heyl Ha'Avir* flew over 7,000 sorties, 2,000 against Syria, the rest against Egypt.

Arab losses are a bit of a puzzle to assess from existing sources, but can be approximately summarised thus: Egypt—220 MiG-21s, MiG-17s and Su 7s, one Tu 16; Syria—130 MiG-21s, MiG-17s and Su 7s. Of the fringe combatants, Iraq lost about 20 aircraft, although they took little part in the fighting, Jordan about eight Hunters and Libya a dozen or more Mirages.

By far the greater part of the combined Arab losses were caused in air fighting, about 250 in all. 25 were brought down by Hawk missiles, 20 by flak, 60 were lost on the ground or in accidents, and the remainder reportedly to friendly fire. If this seems high, quite apart from the missile danger, consider the complications of operating Pakistani aircrews, flying for Libya, based in Egypt, over Sinai, using the same type of aircraft as the Israelis!

16

Aerial wargaming
by Mike Spick

We now come to the nuts and bolts of reproducing the battle, and our first consideration must be how to cover the third dimension. The land battle is, of course, two-dimensional. We could have our aircraft come in at low level at a pre-set height at which they would fly up and down, bombing, rocketing and shooting at targets of opportunity. This will not, however, suffice, as for guns and rockets, and often with bombs, one needs to point the nose of the aircraft at the target to aim. This means that the aircraft will be on a collision course with mother earth, or to use the current attack jockey's expression, hurling one's little pink body at the ground. This is a state of affairs which it is undesirable to continue for too long, but as soon as the aircraft's noise is pulled back up, it no longer has a target, and this is essential to reproduce with some degree of accuracy. We therefore combine the height dimension with the lateral dimension. The land game is set up as normal, and the aircraft are superimposed on it. (See accompanying diagram.)

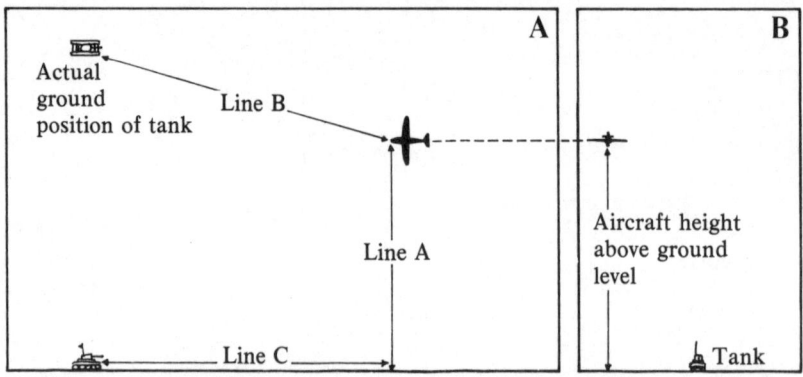

The aircraft entering on the right of the illustration represents two things, its position over the board, and the important one, using the bottom of the playing area as ground level, its height above the ground. Having observed the tank, (see observation section) the aircraft announces that it is attacking. Line A is extended vertically downwards from the nose of the aircraft to establish a point at ground level that the aircraft is vertically above. Line B is then measured from the tank to the nose of the aircraft, this being the exact distance on the ground between the tank and the point which is directly below the aircraft. The distance is then transferred to the base-line, and a duplicate tank set up at the end of it. This gives a precise three-dimensional relationship between the aircraft and the tank. Any hills, trees,

Aerial wargaming, by Mike Spick

buildings, etc, are also set up in duplicate, making sure that their height is directly related to the ground scale. This is to make things as difficult as possible for the aircraft. Diagram B is simply to clarify diagram A a bit.

As we are primarily concerned with the land battle, I have made aircraft handling as simple as possible. The tactics are basic. Aircraft enter at about 3,300 feet (1,000 metres), high enough to get a good view, at a speed varying betwen 340 and 590 mph (550 and 950 km/h). Less than 340 and you are easy meat for the ground defences, more than 590 and you can't hit anything. In the Yom Kippur War, 590 was normal, the ground defences were very good. On spotting a target, nose down and take aim. After bombing or firing, right down on the deck and home, James! The air move is a little different to a land move, as too much can happen in one minute, like travelling six miles (ten kilometres) or more, which is unusable. Our time scale for the air is therefore three seconds per move. This is very convenient, as speed can be related to movement, 500 mph (or km/h) giving a move distance of 250 mm exactly half! If you your playing area is eight feet (2,400 mm) long, this means that even a slow flying aircraft will be off the end in eight moves, a fast one in five, although it may be desirable to perform double moves once the attack is over and the aircraft is homeward bound, to speed things up a little. Each aircraft has been allocated just one radius of turn based on wing loading; this is its minimum radius and it can turn wider than this if required. Tight turning close to the ground is extremely risky, and I have made no attempt to approximate the tightest possible turns. Acceleration/deceleration is covered as simply as possible, being 2.5 per cent of each aircraft's maximum speed at sea level, to be applied at will every move. The power to weight ratio of modern aircraft coupled with their sophistication means that they do not necessarily gain or lose speed in the climb or dive.

Terrain is our next consideration. I feel it would be reasonable to ignore cloud cover in the Middle East, but we cannot forget the sun. Its time in the sky will vary with the time of the year, but at the equinoxes it will be in the sky for 12 hours, moving across at 15° per hour, rising behind the Jordanians and setting behind the Egyptians. The angle of the sun should be shown on the board; aircraft attacking from within 5° either way of the angle of the sun will be much more difficult to see.

Observation is our next consideration. Air-to-air observation is not needed, as it is

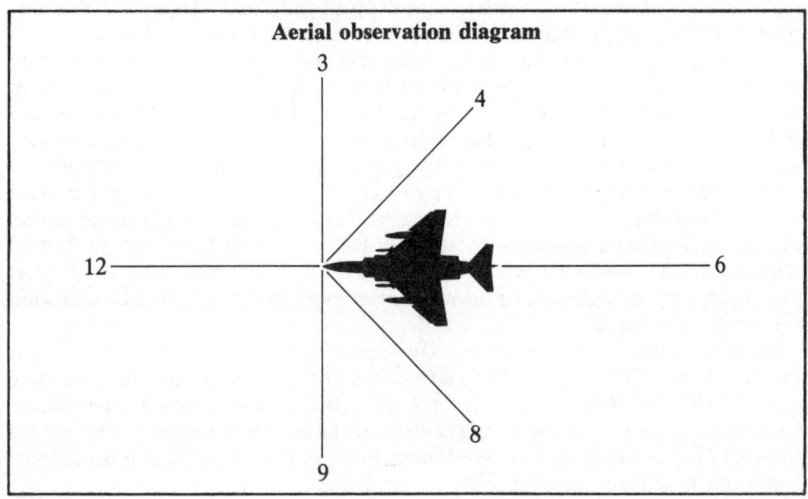

Aerial observation diagram

in no way intended to introduce air fighting, the sole purpose of which would be to gain air supremacy to allow the attack aircraft to operate unmolested. As our attacks are all over in a few seconds, air-to-air combat is irrelevant.

To observe potential targets on the ground, the clock code is used (see illustration). The percentage probability of observing a ground target (and from this point on, all mention of dice refers to percentage dice) are as follows:

12 o'clock to 4 o'clock and 12 o'clock to 8 o'clock—60%. In nearly all modern aircraft, the area between 4 o'clock and 8 o'clock is invisible. Infantry targets count half these probabilities and concealed targets one quarter. Moving vehicles add an extra half to the probability, as do targets marked with smoke. The first target seen will be attacked provided it conforms to the pilot's brief.

Ground-to-air observation is assessed as follows: Units engaged specifically in the anti-aircraft role will always spot the first aircraft coming in. Once they attempt to engage a target, they must stay with it until it a) vanishes off table or b) is destroyed. They will only be distracted by a direct attack from another aircraft. For all other units, the probabilities of spotting are:

		Attacked from	
	Front	Flank	Rear
Engaged units	25	20	5
Units with enemy in sight	40	30	10
Unengaged infantry	100	90	75
Unengaged stationary vehicles	100	90	75
Unengaged moving vehicles	80	60	40

Should the attacking aircraft be coming in within a 5° angle either way of the sun, the above probabilities should be divided by four.

Aircraft weaponry is, in this modern day and age, bewildering in its complexity. Basically it consists of cannon, bombs, rockets and napalm most of which is carried under the innocuous-sounding title of external stores. So varied are the possible loads that it is not unusual for aircraft to have a possible three or four hundred different combinations. We must therefore simplify this considerably, and the only way in which we can do it is to call a bomb-load a bomb-load, dropping it all in one lump. SNEB rocket pods should also be dealt with on the same principle as, while it is perfectly possible to fire them in small batches, it is a much better proposition to let go the lot and try to make sure of hitting something. Cannon fire is, of course, at targets of opportunity, and whilst worthwhile results can often be achieved, it should always be remembered that delivery of bombs and rockets is the primary function of the attack aircraft, and that gunnery is very much second fiddle.

We must now deal with the effect of air-to-ground weaponry. I have not the space here for a detailed exposition of my reasoning: if anyone is interested enough to find out, the basic theory is stated in *Air Battles in Miniature*, although a certain amount of adjustment for modern weaponry has been included. One basic rule. An aircraft must be flying a straight course for a complete move to attack, regardless of what weapon is being used.

Bombing is dealt with very simply. Dive-bombing *à la* World War 2 Stuka was simply not on in 1967 and '73. The method was to come in fast and low, pull up to about 2,500 feet (750 metres), then attack in a shallow dive. Alternatively, release could take place in level flight, particularly if the load was napalm. The impact point is found by using the Low Level Bomb Sight as illustrated, which needs to be drawn out to scale on graph paper.

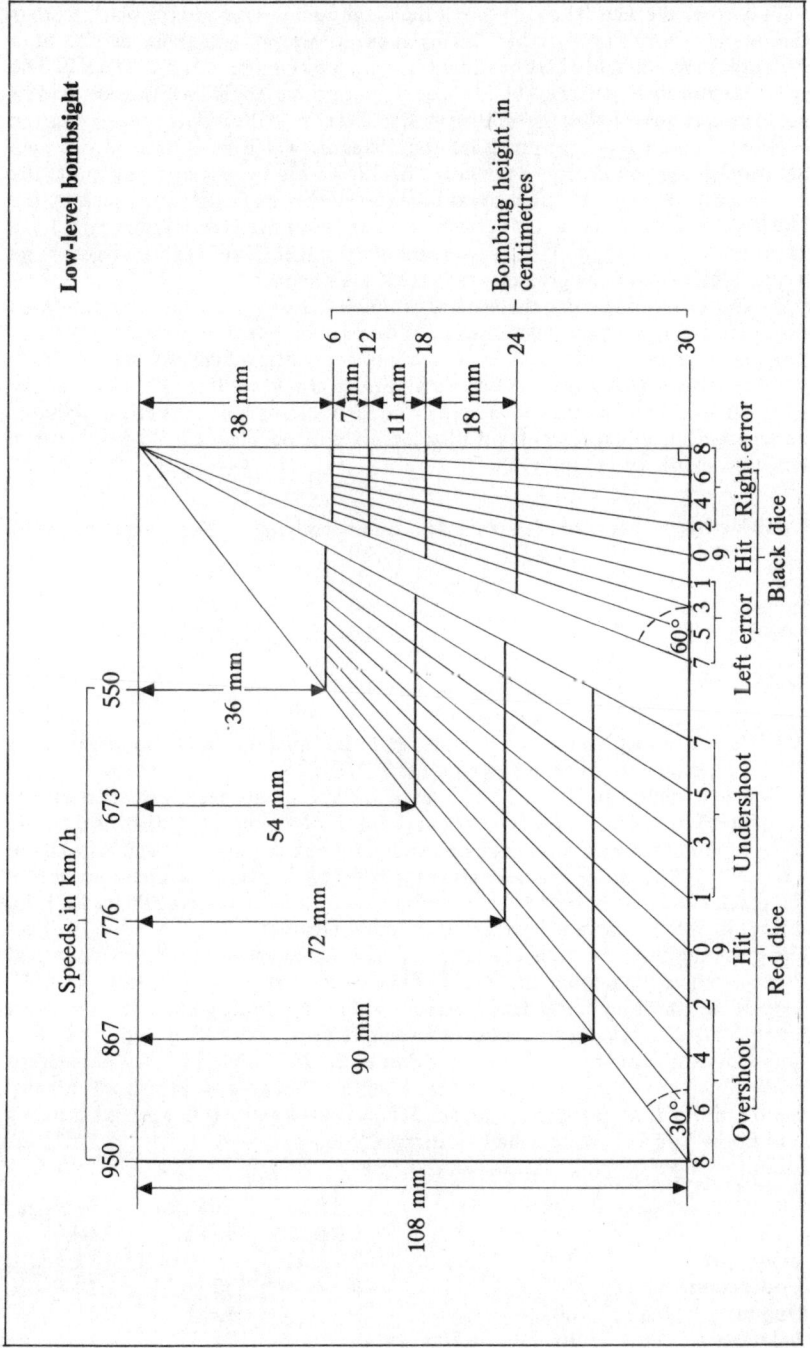

To use, roll the dice. The red score is the longitudinal error and the black score is the lateral error. For example, let us take an aircraft attacking at 420 mph (670 km/h) at a height of six centimetres, with a dice score of red 4, black 2. The speed is close enough to the 673 line (had it not been we would have interpolated it) not to matter, so we follow the oblique '4' line down from the top to where it cuts the horizontal speed line, and measure the distance, which is, if you have drawn accurately, ten millimetres overshoot. Multiply this by ten and you have the overshoot distance on the table. Next take the height, six centimetres, pick up the black die '2' line and repeat the performance, and you have a two millimetre × 10 = 20 mm error to the right of the centrepoint of the target. If either your target or the weapon load is big enough, you may even have scored a hit.

As we are dropping bombs in terms of complete loads, we can, having established the point of impact, postulate a radius of destruction based on the total explosive dropped, a rough rule of thumb being that about half the weight of a bomb is made up of explosive. Working on the assumption that it takes 220 lb (100 kg) of active material to destroy an area 27 yards (25 metres) in radius, our theoretical radius of destruction for varying sizes of bomb loads is given in the following table. Allowance has been made for ground scale.

Bomb load (kg)	Radius of effect (mm)	Bomb load (kg)	Radius of effect (mm)
250	17	2,500	53
500	23	3,000	58
750	29	3,500	63
1,000	34	4,000	67
1,500	41	4,500	71
2,000	47	5,000	75

We now know where the bomb lands, and what area it affects. But what effect does it have on various target categories?

Domestic buildings of brick or stone or bridges of the same construction are destroyed if part of the target lies within two thirds of the radius of effect. I make no differentiation between brick and stone construction as, since Moses' time, there has been plenty of straw available for brick-making. Concrete fortifications need a direct hit with a 250 kg bomb to destroy them, and structural steel bridges a 500 kg direct hit. Soft vehicles are destroyed if any part of them is within the radius of effect (RE), immobilised if within 1¼ times RE and damaged at 1½ RE. Two lots of damage equals immobilised. Light armour is destroyed if within ¼ RE, immobilised if within ½ RE. Heavy armour will need a direct hit to destroy it with a bomb load of 1,000 kg or under, above this it is destroyed if within ⅛ RE, immobilised if within ¼ RE. Infantry casualties are dealt with on a percentage probability basis as the following table. Each bomb-load puts at risk all infantry figures within its radius of effect, and each figure takes a dice roll; a score exceeding that in the table means that he has survived.

	Impact point to ¼ RE	¼ RE to ½ RE	½ RE to ¾ RE	¾ RE to RE
In the open	100	50	25	12
Under cover	80	40	20	10
Dug-in	50	25	12	6
In lorries	95	45	23	12

Napalm is the next weapon to consider. The central point of impact can be determined by use of the bomb sight, and one missile would give a solid patch of flame 18 to 19 yards wide by 65 to 66 yards long (17 metres wide by 60 metres long or 10 mm × 36 mm on the table) which nothing would survive, and so hot that anything nearby would move to at least 110 yards (100 metres, equals 600 mm) away. When clusters of these weapons were dropped, and this was the rule rather than the exception, a certain amount of overlap took place. If we then assume that the overlap is of the order of 50 per cent, we can produce a theoretical pattern to cater for this. The centre of the conflagration caused by the first lot is found by using the bomb sight as described. The second container extends the fire 5 mm to the right, the third container 5 mm to the left. The fourth extends the area of No 1 18 mm to the front; 5 and 6 extend No 4 5 mm left and right respectively. No 7 extends No 4 a further 18 mm to the front, and Nos 8 and 9 extend No 7 5 mm to the left and right again. This gives a maximum load of nine containers, burning up an area 20 mm wide by 72 mm. Nothing within this area survives, as even in a concrete fortification thick enough to withstand the heat, the oxygen in the air would be quickly consumed. The area remains too hot to be entered for at least six hours.

Now for rockets, of which very little in the way of actual operational performance seems to have been written. Generally they are housed in pods hung on external stores stations and the normal method of employment is to ripple-fire the entire content of a pod in a shallow (10°) dive at 1,100 yards' (1,000 metres') range—600 mm on the board. They can be popped off in ones or twos, but the chances of a hit using this method are not very great. Let us take a brief look at a French weapon, the Matra 155 launcher, which carries 18 SNEB 68 mm rockets, and which can be considered reasonably representative. On letting fly with the lot, all 18 rockets clear the pod in 0.8 seconds. Assuming total accuracy, this would give a longitudinal spread of 133 yards (122 metres, or 73 mm on the table) at an aircraft flying speed of 345 mph (550 km/h), and 230 yards (211 metres or 126 mm) at 595 mph (950 km/h), which allows the aircraft to 'spray' the area along the line of flight to a certain degree. The following table gives the percentage probability of scoring a hit on different types of target firing two rockets; roll the dice for each pair of rockets fired.

		Massed infantry Massed vehicles Buildings	Individual vehicles or guns, pillboxes	Individual vehicles or guns in cover
Speed of attacking aircraft	550-700	40	15	05
	701-850	20	07	02
	851-950	0	03	0

Anything hit by rockets is destroyed except for massed infantry, for which one percentage dice is thrown. Divide the score by three, rounding fractions up, and this is the percentage of the troops who become casualties.

Finally we have gunnery. This is almost totally ineffective against heavy armour apart from making tank commandos duck. It is, however, very effective against APCs, soft vehicles, and infantry. The chances of scoring a hit are the same as for rockets plus half as much again, but the maximum range is reduced to 656 yards (600 metres or 360 mm). Strafing deployed infantry, a hit is assumed on the area they occupy every time. All we have to do is to assess the effect.

The chances of knocking out a tank or a pill-box with cannon fire are minimal and for all practical purposes can be discounted. Other armour, such as APCs and SPGs or artillery, is vulnerable. Having achieved a hit, roll one dice. A score of 0 or 1 is superficial damage; the capability of the vehicle or gun is unimpaired. 3, 4 or 5, the vehicle is immobilised, and in the case of the ZSU 23/4, its radar capability is knocked out. 6, 7, 8 and 9 = destroyed. For soft vehicles, a score of 01 or 1 immobilises, anything else destroys. Against massed infantry treat as a rocket hit, and against deployed infantry, dice for each figure at risk. 0 or 1 scores indicate a casualty. Against deployed infantry in cover, only a score of 0 will suffice.

The 'brown jobs' were not, of course, defenceless. They could and did on occasion hit back hard. The main missiles, such as the *Guidelines*, *Gainfuls* and Hawks are not really battlefield weapons and need not be considered here, even though *Gainfuls* were deployed very much up front, as in all cases the launch procedure would be gone through long before the aircraft appears over the table, and the interception would also take place well off-table. We are thus left with anti-aircraft guns, and in the Egyptian and Syrian armies, the SA 7 *Grail*, which was used in the Yom Kippur war only.

Heavy calibre machine-guns were still around, but the likelihood of shooting down a modern combat aircraft with one is almost infinitesimal and can be discounted. Where modern aircraft differ most from their World War 2 counterparts is in their unbelievable toughness. The aerodynamic stresses they are built to withstand are such that their skinning is now so thick that it virtually constitutes a deflector plate. Even if a gunner was lucky enough to aim straight, the chances are that anything less than 20 mm stuff is likely to do little more than bounce off.

Of the guns, the quadruple-barrelled ZSU 23/4 used by Egypt and Syria in 1973 was the most deadly. Self-propelled and with automatic radar guidance, it combined a high rate of fire with admirable accuracy, and in combination with the SA 6 *Gainful*, it gave the IAF a hard time. Hits are scored with anti-aircraft guns as follows: manually laid guns get in one shot every four, five or six air moves, although the first shot can be taken immediately if the aircraft enters within 15° of the angle the gun is pointing initially and is within range. This is to give odds of less than 100:1, which would otherwise require a complex firing chart. Radar-slaved guns, such as the ZSU 23/4 and ZSU 57, and the Israeli 40 mm Bofors L 70, get a shot each air move. This reflects the degree of electronic sophistication built into these weapons. Both the Arab guns have an effective horizontal range of 1,312 yards (1,200 metres or 720 mm on the table) while the Bofors has a horizontal range of 3,280 yards (3,000 metres or 1,800 mm). The one exception to this is when the aircraft comes within 656 yards (600 metres or 360 mm) when the radar is ineffective, unless of course the aircraft is attacking the gun head-on, in which case fire is as normal. Having scored a hit, dice for effect with one die.

Ground-to-air gunnery table

Arab	Air moves per shot	Target speed in km/h				Horizontal scale range
		550 -	650 -	750 -	850 - 950	
ZSU 23/4	each*	08	04	02	01	720
ZSU 57	each*	08	04	02	01	720
Twin 23 mm	4	02	01	00	00	600
Twin 37 mm	5	02	01	00	00	1,200
57 mm/58	6	01	00	00	00	2,000

Israeli
Bofors 40 mm

L 70	each*	09	04	02		01	1,800
Twin 20 mm	4	02	01	00		00	600

*See short-range restriction.

An aircraft is shot down with the following dice throws— ZSU 23/4: 0-5, ZSU 57: 0-3, 40 mm L70: 0-3. Any other guns are 20 mm: 0, 21 to 40 mm: 0-1, 41 to 60 mm: 0-2. Damaged aircraft jettison their stores (if bombs or napalm, treat as an attack but with the aiming point directly under the nose; something might get hit by accident) and buzz off home. Shot down aircraft dip their noses to 30° and plough straight in, causing an effect similar to two napalm containers. If still carrying its ordnance loads, the effect of these should be added to the general mayhem.

Finally in our brief look at ground-to-air weaponry comes the SA 7 *Grail*. This is an infra-red homing missile carried by infantry or mounted for greater effect in batches of six or eight on vehicles. Relatively slow on acceleration, short-ranged (2,150 mm on the board) and not very fast, about 1,060 mph (1,700 km/h) top whack, it can only be fired from a position within a 30° cone to the rear of the target. A further weakness is the size of its warhead, about 2.2 lb (1 kg), which is usually insufficient to do much damage, although quite a few Israeli aircraft returned home with their flues in tatters. To operate a *Grail*, wait until the target turns its back, and therefore its hot exhaust in your direction, then let fly. Throw two dice, the chance of scoring a hit being 04. If a hit is scored, throw one dice, a 0 is a kill, 3 causes damage enough to make the aircraft jettison its load, all other scores are ineffectual.

Aircraft performance data

Israeli

Mirage III. Speed 590 mph-plus (950 km/h-plus), radius of turn on table 320 mm. Armament 2 × 30 mm cannon, 4,410 lb (2,000 kg) bomb-load or four pods of 19 rockets or four napalm containers.
Super Mystère IVB. Speed 590 mph-plus (950 km/h-plus), radius of turn on table 232 mm. Armament 2 × 30 mm cannon, 2,205 lb (1,000 kg) bomb-load or two pods of 19 rockets or two napalm containers.
Mystère IVA. For wargames purposes, as for Super Mystère IVB.
Ouragan. Speed 581 mph (930 km/h), radius of turn on table 208 mm. Armament 2 × 30 mm cannon, 2,205 lb (1,000 kg) bomb-load or two pods of 19 rockets or two napalm containers.
Vautour. Speed 590 mph-plus (950 km/h-plus), radius of turn on table 328 mm. Armament 4 × 30 mm cannon, 4,410 lb (2,000 kg) bomb-load or four pods of 19 rockets or four napalm containers.
Magister. Speed 402 mph (644 km/h), radius of turn on table 152 mm. Armament 220 lb (100 kg) bomb-load or two pods of 18 rockets.
Phantom. Speed 590 mph-plus (950 km/h), radius of turn on table 412 mm. Armament 1 × 20 mm cannon, 11,025 lb (5,000 kg) bomb-load or 11 napalm containers.
Skyhawk. Speed 590 mph-plus (950 km/h-plus), radius of turn on table 376 mm. Armament 2 × 20 mm cannon, 5,950 lb (2,700 kg) bomb-load or nine napalm containers.

Arab

MiG-21. Speed 590 mph-plus (950 km/h-plus), radius of turn on table 334 mm. Armament 2 × 23 mm cannon, two pods of 16 rockets.
MiG-19. Speed 590 mph-plus (950 km/h-plus), radius of turn on table 284 mm. Armament 3 × 30 mm cannon, two pods of 19 rockets.
MiG-17. Speed 590 mph-plus (950 km/h-plus), radius of turn on table 216 mm. Armament 3 × 23 mm cannon, 2,205 lb (1,000 kg) bomb-load or four pods of eight rockets.
MiG-15. Speed 590 mph-plus (950 km/h-plus), radius of turn on table 210 mm. Armament 1 × 37 mm, 2 × 23 mm cannon, 2,205 lb (1,000 kg) bomb-load or two pods of eight rockets.
Su 7. Speed 590 mph-plus (950 km/h-plus), radius of turn on table 360 mm. Armament 2 × 30 cannon, 3,969 lb (1,800 lb) bomb-load or 16 rockets.
Hunter FGA 9. Speed 590 mph-plus (950 km/h-plus), radius of turn on table 208 mm. Armament 4 × 30 mm cannon, 2,205 lb (1,000 kg) bomb-load or two pods of 19 rockets.
Vampire FB V. Speed 537 mph (860 km/h), radius of turn on table 188 mm. Armament 4 × 20 mm cannon, 2,205 lb bomb-load or 16 rockets.
F-104A Starfighter. Speed 590 mph-plus (950 km/h-plus), radius of turn on table 588 mm. Armament 1 × 20 mm cannon, 3,307 lb (1,500 kg) bomb-load.

As far as I have been able to ascertain, the Arab air forces do not use napalm. The Il 28 and Tu 16 bombers are unsuitable for attack missions and have therefore been omitted.

Finally, we need to assess what air strike capability the combatants possess at any given moment. As we saw in the preceding chapter, command of the air is the first essential, followed by, in order of priority, supply routes (tanks cannot go far without fuel) with battlefield support third on the list. We therefore need an approximate assessment of the air superiority phase in order to determine what attack capability is reasonable as the battle progresses.

Both sides commence with their strength as the details given earlier, although due allowance must be made for unserviceability, particularly on the Arab side. In 1967 either side could have launched a pre-emptive strike; the EAF had theirs ready planned. I would suggest if you are running a campaign that you proceed as follows. The probability of the Israelis launching a successful pre-emptive strike against the EAF is 90 per cent. If successful, 50 per cent of the serviceable strength of the EAF is written off on the spot. Israeli losses, including severe battle damage, are assessed as ten per cent of attack strength. The Magisters cannot be used in this phase, so don't count them. The probability of a successful surprise attack by the EAF is 50 per cent causing 25 per cent IAF casualties, their losses being assessed as 15 per cent of attack strength. In the event of a pre-emptive strike failing, the element of surprise is lost and we then enter an air superiority phase. Each side allots a proportion of their forces to airfield attacks and air fighting. The number of Israeli aircraft is multiplied by two to reflect their superior training, and the side with the greatest force inflicts 20 per cent casualties on the weaker force, and sustains ten per cent casualties itself. This process is repeated day by day, and as the opposition weakens, more aircraft can be released for attack sorties.

If you have 80 aircraft assigned to the assault role, assume that half (40) will be employed on behind the lines interdiction, thus leaving 40 for the battlefield attack. Other areas than the one on your table will also need help, so assume one fifth of these (eight) will be available for your sector. They can come on all at once, or in four flights of two. Aircraft have, however, an infuriating habit of turning up at the wrong time or place, so we have to make allowances for this. For each planned strafe, roll the dice. A score of 0-2 for Israelis or Jordanians, 0-4 for Egyptians and Syrians, and 0-6 for the Iraqis means that they have mislaid the battlefield and so do not arrive. In neither war should Iraq participate for more than two days in any case.

This leaves one final loophole which I am about to plug. For every ten per cent difference in the number of aircraft allotted to the air superiority role by either side, the numerically inferior air force adds one to the dice score at which they get lost. This is to simulate the effect of greater interception capability. For example, if the IAF are in an air superiority phase with a numerical inferiority of 20 per cent the chance of their ground strikes not turning up would increase from 0-2 to 0-4. So there we are; instant air campaigns! Seriously though, book-keeping is minimal, and well worth the effort for the results achieveable.

One final word. In 1973, pre-emptive strikes are simply not on, the Israelis partly for political reasons, and the Egyptians because of the low success possibility.

17

The naval war

Naval activity has played only a relatively minor part in the Arab-Israeli Wars, and it may seem odd to include it at all in a book on *tank* battles. There is a reason, however. In a wargames campaign, one or both sides may decide at some point to launch an amphibious assault of some description. Indeed, in 1967 the Israelis had planned and organised one such landing against El Arish, but this was abandoned when it was seen how well General Tal's tanks were performing. In any case, isolated 'nuisance' raids and commando-style operations are a distinct possibility.

The Egyptians have steadily built up the most efficient fleet in this theatre of operations. In 1967 these consisted of seven destroyers, 12 submarines, 18 missile carriers, 32 Motor Torpedo Boats and 12 anti-submarine craft. Since the Israelis only possessed one vintage pre-World War 2 submarine in serviceable condition, the latter may seem rather an extravagance. The main reason for the size of the Egyptian navy, however, was President Nasser's fear of Anglo-American naval forces in the Mediterranean acting on Israeli behalf as they had in 1956. As a result, part of his arms deal with the Soviet Union included several very modern warships.

The Egyptian destroyers are mainly of the Soviet *Skory* Class equipped with 5-inch guns having a range of 14-15,000 metres (16,000 yards), but they also possess one old British 'Z' Class destroyer. Their submarines are Russian also, and include six 'R' Class and six of the large ocean-going 'M' Class. The missile boats are split half and half between the modern *Osa* and older *Komar* Classes. The submarine chasers are of the SO-1 type, the MTBs predominantly of *Shershen* Class. Since 1967 this force has been expanded with the addition of 14 Russian minesweepers.

Against this force, 30 per cent of which was stationed in the Red Sea in 1967 (thanks to an Israeli ruse) and the balance in the Mediterranean, all the Israelis possessed in their 'Cinderella' Service was the one antique submarine mentioned above, three old destroyers (one of them a captured Egyptian ship!), one anti-submarine vessel and eight MTBs. Fortunately, they were not called upon to enter into any pitched naval engagements.

The main Israeli concern was the Egyptian missile boats, which could have bombarded coastal towns. Accordingly, on the night of June 5 1967, an Israeli force including one destroyer and several MTBs attacked the harbour at Port Said with the intention of destroying the Egyptian missile craft and any others they could find. Two *Osa* boats came out to meet them but were driven back by superior firepower and the Israeli vessels sent a frogman task force in to mine the ships. Unfortunately, in the darkness they were unable to find them. However, the raid achieved its objective in that the Egyptians moved their craft back to Alexandria, from where they did not have the range to reach Tel Aviv. Other frogmen released on the same night into Alexandria harbour from Israel's one submarine were captured without inflicting any damage.

The only offensive move made by the Egyptian navy in the Mediterranean was on June 6 when three of their submarines approached the Israeli coast. The Israelis detected all three with sonar and depth-charged them, damaging one and forcing them all to retire.

During the period between the end of the Six Day War and the start of the 1973 campaign, the Israelis modernised their navy through the acquisition of 12 fast, missile-armed patrol boats built in Cherbourg. These are equipped with the Israeli *Gabriel* missile having a range of 19 kilometres (12 miles) and are therefore no match for the Egyptian *Styx* missiles which have a range of 48 kilometres (30 miles). However, the *Styx* is not a particularly accurate weapon, especially against small, fast-moving targets, as was shown in 1970 when the Egyptians attacked an Israeli fishing boat. Four missiles were launched but not one hit! Unfortunately, the fishing boat was nevertheless sunk by a near-miss. Equally unfortunately, the Israelis suffered the loss of two vessels in the inter-war period (the so-called 'War of Attrition')—the destroyer *Eilat* to Egyptian missiles off Port Said, and the submarine *Dakar* lost with all hands en route from England.

Despite their superiority in submarines, the Egyptians achieved nothing positive with them during the Yom Kippur War apart from the sinking of two completely innocent Greek freighters.

The first naval engagement of this war was actually against the Syrians. Like the Israelis, the Syrians had never put a great deal of emphasis on building up a navy. Their total force consists of two ex-Russian *Petya* Class frigates, 12 *Osa* and *Komar* Class fast patrol boats, three minesweepers and eight MTBs (in 1973 they had 11 of the latter but only three *Osa* and six *Komar* Class).

On the night of October 6/7 1973 five of the new Israeli 'Cherbourg' boats were patrolling the Syrian coastline when they observed a single Syrian MTB. They gave chase and came upon a further force of three missile boats and a minesweeper. The Israelis split their forces into two line-ahead columns and flanked the Syrian craft. A missile exchange took place—the first missiles-only naval battle in history—the end result being the total destruction of the Syrian force for no Israeli losses. A similar attempt to draw Egyptian craft out of Port Said on the same night was unsuccessful, although one Egyptian missile boat was sunk by Israeli aircraft.

A second Israeli naval expedition to shell Egyptian coastal positions at Daniette on the night of October 8/9 succeeded in drawing four Egyptian missile boats out to attack and a further exchange of missiles took place during which three of the Arab craft were sunk. Once again, the Israelis suffered no casualties.

On following nights Israeli craft attacked shore positions on the Syrian coastline and succeeded in destroying four more Syrian missile boats as well as the oil tank station at Banias. These harassing operations continued throughout the conflict against both the Egyptian and Syrian coasts but it became rare for the Arab crews to emerge from the protection of their powerful coastal gun and missile batteries.

In the Red Sea and Gulf of Suez the Egyptians took a stronger offensive in support of an amphibious assault on the Sinai coastline, their forces including two *Skory* Class destroyers. The Israelis were aware of the naval build-up, however, and in a surprise raid by two patrol boats shot up a large part of the Egyptian assault force in the bay of Mersa Talamat, creating chaos. A day later another Egyptian missile boat was sunk, and five nights thence five Israeli craft entered the anchorage at Ras Ghareb and sunk 19 Egyptian armed fishing boats.

The 1973 war proved decisively the superiority of the small, fast and highly manoeuvrable Israeli missile boats, crewed by approximately 40 sailors and armed with 40 and 76 mm guns in addition to their missiles, against any of the supposedly modern Soviet-built vessels. Their total casualties were three men killed and 24 wounded. No Israeli craft was sunk in any of the engagements. However, the story could well be different against the same ships in the hands of well-trained Russian crews.

For those wargamers who wish to include the naval side in a campaign, I can do no better than suggest they invest in the boxed game called *Seastrike*. Unlike most games of its type, this can be set up on an ordinary wargames table—it does not rely on a map board. Counters are provided for all the types of vessel which will be required (or small 1:2,400 or 1:1,200 scale model ships can be substituted), and the rules even make provision for designing your own types of boat if you wish. The game mechanics include both conventional gunfire and surface-to-surface missile rules and, although it is now marketed by Philmar, the original game was designed by the Wargames Research Group—which should be good enough for anyone! Amphibious landings can also be staged using this game so it would be presumptuous to include rules for them here, although readers who already have a copy of my previous book in this series on the North-West European campaign can easily adapt the ones contained therein.

Much was made of the Israeli missile boat concept in a lecture delivered by Rear Admiral Benyamin Telem, Navy CO of the IDF, in Tel Aviv in October 1975. The whole concept of Israeli naval policy was, he said, completely transformed by the first appearance of Russian missile boats in the Egyptian navy in 1962. At that time the Israelis had the *Gabriel* missile at the development stage, and the formidable threat posed by the *Komar* Class ships threw it into immediate doubt. In 1967, he continued, the Israeli navy therefore had a seagoing force based on an 'ancient' World War 2 concept but commanded and manned by sailors already geared to the new, fast missile-armed patrol boat concept of warfare. The loss of the *Eilat* brought home the inadequacy of conventional warship classes against these more modern vessels.

Defining the problem, Admiral Telem said that: 'The Israeli operational requirement called for a three-stage engagement technique as follows: *Stage 1*—detect and identify the enemy as early as possible; *Stage 2*—close range and attack when at own effective missile firing range. During the execution of this second stage, out-manoeuvre and avoid being hit by enemy missiles if encountered; *Stage 3*—within own effective range, continue to close range, while firing on missiles. Use guns to finally destroy the enemy.'

In other words, a bit like Matilda tanks charging Flak 88s! However, a crucial factor, especially in Stage 2, is electronic warfare to put the opposing side's tracking and guidance systems off. And it is in this field—which, in terms of close encounters of this kind, every other navy has so far neglected—that the Israelis have subsequently specialised. Their fast patrol boats are capable of detecting similar enemy craft at ranges in excess of 40,000 metres (40 kilometres or 25 miles) whilst the Egyptian craft are apparently only able to detect at 37,500 metres (37.5 kilometres or 23.5 miles). This means that the Israeli ships can begin deploying in battle formation precious seconds, if not minutes, before their opponents, which gives them sufficient 'edge' to negate the superior range of the Russian-designed missiles.

Looking to future needs in this sphere, Admiral Telem said that the 'missile boat as a complete weapon system will have to include the basic answers to the following operational requirements: 1) high cruising speed and good manoeuvrability; 2) a good surface-to-surface missile system; 3) good EW (electronic warfare) equipment; 4) an anti-missile point defence capability.

'It is going to be rather difficult,' he continued, 'in the coming years to work out the right solution for integrating these four contradictory capabilities in a rather small platform.'

So, you *Seastrike* designers, get to it!

Appendix

Availability of model vehicles

1:300 scale or 'micro-tank' wargaming is one of the astonishing phenomena of recent years. When Don Featherstone wrote the first book in this series, it was a courageous venture, and the manufacturers of models suitable for wargaming in this scale could virtually be counted on the fingers of one hand. Since that time the whole hobby has flourished, and micro-tank wargaming with it. Many 'fly by night' companies have appeared on the scene, advertised their wares for a few months, and quietly disappeared. But a few reliable, professional companies remain, most of them producing at least *some* models suitable for Arab-Israeli wargaming.

The most highly detailed and accurate models for this period, if I can say so without giving offence, are the GHQ ones manufactured and designed by New Hope Design, Rothbury, Morpeth, Northumberland, and I would like to acknowledge my thanks to David Winter for the provision of many sample models. Sold in packs of four or five models, this range comes in 'kit' form, usually with separate turrets, gun barrels, etc, which can be cemented in position or left loose to revolve. The other three major manufacturers in this field are Ros and Heroics Figures, of 36 Kennington Road, London SE1; Leicester Micro Models Ltd, of 50 Walcot Walk, Peterborough, PE3 6QF; and Skytrex, 28 Church Street, Wymeswold, Leics. All of these companies run a mail order service and can supply catalogues and/or price lists. Skytrex also market the percentage dice you will require if using my playing rules.

Accessory manufacturers come and go with even greater rapidity than model tank firms, and the only way you can be sure of obtaining specific items is through watching the advertisements in the current issues of *Airfix Magazine*, which I had the pleasure of editing for over six years, *Battle*, *Military Modelling*, *Campaigns*, *Wargamers Newsletter* and other similar publications. One manufacturer of scenic accessories who is still going strong is Micro-Mold, 1-2 Unifax Way, Goring-by-Sea, Sussex whose extensive range of vac-formed products is well worth acquiring, although the company does not (yet) to my knowledge manufacture miniature Suez Canal lengths!

Select bibliography

Brower, K.S.: *Armor in the Yom Kippur War* (1974).
Churchill, R., and Churchill, W.: *The Six Day War* (1967).
Field, Michael (Ed): *Middle East Annual Review* (1978).
Foss, Christopher F.: *Armoured Fighting Vehicles of the World* (1977).
Herzog, Brigadier-General C.: *The War of Atonement* (1975).
Jane's Weapon Systems, 1977 (1977).
Krivinyi, N.: *World Military Aviation* (1976).
Macksey, K.: *Tank Warfare* (1971).
O'Balance, Major E.: *The Third Arab-Israeli War* (1972).
Po, Enrico: *Tanks of the Great Armies* (1969).
RAC Tank Museum: *Fire and Movement* (1975).
Senger und Etterlin, F.M. von: *Taschenbuch der Panzer 1976* (1976).
Sunday Times: The Yom Kippur War (revised edn, 1975).
Teveth, S.: *The Tanks of Tammuz* (1969).
Williams, L. (Ed): *Military Aspects of the Arab-Israeli Conflict* (1975).
Young, Brigadier P.: *The Israeli Campaign, 1967* (1967).

Plus numerous articles in *Armies and Weapons, Battle, War Monthly, Defence, Proceedings, Strategy & Tactics* and other magazines.

Index

(Note: Minor personal and place names, etc, which only occur once in the text, have been omitted from this index due to lack of space.)

A4 Skyhawk - 108, 112, 113, 114, 123.
AA batteries - 73; guns - 111, 113.
Abu Agheila - 20, 23, 24, 25, 26.
Adan, General - 32, 35.
Advisors, Soviet - 20, 31.
Aérospatiale squadrons - 81.
Aérospatiale SA 321 'Super Frelon' - 82.
AFVs, general - 38, 58, 62, 66, 71, 72, 105.
AG 42 - 70, 71.
Aharon, Captain - 13.
Air Battles in Miniature - 7, 118.
Air brigades - 108.
Aircraft weaponry - 118.
Air strikes - 25, 38.
AK-47 - 70, 102.
AKM - 70.
Alexandria - 16, 111, 126.
Alon, Colonel - 10, 11.
Alouette II - 81; III - 81, 83.
Amiel, Professor Saadia - 78.
AML 90 - 87, 90, 92.
Amman - 110.
Ammunition, types of - 92, 93.
Amnon, Colonel - 37, 38.
AMX-13 - 26, 45, 61, 87, 89, 92.
AMX-30 - 44, 45.
AMX M le 50 - 45, 61, 87, 89.
Anti-tank fire - 24; mines - 79, 80; projectiles - 89; towed weapons - 93; ATGWs - 36, 37, 38, 63, 64, 65, 73, 76, 77, 81, 82, 87, 88, 94, 97, 98, 100.
APCs, general - 60, 71, 73, 74, 93, 121.
APHE projectiles - 66, 67, 68, 94.
Arab revolt - 9.
Arab Legion - 10, 27.
Arab Liberation Army - 10, 11.
Armée de l'Air - 107.

Armies of the Middle East - 57.
Armour classifications - 89; plates - 44; thickness for wargaming - 60.
Armoured brigades - 73, 74; divisions - 74.
Ashmura - 28, 29.
Assad, President - 31, 42.
ASU-57 - 62, 90, 93.
Atonement, War of - 36, 40.
Attrition, War of - 30, 31, 111, 112, 127.
Avia C210 - 107.

B-10 - 65.
B-11 - 65.
BA-64 - 59.
Baathist party - 42.
Baghdad - 17.
Baghdadi, Major-General Ali - 112.
Bakr, Field Marshal Hassan al - 42.
Balfour Declaration - 9.
Banias - 114, 127.
BAR - 70.
Bar-Lev, General Haim - 20, 31, 34.
Bazooka - 24, 63, 97.
Begin, Prime Minister - 40.
Beirut - 16.
Bell 205 - 81, 82, 88.
Ben-Ali, Colonel Uri - 19, 20, 29.
Ben-Gurion, David - 18, 21.
Bernadotte, Count - 11.
Besa MG - 70.
Bir Gifgafa - 23, 24, 26, 111, 113.
Bir Hassneh - 24, 26.
Bir Lahfan - 25, 26.
Bir Thamada - 24, 26, 113.
Black September - 41.
Blast radius - 96.
BM-13-16 - 69; BM-14-16 - 69; BM-21 - 69; BM-24 - 69.
BMP-1 - 60, 61, 90.
BO 810 Cobra - 64.
Boeing C-97 Stratocruiser ECM - 112, 113.
Bofors - 113, 122.

Index

Bombs - 118, 123; bombing - 116, 118;
 -load - 118, 120.
BRDM-1, -2 - 60, 72, 90.
Bren gun - 70.
British troops - 10, 88;
 Palestine Regiment - 43.
Browning .5 MG - 13, 22.
BTR-40 - 60, 90; BTR-50 - 60, 61, 90;
 BTR-60 - 60, 61, 90; BTR-152 - 60, 61,
 72, 90.
Bulldozers - 29.

C-97 - 112.
C-130 Hercules - 99, 100.
Cairo - 16, 42, 112.
Canal, bridges - 113, 114; Zone - 78,
 109. (qv Suez.)
Canberra - 107.
Casualty tables - 103, 104.
Centurion tank - 12, 13, 14, 15, 33, 40, 43,
 44, 45, 46, 57, 58, 61, 75, 87, 90, 92.
'Cherbourg' boats - 127.
Chinese Farm - 35, 37, 38.
Chobham armour - 47.
Christie suspension - 58, 59.
Churchill, Randolph and Winston - 180.
Colwill, Ian - 100.
Comet tank - 43.
Commandos - 31, 33, 99, 100, 101, 111.
Conscription - 18.
Corsair, F4 - 107.
Cromwell tank - 43, 87, 89, 92.
Curtis, Steve - 100.

D-30 - 66.
D-44 - 68.
D-74 - 66.
Dakar, submarine - 127.
Damascus - 16, 38, 39, 40, 42, 108, 110,
 113, 114.
Danny, Captain - 13.
Dayan, General Moshe - 12, 21, 27, 33, 36,
 112.
Destruction radius - 96.
Deversoir - 35, 37.
Diaspora, the - 9.
Dimona installations - 40.
Discipline - 30, 43.

Egyptian AF - 107-112, 114, 124.
Eilam, Brigadier Uzi - 63.
Eilat - 23; Gulf of - 23.
Eilat, destroyer - 127, 128.
Elad, Major - 25.
El Arish - 11, 15, 19, 23, 24, 25, 26, 109,
 126.

Elazar, General David - 20, 29, 32, 33, 36,
 63.
Electronic warfare - 86, 112, 128.
El Fatah - 21.
El Qantara - 23, 26.
Entebbe - 99, 100.
Eshkol, Prime Minister Levi - 21.

F4 Phantom - 112, 114, 123.
F4 Wing - 107.
F16 Wing - 107.
F-84 Thunderstreak - 107.
F-104 Starfighter - 113, 124.
Farouk, King - 19.
Featherstone, Don - 12, 57, 100, 105, 130.
Feisal, King - 20.
Fiat G55 - 107.
Field artillery - 66.
Field repairs - 89.
Flail tanks - 79.
Flak - 111, 112, 115.
Flak 88 - 128.
Fluid, inflammable hydraulic - 47.
FN rifle - 70, 71, 75, 102; machine-gun - 71.
'French' Sherman - 92.
Fuel - 25, 47.

Gabriel missile - 127, 128.
Gainful missile - 113, 114, 122.
Gal, Major Uziel - 71.
Galil - 70, 71, 75, 100, 102.
Gavish, General - 31, 32.
Gaza and Gaza Strip - 18, 19, 23, 24, 42,
 99.
Gdud (battalion) - 74.
Gebel Libni - 24, 26.
Geneifa Hills - 35, 38.
Gidi Pass - 33.
Goa missile - 111-114.
Golan Heights - 18, 29, 33, 34, 36, 37, 38,
 39, 87, 110, 113.
Golani Brigade - 39.
Gonen - 28, 29, 39.
Grail missile - 113, 114, 122, 123.
Great Bitter Lake - 37, 38.
Grenades - 102, 104.
Guideline missile - 108-114, 122.
Gunnery, air - 121, 122.

H-35/39 tank - 43, 45, 87, 89, 92.
Haganah - 10, 15, 21.
Haifa - 10, 11, 108, 110, 113.
Hakim - 70.
Harvard armed trainer - 107.
Hativa (brigade) - 74.
Hawk missile - 34, 108, 111, 112, 113, 122.
HEAT shells - 44, 67, 68.

133

Hebron, Mount - 11, 29.
HE fire - 76, 96.
Helicopters - 25, 29, 81-83.
Hennawi, General Mustapha al - 112.
Hermon, Mount - 27, 33, 39, 40, 114.
Herzog, Chaim - 36, 37.
Heyl Ha'Avir - 106, 108, 110, 115. (qv IAF.)
Howitzer battalions - 74.
Huey Cobra - 82.
Hull-down positions - 13, 27, 33, 44, 46, 59, 94.
Hunter, Hawker - 59, 107-110, 113, 124.
Hussein, King - 21, 31, 32, 40, 41, 42.

IAF (Israeli AF) - 29, 30, 33, 107, 109, 111, 112, 114, 122, 124, 125.
IDF (Israeli Defence Force) - 10, 11, 29, 32, 43, 46, 58, 65, 76, 106, 128.
Il-28 - 107-111, 113, 124.
Immigration, Jewish - 9, 10, 11.
Independence, Israeli War of - 15.
Indirect fire - 95.
Infantry - 71, 96-98, 121, 122.
Iraqi AF - 110, 113.
Iroquois helicopter - 83.
IS-II tank - 59.
IS-III tank - 13, 24, 26, 59, 74, 89, 92.
Isherman tank - 44, 87, 89, 92.
Iska, Colonel - 26, 27.
Ismail, General Ahmed - 32.
Ismailia - 13, 23, 26, 27, 35, 37, 38.
ISU-122 - 62, 90, 92.
ISU-152 - 62.

J26 - 107.
Jaffa - 10.
Jane's Weapon Systems - 87, 91.
Jeep - 74, 93, 100.
Jericho missile - 42, 69.
Jerusalem - 9, 10, 16, 18, 27, 110.
Jet Provost - 109.
Jewish Agency for Palestine - 9.
Jewish Brigade - 15.
Jiradi - 25, 26, 29.
Jordan, River - 28, 29, 33, 39.
Jordanian AF - 110, 113, 118.

Kantara (Qantara) - 35, 37.
Katyusha missiles - 26, 59, 69, 73.
Kaukji, Fawzi - 10, 11.
Kennel missile - 113, 114.
Kfir - 113.
Khan Yunis - 23, 24.
Kibbutz, kibbutzim - 15, 20, 21, 29, 30.
Kissinger, Henry - 38.
Knesset - 77.
Komar boats - 126, 128.

Kosygin, Premier - 38.
Kuntilla - 15, 23-26.
Kusseima - 20, 25.
KPV machine-gun - 72.

L-33 - 45, 87, 89.
L70, Bofors - 122.
Laner, Dan - 34, 39, 40.
Laser rangefinder - 93.
LAW (Light Anti-tank Weapon) - 65, 75.
Leadership - 30.
League of Arab States - 42.
League of Nations - 9.
Lee-Enfield rifle - 70.
Leopard tank - 47.
Liberty, USS - 22.
Linear tactics - 75.
Lofgren, General - 63.
Luttwak, Professor Edward - 78.
Lynx helicopter - 83.

M-3 half-track - 48, 74, 87, 90.
M4 Sherman - 43, 44, 48, 57, 58, 61, 67, 87, 89, 92, 94.
M-32 - 45.
M-46 - 67.
M-47 Patton - 13, 14, 15, 29, 75, 76.
M-48 - 46, 47, 48, 57, 58, 61, 87, 90, 92.
M-51 - 69.
M-59 - 67.
M-60 - 44, 47, 57, 58, 61, 71, 87, 90, 92.
M-74 - 45.
M-85 - 71.
M101A1 - 66.
M-110 - 48, 61, 87, 90.
M-113 - 48, 61, 74, 87, 90.
M-114 - 67.
M-125 - 48.
M-577 - 48.
M-1918A2 - 71.
M-1931/37 - 66.
M-1937 - 67.
M-1938 - 66.
M-1943 - 67.
M-1944 - 68.
M-1955 - 68.
M-1974 - 62.
Machine-guns, general - 24, 88.
Magen, General - 33.
Magister armed trainer - 108, 109, 110, 113, 123, 124.
Mandler, General - 33, 34, 35, 36.
Matilda tank - 128.
Matt, Colonel - 37, 38.
Massada - 28, 39.
Matra launcher - 121.
Mauser Kar 98K - 70.

Index

'M' Brigade - 15, 24, 25.
Mecca - 16.
Mechanical reliability - 14, 89.
Meir, Golda - 33.
Men, Colonel - 15.
Merkava tank - 46, 47, 87, 90, 92.
Meteor, Gloster - 107.
MG 34 - 70.
Mi-1 - 81, 88.
Mi-4 - 81, 83, 88.
Mi-6 - 81, 88.
Mi-8 - 81, 88.
MiG-15 - 107-110, 124.
MiG-17 - 100, 106, 108, 110-113, 115, 124.
MiG-19 - 108-110, 113, 124.
MiG-21 - 108, 110-113, 115, 124.
Mines - 24, 78, 79.
Mirage, Dassault - 108, 109, 111-115, 123.
Missiles, general - 48, 94, 111, 114, 126, 127.
Mitla Pass - 19, 23, 26, 32, 35, 37, 110.
Morale - 7, 29, 32, 43, 86, 98, 105.
Moroccan Expeditionary Force - 38.
Mortars - 24, 72, 98.
Mosquito, DH - 107.
Motor Torpedo Boats - 126, 127.
Movement rates - 87.
Mustang fighter - 107.
Muzzle velocity - 91-93.
Mystère, Dassault - 106, 107, 108, 110, 111, 113, 123.
Mystère, Super - 108, 109, 113, 115, 123.

Nakhl - 19, 23, 24, 26.
Napalm - 118, 121, 123, 124.
Nasser, Gamal Abdul - 19, 20, 21, 31, 41, 58, 108, 126.
NBC platoon - 73.
Neguib, General - 19.
Nile, River (and Valley) - 16, 111, 112.
Nixon, President - 31.
Nuclear capacity - 40.

OB 155-50 - 67.
Observation - 90, 91, 117.
Oil embargo - 21.
Old City - 27.
OPEC - 40.
Operation Thunderbolt - 100.
Osa boats - 126.
Ouragon - 107, 108, 109, 113.

Palestine Mandate - 9.
Palestine White Paper - 9.
Palmach - 10.
Panhard AML - 48, 90.
Panzerfaust - 63.

Paratroops, Israeli - 19, 27, 29, 31, 37, 39, 99, 100.
Peel Commission - 9, 10.
Peled, General Benjamin - 33.
Petya Class frigate - 127.
Piper Cub - 111.
Pivka, Otto von - 57.
PK Series - 71.
PLO - 40, 42, 58, 71, 77.
Port Said - 16, 22, 23, 35, 111, 126, 127.
PT-76 - 60, 61, 90, 92.
PzKpfw IV tank - 58, 89, 92.
PzKpfw V Panther - 58, 89.

Qnaitra - 28, 29, 33, 34.

R-35, Renault tank - 45.
Radar stations - 34.
Radio communications - 85.
Radius of destruction - 120.
Rafa - 12, 15, 19, 23, 24, 25.
Ramallah - 10, 29.
Ranges, effective and maximum - 92, 93.
Ramadan, War of - 12, 30, 32, 57, 64, 78, 81, 112. (qv Yom Kippur War.)
Raphoul, Colonel - 15, 24.
Raschid - 70, 71.
Rates of fire - 84, 92, 93.
RBY1 - 48, 87, 90.
Record-keeping - 101.
Refugees, Palestinian - 11, 18, 40.
Reloading time - 102.
Reprisal raids - 100.
Reserves, Israeli - 18.
Retro-rockets - 106.
Rockets, general - 97, 116, 118, 121.
RPG-7 missile - 36.

S/10 Battalion - 24, 25, 26.
S/14 Battalion - 24, 26.
S/23 gun - 67.
Sa 321 - 81.
Sabra tank - 46, 47, 87, 90, 92.
Sadat, President Anwar - 19, 31, 32, 38, 40, 41, 42, 77.
Sagger missile - 36, 37, 60, 62, 63, 64, 65.
SAM (Surface-to-Air Missile) - 31, 38, 108, 112, 113, 115. (qv Individual missile types.)
'S' Brigade - 15, 19, 21, 24, 25.
Scud missile - 31, 69.
Sea Hawk - 107.
Sea Venom - 107.
Sharm el Sheik - 19, 23, 30.
Sharon, General Ariel - 15, 25, 26, 27, 31, 32, 33, 35, 75, 76.
Sheik Zuweid - 13, 24.
Shells - 95, 96.

135

Shillelagh weapons system - 47.
Shmuel, Colonel - 15.
Sikorsky CH-53C - 81, 83; H55 - 81; S-55 - 81.
Simonov rifle - 70.
Sinai, The - 14, 16, 19, 21, 22, 23, 27, 29, 30, 32, 33, 34, 36, 37, 38, 75, 107, 109, 110, 111, 112, 113, 115.
Six-Day War - 12, 30, 32, 41, 44, 81, 111, 127.
Skory Class destroyer - 126, 127.
SLR - 104.
SMGs - 70.
Smoke screens - 114.
Snapper missile - 62, 64.
SNEB rocket pods - 118, 121.
Soft-skin vehicles - 87, 96, 120, 121.
Soltam/Tampella - 48, 67.
SP 120 mm mortar - 74.
SPG (general) - 66, 67, 73, 121.
Spick, Mike - 7, 22, 81, 88.
SS-10 missile - 48, 64.
SS-11 missile - 48, 64, 82.
Staghound armoured car - 48, 87, 90, 92, 94.
Stalin tank - see IS-III.
Steamroller tactics - 33.
Stern Gang - 11, 15.
Styx missile - 127.
Su-7 - 108, 110, 111, 115, 124.
SU-76 - 62, 90, 92.
SU-85 - 62, 90, 92.
SU-100 - 13, 62, 74, 90, 92.
Super Sherman - 87, 89, 92. (qv M-4.)
Supply - 15.
Suez - 16, 23, 26, 35, 38; Canal - 18, 19, 26, 27, 29, 30, 38, 41, 76, 77; Crisis - 44; Gulf of - 23, 35, 37, 127. (qv Canal.)
Swatter missile - 62, 65.
Syrian AF - 108, 113, 114.

T-10 tank - 59, 61, 72, 74, 89, 92.
T-34 tank - 13, 58, 59, 89, 92.
T-44 tank - 59.
T-54 tank - 26, 57, 59, 60, 61, 89, 92.
T-55 tank - 13, 14, 33, 59, 61, 89, 92.
T-62 tank - 34, 38, 59, 60, 61, 89, 92.
Tactics, general - 14, 18, 20, 24, 30, 36; aerial - 117.
Tal, General Israel - 12, 15, 20, 21, 24, 25, 26, 31, 33, 46, 75, 91, 126.
Tank design - 12, 43.
Tanks of Tammuz, The - 12, 19.
Tel Aviv - 10, 16, 22, 108, 126, 128.
Terrorism, terrorists - 10, 15, 30, 99.
Teveth, Shabtai - 12, 19, 22.
Tewfik, Port - 36, 112.

Tiger tank - 89.
Tiran, Straits of - 19, 21.
TOW system - 47, 64, 65.
Training - 18, 20, 30, 43.
Tu-16 - 108-111, 113-115, 124.
Type D rifle - 71, 102.

Ugdah (division) - 74.
United Nations - 10, 11, 19, 21, 30; Security Council - 29.
Unit identification signs - 57.
Units: 1st Armoured Division - 33, 34; 1st Army Reserve - 32; 2nd Army - 32, 37; 2nd Infantry Division - 22, 24, 25, 32; 3rd Armoured Division - 34; 3rd Army - 32, 37, 58; 3rd Infantry Division - 22; 3rd Mechanised Division - 32; 4th Armoured Division - 22, 24, 32; 5th Infantry Division - 33, 34; 6th Infantry Division - 22, 24; 6th Mechanised Division - 32; 7th Armoured Brigade - 33, 34, 39; 7th Infantry Division (Egyptian) - 15, 22, 24, 32; (Syrian) - 34; 8th Army - 12, 22; 9th Division - 33; 14th Brigade - 34; 16th Division - 37; 18th Infantry Division - 32; 19th Brigade - 34; 19th Infantry Division - 32; 20th Brigade - 34; 20th PLA - 22, 23; 21st Division - 37; 23rd Mechanised Division - 32; 25th Independent Armoured Brigade - 32; 137th Armoured Brigade - 33; 202nd Airborne Brigade - 100.
Ural 375D - 69.
Uzi SMG - 70, 71, 75, 100, 102.

Valiant bomber - 107.
Vampire fighter - 107, 108, 124.
Vautour - 108, 109, 111, 113, 123.
Vickers 105 mm L/51 - 45, 46, 47, 57.
Vulcan cannon - 72.
Vz 58 rifle - 71.

Watch and dodge tactics - 76.
Weapon values - 105.
Weapon loads - 120.

Yagouri, Colonel - 36, 44.
Yoffe, General Abraham - 15, 22, 25, 26, 27, 75.
Yom Kippur War - 12, 30, 32, 57, 63, 64, 78, 81, 112, 117, 127.

Zahal - 10, 15, 18, 20, 21, 30, 32, 46, 91.
'Z' Brigade - 15, 24.
Zeira, General Eli - 33.
ZSU-23-4 - 61, 74, 113, 114, 122, 123.
ZSU-57 - 122, 123.